CONTENTS

4 WHEN THE PEN IS MIGHTIER THAN THE PUTTER

5 GOLF COURSES OF GREAT BRITAIN AND IRELAND

6 1990: A YEAR OF GOLF

FOREWORD

by Gordon Brand Jnr

If I had to pick two highlights from my golfing year in 1989, they would be helping Europe to retain the Ryder Cup at The Belfry and winning the Benson and Hedges International tournament at Fulford. I am sure it will not surprise anyone to learn that my major goal for 1990 is to win the Open Championship at St Andrews, but you can be certain that I will be trying my utmost to retain my Benson and Hedges title at St Mellion in May – I have grown rather fond of that gold trophy!

I can confidently say that among my fellow professionals on the European circuit the Benson and Hedges International is one of the most eagerly awaited tournaments we play in: it is also unquestionably one of the most popular. Naturally I am proud to have won the last tournament staged at Fulford, and it would make a great double if I could win the first to be held on the Jack Nicklaus course at St Mellion. They are two very different golf courses, and although I will undoubtedly miss the Yorkshire course, I relish the prospect of playing Jack's Cornish creation. It is going to be quite a challenge.

I am honoured to provide the Foreword to this first edition of the *Benson and Hedges Golf Year*. 1989 was such an extraordinary year in so many ways, and this book will serve as an exceptionally colourful and interesting reminder of how the world of golf looked at the end of one decade and the beginning of another.

As well as its fierce competition, and despite the odd serious face you may have noticed when watching televised events, professional golf does have its lighter moments and I am delighted to see that the *Benson and Hedges Golf Year* contains many humorous touches. I think it is a book that will make all of us smile.

Gordon Brand Jnr

SPONSOR'S MESSAGE

Benson and Hedges have long been enthusiastic supporters of golf both through the sponsorship of the Benson and Hedges International at Fulford, which this year moves to St Mellion, Cornwall, and through our association with the *Benson and Hedges Golfer's Handbook*.

We are therefore delighted to further our association with golf through this first edition of the *Benson and Hedges Golf Year*. Superbly produced by editor Nick Edmund, I am confident it will prove invaluable to all golfing enthusiasts. This comprehensive publication carries all the important facts and statistics of the past year interspersed with lively features and articles from some of the sport's top writers on the game's major tournaments and personalities.

We are particularly pleased also that our current 1989 Benson and Hedges International Golf Champion, Gordon Brand Jnr, has kindly agreed to write the foreword to this magnificent book, which we hope will give you many hours of pleasure through your 1990 season.

Barry Jenner
Marketing Manager
Benson and Hedges

INTRODUCTION

This first *Benson and Hedges Golf Year* does not pretend that it can in any way help improve the golf swing. Not a jot. However, we do hope that for anyone hooked on the game it will provide many hours of pleasure and entertainment off the fairways.

1989 was a year well worth remembering and 1990 undoubtedly a year to look forward to. That is essentially what this golf book is all about. It is a review of the golfing season in all its aspects, although we believe it to be especially colourful and informative and completely unlike any review you will have seen before; after all, not many golf year books quote Disraeli and the Earl of Stockton or mention Caesar and Alexander the Great!

For easy reference, the book has been divided into six main sections. An opening editor's review is followed by a detailed look at golf's major championships. We have included pieces on each of the four Majors written by some of the game's most prominent scribes and we have also explored how each of these Majors was won and lost in 1989, together with all the necessary vital statistics.

Section 3, entitled 'The World of Golf', is a comprehensive record and analysis of results from all four corners of the globe. It tells the story of how the Walker Cup was won and the Ryder Cup halved; it also includes full results and a comment on the Women's European Tour in 1989. A large proportion of the book's colour pictures are to be found in this section, illustrations which range from a view of golf in the shadows of Mount Fuji to the dazzling fairways of Augusta.

In Section 4 we really let the armchair experts loose. We have gathered a collection of articles from golf's leading journalists based on the theme of 'greatness': from the greatest championship moments to the greatest eighteen holes of golf, and from the greatest mistakes to the greatest women golfers.

The fifth section is a directory of all golf courses and clubs in Great Britain and Ireland, providing telephone numbers, addresses and course yardages, while the final section is a colourful global golfing diary pinpointing many of the highlights we can all look forward to in 1990.

Finally, as Editor, I would like to take this opportunity to express my considerable appreciation for the help I have received from a number of people in the compilation of this book. Particular thanks are owed to Debbie Beckerman and Judith Wardman at Partridge Press for their patience and support; Bob Brand for his guidance in a number of areas; Dave Cannon for providing such outstanding photography and invaluable selection advice; and to my wife Teresa for allowing me to turn our living room into a scene reminiscent of the press tent at Troon – the morning after the Open. And I mustn't forget you either, firstly for having purchased this book and secondly for telling all your friends to do the same.

Nick Edmund
1 January 1990

Benson and Hedges
GOLFER OF THE YEAR

Tom Kite

Curtis Strange

Mark Calcavecchia

Payne Stewart

Nick Faldo

Ronan Rafferty

Faldo's Five – 1989 Winner of the US Masters, Dunhill British Masters, Volvo PGA Championship, French Open and Suntory World Matchplay Championship

The man who rebuilt his swing to become a Master, and the man who controlled his temper to become a double Champion. The short, bespectacled gent from Texas, and the stocky cocksure Nebraskan. The young Irishman who at last fulfilled his promise and the All American Boy who finally emerged from the elongated shadow of his knicker-bockers. Faldo, Strange, Kite, Calcavecchia, Rafferty and Stewart. Six of the best, and in our opinion worthy candidates for the title Golfer of the Year. Let us examine their credentials, starting with the All American Boy.

Before the 1989 season got under way, Payne Stewart had already amassed a fortune from America's dollar-laden fairways and had won himself many friends with his colour-ful and affable approach. Unfortunately he hadn't won too many golf tournaments. In 1989 Stewart landed one of the big ones, the USPGA, thanks to a stunning finish of four birdies in the final five holes. He also beat a strong field to win the Heritage Classic by five strokes and but for a poor finish in the Nabisco Championships — he slipped to a back-nine 37 after having scorched to the turn in 29 — Stewart would have topped the US Money List last year. Still $1.2 million and a scoring average of 69.48 doesn't look too bad in the record books.

The man who pipped Stewart to win the Nabisco and head the Money List was Tom Kite. The Texan's greatest win of the year (and of his career to date) was his victory in the much-vaunted Players Championship in March. When Kite later 'threw away' a golden opportunity to add the US Open Championship at Oak Hill, he put a brave face on things by claiming that his Florida success was equivalent to winning a Major. Well, a gentleman he certainly is, but do you think he'd pass a lie-detector test?

As for the one that got away from Kite, this was won for the second successive year by Curtis Strange, a man who is said to have once possessed a formidably short fuse. A great degree of patience is required to win one US Open, never mind two: perhaps that is why a certain mercurial Spaniard has yet to win this championship.

Strange's historic win was arguably the greatest single achievement of the year, and his finish at The Belfry to defeat Ian Woosnam possibly the most spectacular; but for once Strange failed to dominate the US Tour, and his only other victory came at the beginning of the year in Australia.

On the golf course at least, Mark Calca-vecchia is the antithesis of Curtis Strange. 'Heave-ho have-a-go', that's his method. In 1989 it paid dividends in a major way. Calcavecchia described the 5-iron he hit out of the rough to the final hole in the Open play-off as 'the best shot I ever hit'. In addition to his triumph at Troon he won twice on the US Tour, including a seven-stroke victory in the Phoenix Open, where he produced rounds of 66–68–65–64. In America they are describing Calcavecchia as the next Palmer — well, we shall see, perhaps at St Andrews.

Calcavecchia's notable (and somewhat un-ruly) scalp was one of several collected by Ronan Rafferty in 1989. That particular am-bush took place in the Ryder Cup; a month later the Ulsterman was punching the air with delight at having clinched the European Order of Merit title by virtue of a thrilling win over Faldo and Olazabal in the Volvo Masters at Valderrama. It was Rafferty's third victory of the year, to go with his wins in the Italian and Scandinavian Opens. Golfer of the Year? Not quite — or at least not yet. The standard required to claim such an award must include at least five wins during the year on more than one continent. It helps if one of those wins is in a major championship, and it also helps if the golfer has proved himself a champion both at stroke-play and at match-play. In other words, there can only really be one winner . . .

ST MELLION
and the Benson and Hedges International

To begin a tournament by shooting an eight-under-par round of 64 has to be immensely satisfying. To finish the same event with a second 64, and so win by a stroke, and in the process book a place in the European Ryder Cup side, must give cause for ample celebration. To find out, we should ask Gordon Brand Jnr, for that is precisely what he did in the Benson and Hedges International at Fulford last August.

As worthy a challenge as the Yorkshire course is, one suspects that the defending champion, or anyone else in the field for that matter, will be hard-pressed to return such par-shattering scores when the twentieth Benson and Hedges International is staged at St Mellion in May (4th–7th). The tournament has already visited Cornwall once, in the mid-seventies, but that was before Jack Nicklaus had built his imposing masterpiece. So, a new date in the calendar and a splendid new venue to look forward to.

You would think it reasonable to suppose that the county of Cornwall and the American state of Georgia had precious little in common: after all whoever heard of a red-neck

pixie? Yet St Mellion has been described by many observers as having more than a hint of Augusta about it. Nicklaus, who triumphed six times at Augusta, may well have had Georgia on his mind when he designed some of the holes. The spectacular par-three 11th, for instance, with its demanding tee shot over a small lake to an angled green, followed by the glorious downhill par-five 12th – surely that's Rae's Creek in front of the green – are more than a little reminiscent of the 12th and 13th at Augusta, and most who have played both would agree that they are every bit as good.

St Mellion is very much an American type of course: plenty of water, beautifully manicured fairways that gather the drive, and lightning-quick greens. Several elevated tees also give the course a distinctive Nicklaus feel. Although officially opened less than three years ago it is already being hailed as one of the finest courses in Europe. Moreover, the Master himself is most impressed with his creation.

For all the comparisons with Augusta and Nicklaus's best courses in North America, the golfer only has to lift his eyes and look around to be reminded where he is. The accompanying scenery is unmistakably Cornish: the rolling green fields, the village church, the babbling brook with its kingfisher, and the gnarled trees that huddle around many of the greens and look as if they've endured a million Cornish winters.

With the strong field that has been assembled for this year's International we can anticipate some exciting golf, which will be all the easier to follow from the many natural vantagepoints of this stadium course. Whoever lifts the gold trophy at the end of the week will know that he's triumphed on one of golf's toughest challenges and will clearly deserve to see his name added to an impressive list of past winners, which includes no fewer than five Open champions – Messrs Jacklin, Trevino, Weiskopf, Norman and Lyle. So, fingers crossed for a blue sky and just a touch of a Cornish breeze.

I

1989
A YEAR TO REMEMBER

1989 – THE YEAR THAT WAS . . .

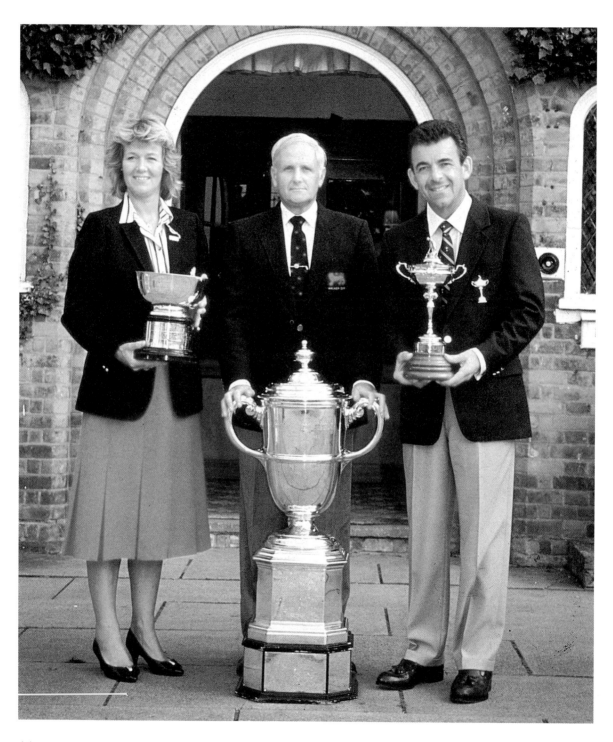

'First of all the Georgian silver goes, then all that nice furniture.'

The Earl of Stockton actually made the remark, but it might just as well have come from the golf governing bodies of the United States. Never before has so much silverware resided on this side of the Atlantic; more specifically, 1989 was the first time that all three team trophies, the Ryder, Walker and Curtis Cups, were in the safe keeping of teams from the 'Old World'.

Political commentators have not surprisingly described 1989 as an *annus mirabilis*. On the fairways of life it was not so much a year of wonders as a decade of miracles – at least so far as British and European golf is concerned. British golf had struggled through the seventies without a single home-grown Open Champion, no Ryder Cup victories, no World Matchplay champions and certainly no sight of a Women's US Open Champion. What a difference ten years can make!

As we approach the 1990s, women golfers in Europe are competing in as many countries and for as much prize money as the men did a decade ago, while the Seves and Faldos will be playing for more than ten times as much in 1990 as they did in 1980. From the jet-setting pros to the starry-eyed junior players, golf has become the fastest growing sport in just about every western European country. No wonder Uncle Sam is a-quaking in his boots.

But perhaps we Euro-Brits have allowed the taste of success to go to our heads. Open an American golf magazine or a USPGA Tour Yearbook and you'll read how the eighties have been a triumphant decade for American golf. 'There is not a sport in America that has accomplished as much as the PGA Tour has in the past decade,' *Golf* magazine claimed in its January issue.

What we really have witnessed in the eighties is a shift towards equality. Golf now has its own balance of power. At the beginning of the decade American golfers were all-conquering. The US Ryder Cup side

that visited Walton Heath in 1981, headed by Watson, Nicklaus, Trevino, Irwin and Floyd, was arguably the strongest ever assembled; yet by 1989 the score for the decade read 2½–2½. Ten years ago there had never been a European Masters champion; again, by 1989 the score for the decade was USA 5, Europe 5. America's resurgence, however, was clearly evident at Troon, and of the four Major winners in 1989, three paraded the stars and stripes. Interestingly, only two Americans so triumphed in 1979 – an unusual year, one might say, when the Masters champion bore the name Fuzzy and the US President was called Jimmy. Times have changed, and tradition now reigns, for the Americans have a President named George, an English Masters champion and USPGA champion who strides the fairways in plus-twos.

Captains and Cups: The Curtis, Walker and Ryder Cups all on British soil

Like all good things, they went up with the Stewarts

17

'Britain enjoys warmest weather since 1659 – official', reported the *Sunday Times* on 31 December 1989. Yet more evidence of global warming, scientists were claiming.

Those seeking proof that man has well and truly screwed up the Earth's climate could do a lot worse than to take note of the conditions that prevailed in golf's major championships of 1989. During our sweltering British summer, firemen were called out to the 'breezy links o'Troon', and in the United States snorkels and flippers were the order of the day, with all three of America's 'big events' being suspended at one time or another because of torrential rain and thunderstorms.

It wasn't just the Majors either that were affected. Golf's World Cup in Spain had to be shortened to a thirty-six-holes affair, and wags were claiming that the Australian team won only because they had the best surfers. In November 1990 the World Cup is to be played at Grand Cypress in Florida – no problems here surely ... In 1989 Florida enjoyed its first white Christmas!

The 1989 US Open

The 1989 Open Championship

Some golfers seem to wallow in difficult conditions. Hands up who remembers Palmer in the 1961 Open at Birkdale? Woosnam is another who relishes a challenge, and few will forget his performance in gale-struck Hawaii during the 1987 World Cup. Woosnam played some of his best golf in 1989 at the US Open, where a birdie on the final hole (450 yards – 'a drive and a flick with a nine-iron'!) left him only one behind champion Curtis Strange. A good case of what might have been.

Many have suggested that 1989 was a year when all four Majors were lost rather than won. But for a few missed short putts and the odd attack of 'Hell's bells, I'm leading a Major', the four champions could so easily have been Hoch, Kite, Grady and Reid. This may be true but it hardly does justice to the heroics of Messrs Faldo and Co. It overlooks the fact that Faldo 'won' the Masters with a brilliant final-round 65, that Stewart grabbed

Ian Woosnam at the US Open

The Volvo Tour's most popular winner –
Andrew Murray at the European Open

Alison Nicholas, a triple winner on the
Women's PG European Tour

his first Major with a superb back nine of
31, and that Strange set up his repeat US
Open win with a second-round 64. As for
Calcavecchia, forgive him the fluke at the
12th – he alone could birdie the 18th, not
once but twice on that thrilling Sunday afternoon.

1989 was a year of smiles and trials. While
the widest grins (and greatest leaps) undoubtedly belonged to Faldo, for Sandy Lyle it was
a year of trial and tribulation. Not once was
he asked to make a victory speech; instead
the golfing world watched as the kilt-clad
Scotsman helped put a green blazer on to
the back of his great English rival.

Trials of a different nature were being
threatened in 1989. The Ping square-grooved
controversy raged for much of the year, writs
and law-suits being filed against the R & A
and the USGA; the giant putter that Jack

Nicklaus used to win the '86 Masters was at the centre of another legal entanglement; and at Wentworth the members were up in arms at what they regarded as 'a Japanese take-over by the back door.'

Fortunately the tales of woe were easily outnumbered by the happier faces of 1989. The women's professional tour took one step backwards at the start of the year, then at least five strides forward – nobly supported, it might be added, by the IMG organization, who rarely receive the kind of press their efforts so often merit. Spanish eyes and Irish eyes were smiling both at the Belfry, where Christy O'Connor hit the shot of the year and Canizares holed the putt that retained the Cup, and at Valderrama in southern Spain, where Rafferty pipped Olazabal to capture the European Order of Merit title.

For many Americans their most sacred memory was the sight of Arnold Palmer (who ceased winning Majors long before Olazabal was born) charging to the turn in 31 during the first round of the USPGA Championship. Mitchell Platts described the scene in *The Times*: 'Arnie's Army was on the march again as its hero, looking every bit like Indiana Jones on his last crusade as he strode the fairways in his straw hat, hitched up his pants and reminded all of yesteryear.' Marvellous stuff.

As 1989 drew to a close, Lee Trevino turned fifty and the US Seniors Tour prepared for the Super Mex–Golden Bear assault. Nick Faldo was named BBC Sports Personality of the Year, and Bernard Gallacher was invited to succeed Tony Jacklin (CBE) as captain of the Ryder Cup team. Oh, and I nearly forgot ... the first *Benson and Hedges Golf Year* was knocked into shape.

Arnold Palmer and The Last Crusade

Lee Trevino – 'It's got to be easier on the Seniors Tour'

GOLF'S BIG TWO OF THE EIGHTIES, BALLESTEROS AND NORMAN

THE HIGHS AND LOWS

Ballesteros – The young matador of '79

Norman – Hail the conquering hero

Seve Ballesteros opened the decade as Open Champion; Greg Norman should have closed it as Open Champion. For much of the eighties this was the story of golf's most brilliantly talented duo: a decade that will largely be remembered for the fabulous achievements of Ballesteros and for the near misses of Norman.

If fortune had truly favoured the brave, the Australian could so easily have won seven major championships including a grand slam. The ones that got away were the US Open in 1984 – Norman lost a play-off to Zoeller; the

Masters of 1986, '87, and '89 – where on each occasion a birdie on the final hole would have given him outright victory; the USPGA of 1986 – stolen from him by Bob Tway; and most recently the 1989 Open. At the end of the decade the score in major championships read Ballesteros 5, Norman 1.

Much better luck, perhaps, but few would argue that Ballesteros has achieved everything expected of him in the eighties. Twice, first in 1980 after he had become the youngest ever Masters champion, and again in 1984, when he defeated Watson at St Andrews, the

Ballesteros: If looks could kill

Norman: 'Destiny hasn't been too kind to me'

Spaniard appeared to have the golfing world at his feet; yet he has added only one Major in the past five years, and unlike his Australian rival his near misses have been confined to Augusta. The truth is, we probably expect far too much from our heroes! Since 1985 both Norman and Ballesteros have claimed over twenty victories worldwide, records which compare very favourably, for instance, with Watson's single tournament win. At their best and in full flow, Norman and Ballesteros are golfers apart.

In Europe we have seen much more of Seve, and as an Australian Norman of course hasn't taken part in the decade's classic Ryder Cup encounters in which the Spaniard has played a starring role. Perhaps the biggest regret is that we have never seen the two really battle it out in a head-to-head situation over the back nine holes of a major championship.

Between 1980 and 1986 the 'Big Two' shared all seven World Matchplay Championships at Wentworth, yet strangely never met in a final.

Norman's greatest year was unquestionably 1986, when he won a staggering ten tournaments, including six in succession. Practically unbeatable in Australia, he headed the US Order of Merit (the first non-American to do so for a quarter of a century), in Europe he won the Open, European Open and World Matchplay and led Australia to victory in the Dunhill Cup, and he led all four Majors going into the final day's play – perhaps the closest any golfer has come to winning golf's modern grand slam. Seve has had several momentous years in the eighties, perhaps none as singularly spectacular as Norman's 1986, but in 1988 he won seven titles in seven different countries, including his third Open Championship.

1989 was a fine year for Norman. He won five times and came very close in two Majors. His final round of 64 at Troon was described by Tony Jacklin as 'simply incredible' and the Open is such that, had Norman won the play-off, we might be heralding him and not Faldo as the Golfer of the Year.

Ballesteros's golf in 1989 might be described as 'chaos illuminated by flashes of lightning'. The lightning struck most notably at St Pierre, where he played brilliantly to win the Epson Grand Prix title; there were also wins in Spain and Switzerland, but a frustrating year was perhaps typified by the way he lost his singles match to Paul Azinger in the Ryder Cup.

If Seve ended the eighties on a fairly low note, Norman ended it on a high note, being named as Australia's 'Athlete of the Decade'. On receiving the prize Norman declared: 'The way I see it, the 1980s were my front nine and the 1990s are going to be my back nine. I feel that I shot something like a 33 coming out but I want to come back in 31 or better.' You can bet your last peseta that Seve will be trying to shoot 30.

YIPS, GRIPS AND GRIPES

PUTTERS AND PROBLEMS

Langer's somewhat unorthodox grip

Bobby Jones could

Ben Hogan couldn't

Bobby Locke, Bobby Jones and Bob Charles were three of the best; Tony Jacklin, Peter Alliss, Arnold Palmer and Ben Hogan all suffered terribly: putting, the game within the game, the most significant yet most frustrating aspect of golf. How many major championships must have been determined by the missing of a short putt, the tweaking of a tiddler? Would Tom Watson still be winning major championships if he could putt the way he used to? And will Bernhard Langer ever rid himself completely of the dreaded yips?

1989 was a famous year for the putter. In April Scott Hoch snatched from Doug Sanders the reputation for having missed the shortest ever putt to win a Major, Mike Reid three-putted from 15 feet at the 17th, and then missed a five-footer at the 18th to hand the USPGA Championship to Payne Stewart on a silver platter; and then the same grateful recipient himself three-putted the final hole of the Nabisco Championship in October to

present Tom Kite with a cheque for $450,000.

Bernhard Langer is a golfer worthy of our admiration and utmost sympathy. Twice in his career he has been afflicted by the professional golfer's worst nightmare, the yips (for the uninitiated, these are the unwelcome gift of being able to send, or rather twitch, a three-foot putt six feet past the hole). They first struck the German golfer in the early 1980s, but courageously he overcame them to top the European Order of Merit in 1984 and win the US Masters the following April. By the middle of the decade, Langer held a strong claim to being the world's leading golfer. Then in early 1988 the yips returned with a vengeance. Langer's long game remained a match for anyone, but on the greens three-putting became commonplace; at times he four-putted, even five-putted.

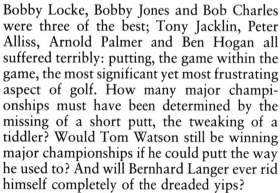

Torrance believes he's found the answer

1989 came and many were predicting the unthinkable – that Langer would lose his place in the Ryder Cup team. But of course the doubters were underestimating the man's incredible resolve. How many putters he must have tried, and what an amazing grip he introduced to the world! Two tremendous wins, in the Spanish Open and the German Masters, showed that Langer is once more getting the better of the golfing curse. If he fully recovers in 1990 we can expect him to be challenging strongly once more for golf's major prizes.

Langer wasn't the only European Ryder Cup player having a wretched time on the greens. At the start of the year Sam Torrance was so desperate he'd have tried anything if he thought it might help. Eventually the answer to his prayers came in the shape of a broom handle – the so-called broom-handled putter. So effective did it prove that many fellow sufferers converted. Most successful of these was Peter Senior, who used his newfangled device – almost as tall as himself – to claim three end-of-year victories, including the Australian Open.

Yet not all golfers, it seems, have been swept off their feet. Denis Durnian, who just missed out on a Ryder Cup place, when asked what had become of his broom-handled putter explained: 'I smashed it against a wall in Portugal, threw the head in the swimming pool and buried the shaft in the garden. I wanted to make sure it was never used again.' Who ever described golf as a gentle art?

THE SONY WORLD RANKINGS

31 December 1989 (The Top 60)

Greg Norman

Pos.	Player	Circuit	Points average
1	Greg Norman	ANZ	17.76
2	Nick Faldo	Eur	16.25
3	Seve Ballesteros	Eur	15.03
4	Curtis Strange	USA	13.79
5	Payne Stewart	USA	12.82
6	Tom Kite	USA	12.41
7	J.-M. Olazabal	Eur	12.00
8	Mark Calcavecchia	USA	11.81
9	Ian Woosnam	Eur	11.56
10	Paul Azinger	USA	10.95
11	Chip Beck	USA	10.49
12	Masashi Ozaki	Jpn	10.00
13	David Frost	Afr	9.39
14	Sandy Lyle	Eur	9.37
15	Fred Couples	USA	8.85
16	Bernhard Langer	Eur	8.47
17	Ben Crenshaw	USA	8.31
18	Mark McCumber	USA	8.04
19	Larry Mize	USA	7.08
20	Tom Watson	USA	6.81
21	Ronan Rafferty	Eur	6.73
22	Mike Reid	USA	6.57
23	Larry Nelson	USA	6.46
24	Scott Hoch	USA	6.42
25	Lanny Wadkins	USA	6.35
26	Peter Senior	ANZ	6.35
27	Mark O'Meara	USA	6.20
28	Steve Jones	USA	6.09
29	Craig Parry	ANZ	6.03
30	Craig Stadler	USA	5.90
31	Mark McNulty	Afr	5.82
32	Bruce Lietzke	USA	5.68
33	Ken Green	USA	5.47
34	Isao Aoki	Jpn	5.45
35	Tim Simpson	USA	5.44
36	Scott Simpson	USA	5.33
37	Mark James	Eur	5.27
38	Nick Price	Afr	4.87
39	Don Pooley	USA	4.75
40	Bob Tway	USA	4.69
41	Steve Pate	USA	4.67
42	Wayne Grady	ANZ	4.62
43	Rodger Davis	ANZ	4.42
44	Dan Pohl	USA	4.36
45	Blaine McCallister	USA	4.30
46	Peter Jacobsen	USA	4.28
47	Fuzzy Zoeller	USA	4.22
48	Naomichi Ozaki	Jpn	4.20
49	Jodie Mudd	USA	4.17
50	Bill Glasson	USA	4.15
51	Joey Sindelar	USA	4.07
52	Gordon Brand Jnr	Eur	4.07
53	Eduardo Romero	SAM	3.96
54	Peter Fowler	ANZ	3.94
55	Jeff Sluman	USA	3.93
56	Graham Marsh	ANZ	3.92
57	Howard Clark	Eur	3.83
58	Hal Sutton	USA	3.79
59	Ian Baker-Finch	ANZ	3.76
60	Sam Torrance	Eur	3.74

WORLD RANKINGS AND A WOULD-BE WORLD TOUR

How they stand and how it could look

Jones, Hogan, Palmer and Nicklaus had at least one thing in common – each at the peak of his powers was the undisputed world number one. Nicklaus's last great year was 1980, when he captured two of golf's four major titles, but by then Tom Watson had in most people's opinion superseded him as the game's leading player.

The first year of the decade was undoubtedly a vintage year for golf and if in winning his third Open Championship so emphatically at Muirfield Watson established his hegemony, three months earlier at Augusta Ballesteros had signalled to the world that the American golfer wasn't going to have everything his own way in the next few years. Indeed throughout the early eighties arguments raged as to who was the better player, and it was in part because it was so very far from clear-cut that in the middle of the decade the Sony World Ranking system, an IMG brainchild, was set up.

Ironically, since its inception neither Watson nor Ballesteros has spent much time in the number-one position; instead Greg Norman has spent easily the greatest number of weeks surveying the golfing world from this lofty perch.

A lot of thought and effort has gone into refining the Sony ranking system, and most would agree that it is now a very good measure. However, while just about every informed commentator would concur that on 31 December 1989 Norman, Faldo, Ballesteros and Strange are the world's top four golfers, a sizeable number (particularly on the other side of the Atlantic!) might still wish to debate the precise pecking order. The ranking system isn't helped by the fact that the game's leading players compete against one another in only a handful of tournaments

each year. The idea of a world tour is hardly an original one, but there can be little doubt that any golfer dominating such a tour could justifiably claim the title 'world champion'.

Various arguments have been propagated against the formation of a world tour; currently the one most frequently heard is that the four major professional tours, the US, European, Japanese and Australian, have grown so strong that it isn't in their individual interests to encourage the 'creaming off' of their major tournaments and star players. There is a great irony in this argument, for it is precisely because golf has grown so strong in all corners of the globe that the demand for a genuine world tour has gained momentum.

Rather than being a separate entity from the four major tours, surely a world tour could be complementary to them if it were constructed within the framework of the existing tour schedules. By visiting each of the four tours at various times of the year, international attention would be focused firmly on the particular tour visited and its leading events would be highlighted. Provided a world tour didn't run from the beginning of January to the end of December, covering forty-plus tournaments, a flexible itinerary could be built around existing events. A schedule of, say, 28 tournaments in a 42-week span (as in our not-to-be-taken-too-seriously example on p. 32), with a minimum playing requirement of fifteen events and a rough balance in the spread of events between Europe, America and Japan/Australasia, would seem to fit the bill. Players competing on the world tour could still easily meet their obligations to their home tour, as many of these 'home tour events' would also be part of the world tour.

In addition to giving our would-be world

Nick Faldo

Seve Ballesteros

tour a geographical balance, we have also designated nine events as 'majors'. Naturally the existing four major championships are given this special status, and it would also extend to the Open Championships of Australia, Japan, Canada and Europe, plus The Players Championship. The idea would be to encourage the game's great players to demonstrate their skills around the world in the premier championships of the world. A points system would determine the world tour order of merit, and the 'big nine' events would simply attract greater ranking points. A top European golfer could compete in the eight European tournaments and play in each of the nine majors, and in so doing would have entered fifteen world tour events. The position for the US tour player is similar, and although Australian and Japanese golfers might have to travel a little further, at least their countries would possess a 'major' and host more international events.

Again, to give the tour added international flavour we have included in our itinerary events in Hong Kong, Hawaii and South

America. It tees off in New Zealand, crosses the Atlantic twice, the Pacific three times, and finishes in Australia. In all, fifteen countries are visited (not to mention several spectacular locations), and the nine major events are spread nicely across the calendar. Because we have had the opportunity to start from scratch, so to speak, our European Open would be staged on the Continent, and at least two of the events (including the USPGA) would be match-play tournaments.

Of course having nine majors would play havoc with the history books! But interestingly only Nicklaus has won as many as six of our nine events, while Tom Kite, with his European Open and Players Championship wins, could now rest happily in the knowledge that he has two 'world majors' to his credit.

Pure pie in the sky? Quite probably, but it brightens up the winter months here and, hand on heart, what golfer wouldn't like to see the world's best battling it out on such a stage?

THE MAGICAL-MYSTERY WORLD TOUR 1990

January	4		July	5	
	11			12	Irish Open
	18				*(Portmarnock)*
	25			19	THE OPEN
					(St Andrews)
February	1			26	The International
	8	New Zealand Open			*(St Mellion)*
		(Auckland or Wellington)			
	15	Australian PGA	August	2	European Masters
		(Queensland or South Australia)			*(Switzerland or Germany)*
	22	AUSTRALIAN OPEN		9	
		(Royal Melbourne)		16	
				23	EUROPEAN OPEN
March	1				*(Holland or Sweden links)*
	8	South American Open		30	French Open
		(Brazil or Argentina)			*(Chantilly)*
	15	[World Cup]			
	22	PLAYERS CHAMPIONSHIP	September	6	Spanish Open
		(Florida)			*(El Soler)*
	29	Colonial Invitational		13	PGA/Matchplay
		(Texas)			*(Wentworth)*
				20	
April	5			27	
	12	THE MASTERS			
		(Augusta)	October	4	Canadian PGA
	19	Memorial Tournament			*(Vancouver)*
		(Muirfield Village)		11	USPGA
	26				*(Pebble Beach)*
				18	Kapalua/Hawaiian Open
May	3	Hong Kong Open		25	
	10	Asia-Pacific Masters			
	17	Japan PGA	November	1	[Four Tours Championship]
	24			8	JAPAN OPEN
	31			15	Japan Masters
				22	Australian Masters
June	7	US OPEN			*(Sydney)*
		(Medinah)		29	
	14	Western Open			
		(Chicago)	December	6	
	21	CANADIAN OPEN		13	
		(Glen Abbey)		20	
	28			27	

2

THE MAJORS

'Laugh and the world laughs with you; Weep and you weep alone'
(Ella Wilcox)

THE MASTERS
THE US OPEN
THE OPEN
THE USPGA

THE MASTERS

The 13th at Augusta – home of the Masters

Reds and yellows and pinks and greens, oranges and purples and blues.

Augusta is every golfer's rainbow. It is our dream course and the one we all like to play each year from a seated position, sometimes well into the early hours of a weekend in early April. The brilliant shades of Augusta waken us from a long winter. Eight months since the last major championship, no golf tournament is more eagerly awaited than the Masters.

For the players, to win the Masters is to find the pot of gold at the end of the rainbow.

As Peter Alliss said when Larry Mize holed his miraculous pitch shot a few years ago, 'and the meek shall inherit the earth'.

Michael Williams, golf correspondent of the *Daily Telegraph* is a fortunate man, for he is on close personal terms with Augusta. In his introduction to the Masters he takes us behind the scenes of this, one of the world's greatest tournaments, and he explains why Augusta National is in not just a class but a world of its own.

THE MASTERS

Michael Williams, *Daily Telegraph*

The Masters is unique in that it is the only one of the year's major championships that is played every year on the same course, Augusta National. It is also the only one of the quadrilateral that does not claim to be a championship. The club has always called it a tournament, but the rest of the world takes no notice.

Strictly speaking, participation in the Masters is by invitation only; at least that was how it began in 1932 when the late and great Bobby Jones decided to hold 'a tournament for a few of my friends'. Since then the invitations have tended to hinge much more on qualification, such as American tournament winners over the past 12 months and the top 24 in the previous year's Masters. Even so the club still reserves the right to make a few choices of its own.

Another factor that distinguishes the Masters from the Open Championship, the US Open and the USPGA is that its field is considerably smaller: it varies between 70 and 90, whereas the other three usually exceed 150. Consequently play – traditionally in pairs – never begins earlier than the very civilized hour of 9 am, by which time the members have had time to digest their breakfasts.

A half-hour flight from Atlanta, Augusta National rates as one of the most beautiful courses in the world. This is not surprising: previously it was a nursery, known as Fruitlands and owned by a Belgian horticulturalist, Baron Berckmans. One look at it was enough to persuade Bobby Jones, who by then had retired from competitive play, that this was the perfect piece of ground for a golf course. He elicited the help of Alister Mackenzie, who had also designed Cypress Point and Royal Melbourne, and together they created a masterpiece.

Augusta National is also one of the most exclusive golf clubs in the world, with a membership of only a little over 200, very few of them from Augusta itself. Annual dues are never divulged, and there is probably something in the suggestion that whenever the club feels the need to make a course improvement, they just add it on the annual account. The members are well enough endowed not to notice, and certainly do not complain.

Though much of the credit for Augusta National's eminence goes to Jones, the motivating force behind the Masters event was largely the club's chairman, Clifford Roberts. A hard-headed businessman who picked his sentences as carefully as he laboriously delivered them, his word was law. Nothing was done without his consent, and until recently prize money was announced reluctantly and only after the event.

Television commentators were forbidden to reveal in their broadcasts the names of other tournaments that players had won because it constituted advertising and when one of them inadvertently spoke of 'the mobs running', he was informed by Roberts that there were no mobs at Augusta and they certainly did not run. He was accordingly suspended from his television duties.

When Roberts was discovered to be suffering from cancer, he took his own life in a quiet spot on the nine-hole par-three course where a curtain-raising garden party event is held each year on the eve of the Masters. His successor, the much younger and more far-sighted Bill Lane, died after only a short spell in office, and the chairman of the club is now Hord Hardin, who, in his own way, is almost as inflexible as Roberts (though I doubt that Roberts would ever have agreed, as Hardin has done, to television's demand to put the leaders out last as early as the second day!).

The Masters is run entirely by club members, their badge of office being the distinctive green blazer with its crest of Augusta National, an outline of North America with a flagstick protruding from the rough location of Georgia. This same blazer is presented to the winner of the Masters each year by the previous winner and carries with it honorary membership of the club.

The clubhouse, largely single-storey, is all green and white and lies at the end of Magnolia Drive, immaculate practice grounds on either side. The verandah, back and front, is carpeted in green; black waiters in mustard-coloured jackets hover, attending the needs of the assembled company. The great gathering point is the lawn overlooking the course, which drops away to its furthest point, the 11th, 12th and 13th, known as Amen Corner because of the menacing Rae's Creek which winds its way around each of these greens.

Nowhere is there such a sense of well-being as there is at Augusta, and the Masters has long been an all-ticket occasion, people returning year after year to take up their places behind some favourite green, even though it may be three or four hours before they actually see any play.

The favourites are the 13th and 15th, both par fives. It is here that scores are either made or ruined. Each can usually be reached in two shots by all except the shortest hitters, but it is still a gamble, with Rae's Creek at the front of the 13th green and a broad pond at the mouth of the 15th. Come the Sunday afternoon of the Masters, these two holes invariably have a telling bearing on the outcome.

Seldom does the Masters not throw up some dramatic finish, the fashion indeed being set in the second Masters in 1935, when Gene Sarazen holed a four-wood second shot at the 15th for an albatross two, tied Craig Wood and then beat him in a play-off. Since then many great names, from Byron Nelson, Ben Hogan, Sam Snead, Arnold Palmer, Jack Nicklaus, Gary Player, Tom Watson to Severiano Ballesteros, have triumphed at one of the great shrines of golf.

It was not until the eighties that a European golfer finally got on to the Masters roll of honour, Ballesteros winning in 1980 and again in 1983. Two years later Bernhard Langer followed suit, and in 1988 Sandy Lyle became the first British champion. The 7-iron he hit from a fairway bunker at the 18th, and then the birdie putt that followed to beat Mark Calcavecchia by a stroke rank as probably the most thrilling finish of all time – that is, of course, unless one's name happens to be Nick Faldo. . . .

THE 1989 US MASTERS

The Major season would close with Arnold Palmer turning back the years in the USPGA; it began at Augusta with 49-year-old Lee Trevino leading the US Masters after a first-round 67. It was good enough for a one-shot lead over Britain's Nick Faldo. Paired together on Friday, Faldo, thanks to a putt of fully 100 feet at the 2nd, went out in 34 and led the tournament by three strokes. He then missed several putts on the back nine and ended the day with a 74, but still shared the lead with Trevino on 141. Ballesteros looked menacing on 143, tied for third with four Americans, Crenshaw, Reid, Green and Hoch. The only other player who was to take a prominent role in the 1989 Masters was Greg Norman. He was way back on 149, but typically would play his second 36 holes in 14 shots fewer than he had played his first. Sadly the defending champion Sandy Lyle missed the halfway cut.

Rain had been in the air throughout the week, but on the third day it didn't just rain, it poured. Ballesteros hates playing in a deluge more than most, and his challenge started to slip as the weather deteriorated. So too did Faldo's who was having a torrid time on the greens. Only Crenshaw was thriving in these conditions, and when play was suspended with the leaders only two-thirds of the way around the likeable Texan held a commanding lead.

The round was completed on Sunday morning. Crenshaw clearly hadn't slept well on his lead and he came back to the pack. Ballesteros made three birdies in his five remaining holes and began the final day only three shots behind Crenshaw. Hoch and Reid were only one off the pace, but Faldo was five back, having again played poorly in the morning to conclude a disappointing third round of 77. He had, it seemed, left himself far too much to do on the Sunday afternoon.

Ballesteros – nice legs, shame about the place

It was Ballesteros who first decided to grab the tournament by the scruff of the neck. Five birdies saw him out in 31, and the name that just about every golfer in the world fears was sitting atop the leader board. Faldo, it seems, is the exception; he fears no one, and he was out in 32 and back in the thick of things. At this point the magic deserted Ballesteros; his only birdie on the back nine came on the 18th, but that was soon after a double bogey 5 at the 16th had seen his hopes of a third Masters' victory vanish in a watery grave.

It wasn't even this long! – Hoch's play-off despair

Nick Faldo finds his pot of gold

As the drama of the back nine unfolded, the unlikely figure of Reid appeared at the top of the leader board. However, at the 14th Reid missed from three feet for a par and at 15 he walked off the green having taken a seven. Faldo continued his relentless charge up the leader board and, after a dropped shot at 11, he made birdies at 13, 14, 16 and then holed a monster putt at 17 for his eighth birdie of the round. He finished with a 65, five under par, and set a target that all the others had to shoot at.

Greg Norman was the first to try. On the back nine he had made birdies at 10, 13, 15 and 16; at 17 he put his second to within two feet of the flag and was now five under par. As in 1986, not only was the birdie that he needed to win the championship beyond Norman, but so too was the par to tie, and another Major had slipped away. Minutes lat-

er both Hoch and Crenshaw came to the 18th also needing fours to tie. Only Hoch could do it and so it was to be a play-off, Hoch versus Faldo.

For Faldo it was a chance to avenge his play-off defeat by Strange in the previous year's US Open, but when Hoch stood over a putt of less than two feet on the first sudden-death play-off hole it looked highly improbable. But golf is a funny game, and Hoch did a Sanders. The missed putt opened the door for Faldo, and he responded with a brilliant 3-iron shot to the next green. It was almost dark by the time the 30-foot birdie putt rattled the back of the hole. Faldo threw his arms into the air and looked towards the heavens. For the fifth time in ten years a European golfer had caught the Americans bathing and had walked away with their clothes.

THE 1989 MASTERS
FINAL SCORES

*N. Faldo	68	73	77	65	283	$200,000
S. Hoch	69	74	71	69	283	120,000
G. Norman	74	75	68	67	284	64,450
B. Crenshaw	71	72	70	71	284	64,450
S. Ballesteros	71	72	73	69	285	44,400
M. Reid	72	71	71	72	286	40,000
J. Mudd	73	76	72	66	287	37,200
J. Sluman	74	72	74	68	288	32,200
J.M. Olazabal	77	73	70	68	288	32,200
C. Beck	74	76	70	68	288	32,200
M. O'Meara	74	71	72	72	289	25,567
F. Couples	72	76	74	67	289	25,567
K. Green	74	69	73	73	289	25,567
T. Watson	72	73	74	71	290	19,450
D. Pooley	70	77	76	67	290	19,450
I. Woosnam	74	76	71	69	290	19,450
P. Azinger	75	75	69	71	290	19,450
J. Nicklaus	73	74	73	71	291	14,000
C. Strange	74	71	74	72	291	14,000
J. Ozaki	71	75	73	72	291	14,000
L. Trevino	67	74	81	69	291	14,000
D. Frost	76	72	73	70	291	14,000
T. Kite	72	72	72	75	291	14,000
P. Stewart	73	75	75	70	292	10,250
T. Purtzer	71	76	73	72	292	10,250

* Winner in play-off.

Nick Faldo the '89 Master

THE MASTERS
PAST WINNERS

1934	Horton Smith
1935	*Gene Sarazen
1936	Horton Smith
1937	Byron Nelson
1938	Henry Picard
1939	Ralph Guldahl
1940	Jimmy Demaret
1941	Craig Wood
1942	*Byron Nelson
1943-5	No Tournaments
1946	Herman Keiser
1947	Jimmy Demaret
1948	Claude Harmon
1949	Sam Snead
1950	Jimmy Demaret
1951	Ben Hogan
1952	Sam Snead
1953	Ben Hogan
1954	*Sam Snead
1955	Cary Middlecoff
1956	Jack Burke, Jr
1957	Doug Ford
1958	Arnold Palmer
1959	Art Wall, Jr
1960	Arnold Palmer
1961	Gary Player
1962	*Arnold Palmer
1963	Jack Nicklaus
1964	Arnold Palmer
1965	Jack Nicklaus
1966	*Jack Nicklaus
1967	Gay Brewer, Jr
1968	Bob Goalby
1969	George Archer
1970	*Billy Casper
1971	Charles Coody
1972	Jack Nicklaus
1973	Tommy Aaron
1974	Gary Player
1975	Jack Nicklaus
1976	Ray Floyd
1977	Tom Watson
1978	Gary Player
1979	*Fuzzy Zoeller
1980	Seve Ballesteros
1981	Tom Watson
1982	*Craig Stadler
1983	Seve Ballesteros
1984	Ben Crenshaw
1985	Bernhard Langer
1986	Jack Nicklaus
1987	*Larry Mize
1988	Sandy Lyle

* **Winner in play-off.**

Nicklaus follows Langer in '86

Larry Mize, winner in '87

COMMENTARY:

Faldo – a Golfer Apart

In 1987 they said Nick Faldo was a golfing machine: a fine player who could string eighteen pars together to win a British Open. In 1988 they said he was a very fine player: good enough to have the most consistent record in the year's four major championships, and after all he had come second in the US Open, third in the British Open and fourth in the USPGA.

Yes, they all agreed that Nick Faldo was one of the best, but the tall Englishman wasn't the sort of golfer who could shoot an eight-birdie 65 to win the Masters, was he? Well, they got it wrong.

Nick Faldo is an extraordinary golfer. He has the ambition and determination to succeed of a Gary Player, and he strikes the ball with a relentless precision reminiscent of Ben Hogan in his prime. One of the major factors that distinguishes Faldo from his peers is his ability not to let the inevitable bad shots and bad breaks get to him. When Faldo is out on the course he seems utterly cocooned in concentration. If he doesn't seem too warm to surrounding spectators, it is probably because he is only vaguely aware of their presence. One of the keys to Faldo's win at Augusta was that he didn't let his third-round 77 and all those missed putts upset his rhythm or his resolve. It is this, perhaps, that is the one chink in the Ballesteros armour, as witnessed during the last round in the Masters and again in the USPGA Championship. Although Ballesteros went out in 31 at Augusta he grew frustrated when the putts failed to continue dropping on the back nine, and he eventually lost his way. But Ballesteros, of course, has more than a touch of Arnold Palmer about him, and one cannot imagine Faldo throwing away a seven-shot lead on the back nine at a major championship as Palmer once did. Faldo is more of a Nicklaus than a Palmer, and it will be interesting to see who wins more major championships during the nineties – Ballesteros or Faldo.

Faldo regards his Masters triumph as his greatest victory: more satisfying even than his Muirfield win, because of the dramatic style in which he did it, and a finer achievement because 'it is more difficult to win away from home'. It was indeed a stunning victory and, coming, as it did, immediately on top of Lyle's Masters win, a tremendous sight for British eyes. To see a home player winning the Masters for the first time ever was momentous enough, but then twelve months later to witness a Scotsman, kilt and all, helping an Englishman into a second green jacket was something beyond most of our wildest dreams. Whatever next – the Scotsman, the Englishman and the Welshman? It may happen sooner than we think, for in Faldo, Lyle and Woosnam Britain can boast three of the world's top ten players. Things haven't been so rosy since the days of Vardon, Braid and Taylor.

THE US OPEN

Tom Watson at Pebble Beach, 1982

The new decade will mean many things to many people; to golfers the world over it signifies 40 major championships, including, of course, ten US Opens. If Curtis Strange had not created history at Oak Hill Country Club last year by becoming the first champion to defend his title successfully since Ben Hogan in 1951 – there would have been ten different US Open winners during the eighties, proving just how difficult a championship this is to win.

To the majority of American players, the US Open is the most important of all the majors. Lining up five-feet putts when they are barely four feet tall, they say, 'This one for the US Open.' Patriotic thoughts aside, a great event it certainly is, and a title very much cherished by European golfers. It is also a title that has eluded their grasp for twenty years, although both Nick Faldo and Ian Woosnam have recently come close to emulating the achievement of their Ryder Cup captain, Tony Jacklin.

Our guide to the US Open is **Tim Glover**, golf correspondent of *The Independent*. He takes us on a little trip down the US Open's own memory lane – a painfully narrow road, bordered by thick rough dense forest . . . .

THE US OPEN

Tim Glover, *The Independent*

The first United States Open Championship was staged in 1875 at Newport Golf Club in Rhode Island on the same nine-hole course that had been the site of the inaugural US Amateur Championship a few days earlier. Out of a field of 10 professionals and one amateur, Horace Rawlins, a 21-year-old assistant professional at the host club, won with a 36-hole total of 173. He received custody of the cup, 150 dollars and a gold medal. It was the first time that prize money had been offered in a golf tournament in America, and it was to have enormous consequences.

The early US Opens were dominated by the British, either emigrant professionals from Scotland or eminent Englishmen . . . Vardon, Anderson, Auchterlonie, Ross, McLeod. The spell was broken and a new one cast in 1913 by a 20-year-old store clerk. The venue was the Country Club in Brookline, a suburb of Boston, and it happened to be the home of Francis Ouimet. After four rounds the young American found himself tied with the Englishmen Harry Vardon and Ted Ray, figures so dominant in the game that the USGA had moved its June date to September to accommodate them. What was extraordinary about Ouimet's performance was not just his tender age and amateur status, it was the substance of his play. In the play-off over 18 holes, Ouimet, accompanied by his 13-year-old caddie, scored a brilliant 72. Vardon had a 77 and Ray a 78. Bernard Darwin, a grandson of the naturalist Charles and the then golf correspondent of *The Times*, said that Ouimet's round on a muddy, wet day was by far the most enthralling game he had ever seen.

Ouimet's achievement was the origin of the species. The realization of an American dream catapulted golf into the public imagination, shattered its image of exclusivity, and changed the course of its history. Ouimet, dressed in a crumpled jacket done up with two buttons, cloth cap and plus-fours, was an unlikely-looking hero. His reward was historical, not monetary. Seventy-five years later, when, on the same course, Curtis Strange followed Ouimet's footsteps and won the 1988 US Open by beating Englishman Nick Faldo in a play-off, he was already a multi-millionaire.

In between the unrecognizable worlds of Ouimet and Strange, the US Open Championship established its hallmark. Played on the nation's most demanding courses – the fairways are traditionally mean and narrow and are bordered by rough that knows the meaning of the word, and the greens are exceptionally fast, putting a premium on the accuracy of approach shots – the US Open traditionally produces a pedigree champion and the roll of honour reads like a who's who of golf.

However, one of the game's greatest names is missing from the list: Sam Snead never won the US Open. Take 1939. Snead needed two pars over the last two holes to win by two strokes: surely he could do that blindfolded? What happened? He dropped a shot at the 71st and then, incredibly, scored a three-over-par eight at the last. Bob Sommers, in his book *The US Open*, wrote: 'Women's eyes watered and men patted him softly on the back.' Snead was destined to finish runner-up on four occasions.

By contrast, Snead's greatest rival, Ben Hogan, like Bobby Jones, won four US Opens, most memorably in 1950. It was the golden anniversary of the US Open, and it was also the year when the extraordinary Hogan came back after a car crash which had threatened to end his life, never mind his golfing career. Heavily bandaged and limping on both legs, Hogan forced himself into a tie with Lloyd Mangrum and George Fazio and then went on to win the play-off by four strokes.

1960 was the year of the famous 'Palmer charge'. He began his final round by driving the first green and then proceeded to gatecrash his way through the field with six birdies in the first seven holes. It was to be Palmer's only win in the championship – six years later he frittered away a seven-shot lead over the final nine holes, handing a second championship to Billy Casper.

There was no such collapse in the 70th US Open at Chaska, Minnesota, when Tony Jacklin, who the previous year had won the Open at Lytham, pulled away from a strong field on the final day to win by seven strokes. His victory was the first by a Briton in 50 years.

If 1970 was Jacklin's year, then 1980 was Jack Nicklaus's. It was five years since the 'Golden Bear' had won a US major, two years since he had won anything at all, and at Baltusrol Golf Club in New Jersey they were talking about him in the past tense. After all the man was virtually in his dotage. They spoke too soon. Nicklaus not only won but set a 72-hole record, and, as if to rub salt into his critics' wounds, two months later he triumphed in the USPGA Championship.

Baltusrol provided Nicklaus with his fourth US Open, and only a shot in a million at Pebble Beach deprived him of a record fifth championship win. Nicklaus was sitting pretty in the clubhouse after a fourth-round 69 had put him four under for the 72 holes. Only one man could beat him, but at the 71st hole that man was up to his neck in trouble on the Monterey Peninsula. Tom Watson was in the long grass, on a downslope facing a green faster than a marble staircase. Nicklaus was already thinking of his victory speech when Watson chipped the ball into the hole for a birdie. With his sand wedge for a partner, Watson danced deliriously around the green. 'You little son of a bitch,' Nicklaus told him a few minutes later, 'you're something else.' So was the chip. So is the US Open.

THE 1989 US OPEN

Strange – following in Hogan's footsteps

'I'm either gullible enough or dumb enough to believe that I can still win.' This is how Jack Nicklaus summed up his chances in the '89 US Open after an opening 67 had left him only a stroke off the early pace set by Payne Stewart, Jay Don Blake and Bernhard (8 birdies) Langer. The four-time champion is something of a specialist at Oak Hill, for it was here, nine years earlier, that he had spread-eagled the field to win his fifth USPGA Championship by seven strokes. But Nicklaus, dare one say it, is not the golfer he then was and his dream was soon to fade; however, it was fun while it lasted and it brightened up what so often seems a very serious championship.

Golf or poker? Four aces at the 6th

Much of the pre-tournament chatter had centred on whether Nick Faldo could add the second leg of the big four to his Masters triumph and set up a possible Grand Slam. Whenever a 'good player' wins the Masters, he has to carry this impossible burden for two months or so, and we have to go back to 1972 to find a year when a golfer (Nicklaus, as it so happens) was able to win the first two legs of the quadrilateral. Suffering from a minor virus Faldo was never able to produce his best form at Oak Hill, and his first-round 68 only flattered to deceive. Instead the European challenge would be led by Ian Woosnam, who opened his account with a 70 and then added an excellent 68.

Besides Faldo, the other golfer commanding pre-championship centre stage was Curtis Strange. He had begun the defence of his title with a 71, solid enough, but still leaving him five shots behind the leading trio. By Friday evening Strange had forced himself to the top of the leader board. His 64, witnessed in full by Ballesteros, stands as one of the US Open's greatest rounds, and it is only one stroke more than the championship record set by Johnny Miller back in 1973. The second day of the US Open would in fact be remembered for two things: Strange's 64 and the extraordinary happenings on the par-three 6th hole, where no fewer than four aces were recorded.

Woosnam birdies the 18th

One man at least was determined that Strange should not have things all his own way. Tom Kite lay only a shot behind after 36 holes, and as the champion struggled to a third-round 73, Kite returned his third consecutive sub-70 score. After three rounds Kite led on 205, one ahead of Scott Simpson, the 1987 champion, with Strange on 208. It looked to be a three-horse race; Woosnam had slipped to a 73 and trailed six shots behind Kite on 211.

Texan Tom wears a tag around his neck which reads 'Greatest golfer never to have won a Major.' The 1989 US Open was Kite's for the taking. Early in the final round he found himself three ahead of Simpson and four ahead of Strange. He had been playing beautiful golf when he stepped onto the 5th tee. When he left the 5th green, however, his lead had gone. Kite would never recover from his horrific treble bogey seven; in fact he merely proceeded to leap from the frying pan straight into the fire. His despair seemed to rub off on playing partner Simpson, who also frittered away shots, and at the end of the day, Kite signed for a 78, Simpson for a 75.

Of that original leading trio only the defending champion was playing par golf — very much so in fact: Strange parred the first 15 holes of the final round. The inevitable last-day surges came from Chip Beck (68), Mark McCumber (69) and Woosnam, who opened with two birdies and ended in style on the last green holing a 12-foot putt for a 3. Beck, McCumber and Woosnam waited in the clubhouse knowing that only one man could overhaul them. That man was Curtis Strange, and his birdie at 16 decided the issue; it even gave him the luxury of being able to take three from the back of the 18th green. Woosnam had won himself many friends and was happy to have played so well and come so close; Kite was devastated; Strange was, not unnaturally, euphoric.

THE 1989 US OPEN
FINAL SCORES

C. Strange	71	64	73	70	278	$200,000
I. Woosnam	70	68	73	68	279	67,823
M. McCumber	70	68	72	69	279	67,823
C. Beck	71	69	71	68	279	67,823
B. Claar	71	72	68	69	280	34,345
S. Simpson	67	70	69	75	281	28,221
M. Ozaki	70	71	68	72	281	28,221
P. Jacobsen	71	70	71	70	282	24,307
J.M. Olazabal	69	72	70	72	283	19,969
T. Kite	67	69	69	78	283	19,969
H. Green	69	72	74	68	283	19,969
P. Azinger	71	72	70	70	283	19,969
L. Nelson	68	73	68	75	284	15,634
P. Stewart	66	75	72	71	284	15,634
T. Pernice Jnr	67	75	68	74	284	15,634
S. Hoch	70	72	70	72	284	15,634
M. Lye	71	69	72	72	284	15,634
D. Frost	73	72	70	70	285	13,013
N. Faldo	68	72	73	72	285	13,013
J.D. Blake	66	71	72	76	285	13,013
D.A. Weibring	70	74	73	69	286	11,306
N. Henke	75	69	72	70	286	11,306
B. Glasson	73	70	70	73	286	11,306
F. Couples	74	71	67	74	286	11,306
S. Elkington	70	70	78	68	286	11,306

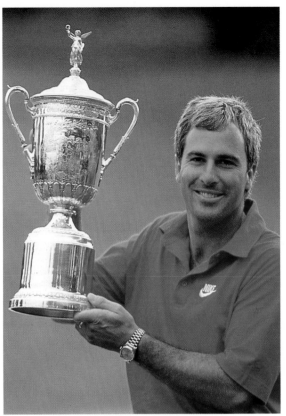

Curtis Strange, the '89 US Open Champion

THE US OPEN
PAST WINNERS

Ray Floyd, Champion in '86

1895	Horace Rawlins
1896	James Foulis
1897	Joe Lloyd
1898	Fred Herd
1899	Willie Smith
1900	Harry Vardon
1901	*Willie Anderson
1902	Laurie Auchterlonie
1903	*Willie Anderson
1904	Willie Anderson
1905	Willie Anderson
1906	Alex Smith
1907	Alex Ross
1908	*Fred McLeod
1909	George Sargent
1910	*Alex Smith
1911	*John McDermott
1912	John McDermott
1913	*Francis Ouimet
1914	Walter Hagen
1915	Jerome Travers
1916	Charles Evans, Jr
1917-18	No Championships
1919	*Walter Hagen
1920	Edward Ray
1921	James M. Barnes
1922	Gene Sarazen
1923	*Robert T. Jones, Jr
1924	Cyril Walker
1925	*W. MacFarlane
1926	Robert T. Jones, Jr
1927	*Tommy Armour

1928	*Johnny Farrell
1929	Robert T. Jones, Jr
1930	Robert T. Jones, Jr
1931	*Billy Burke
1932	Gene Sarazen
1933	Johnny Goodman
1934	Olin Dutra
1935	Sam Parks, Jr
1936	Tony Manero
1937	Ralph Guldahl
1938	Ralph Guldahl
1939	*Byron Nelson
1940	*Lawson Little
1941	Craig Wood
1942-5	No Championships
1946	*Lloyd Mangrum
1947	*Lew Worsham
1948	Ben Hogan
1949	Cary Middlecoff
1950	*Ben Hogan
1951	Ben Hogan
1952	Julius Boros
1953	Ben Hogan
1954	Ed Furgol
1955	*Jack Fleck
1956	Cary Middlecoff
1957	*Dick Mayer
1958	Tommy Bolt
1959	Billy Casper
1960	Arnold Palmer
1961	Gene Littler
1962	*Jack Nicklaus
1963	*Julius Boros
1964	Ken Venturi
1965	*Gary Player
1966	*Billy Casper
1967	Jack Nicklaus
1968	Lee Trevino
1969	Orville Moody
1970	Tony Jacklin
1971	*Lee Trevino
1972	Jack Nicklaus
1973	Johnny Miller
1974	Hale Irwin
1975	*Lou Graham
1976	Jerry Pate
1977	Hubert Green
1978	Andy North
1979	Hale Irwin
1980	Jack Nicklaus
1981	David Graham
1982	Tom Watson
1983	Larry Nelson
1984	*Fuzzy Zoeller
1985	Andy North
1986	Ray Floyd
1987	Scott Simpson
1988	*Curtis Strange

* Winner in play-off.

COMMENTARY:

Nerves of Steel

Any lingering doubts as to whether the name Curtis Strange could be mentioned in the same breath as Severiano Ballesteros and Greg Norman were emphatically dispelled on the rain-sodden fairways of Oak Hill, New York, last June.

Golfing commentators around the world – and, let's face it, the Europeans had been particularly guilty – had rather smugly proclaimed that since the decline of Tom Watson America no longer had a world-class player.

Yet no post-war European golfer has been able to win a major title back-to-back as Strange has now done, and not even Jack Nicklaus, Arnold Palmer or Watson at the height of their powers could win two US Opens in succession. This latter fact at least should put Curtis Strange's achievement into perspective.

'American players can only perform in their own back yards.' This is the other unkind jibe that has often been levelled at American players recently, yet Strange's fellow countryman Mark Calcavecchia has surely put matters right in this department; and of course many of us seem to forget, or perhaps prefer to overlook, that it is Curtis Strange who holds the course record at St Andrews.

There were two reasons behind American Ryder Cup captain Ray Floyd's decision to put Curtis Strange last out in the final day's singles at the Belfry. Firstly if, as he guessed rightly, it was going to be a close finish he wanted to have his best golfer playing the anchor role; and, secondly, Floyd knew that he could rely on Curtis Strange when the going got tough. Strange has nerves of steel. It was Floyd's best decision of the week, and although Strange hadn't played well in the earlier matches, he produced the necessary birdies when it mattered most.

At Oak Hill the pressure on Strange as defending champion must have been immense and to shoot a round of 64 while playing in the company of Ballesteros was the mark of a true champion.

In 1985 Strange had led the Masters by 4 strokes with 9 holes to play (this despite an opening 80 – after which he played the next 45 holes in 15 under par) but contrived to throw away the championship by twice hitting his ball into water. It was a different man altogether who teed up on the 16th hole in the final round at Oak Hill knowing that he needed three pars, or the equivalent, to become the first player since Ben Hogan to successfully defend his Open title. It was an almighty challenge, yet there seemed an air of inevitability as Strange played out the final scenes of the 1989 US Open. Such is the measure of the man.

THE OPEN

Seve Ballesteros at St Andrews, 1984

The Open Championship is the oldest and, at least for anyone born outside the United States, unquestionably the greatest of all golf's championships. Ironically it was an American who helped bring this situation about; Arnold Palmer's attendance (and near triumph) at the Centenary Open at St Andrews in 1960 gave the championship the uplift it then needed.

Today few people would suggest that the Open is in need of an uplift, yet there have been rumours that it might one day be brought inland, away from the traditional golfing links courses hard by the sea. How could they? It would be like playing Wimbledon on clay. And the Jack Nicklauses and Ben Crenshaws of this world would probably stop coming anyway.

The history of the Open is the history of our great links courses. We do not remember that Gene Sarazen holed in one during the 1973 Open; we remember that he holed in one at Troon's Postage Stamp.

And what Greg Norman would have given for Sarazen's ace last year!

In 1990 the Open Championship returns to St Andrews. Norman may have another chance to conquer. One thing is for sure, the winner will feel an extraordinary sense of history when he walks the 18th fairway towards the Valley of Sin, the 18th green and the Home of Golf beyond. 'My greatest experience in golf,' said Jack Nicklaus in 1978. But to hole a winning birdie putt on that final green? Words were not necessary in 1984.

THE OPEN CHAMPIONSHIP

Nick Edmund

Funny how the mind plays tricks with time. Often events of twenty, even thirty years ago can appear very recent, so fresh are they in the memory. The Open is a curious animal: it often cheats the other way. As a championship it exudes infinitely more charm and more tradition than any other, and there is a feeling that it has existed since time immemorial. The age of the Parks, the Morrises and the Straths seems to belong deep in the cobwebbed annals of history, indeed to another world.

The first Open was held in 1860, played over a twelve-hole course at Prestwick on the west coast of Scotland. It started and finished on the same day and was won by Willie Park, who defeated seven players to earn himself temporary possession of a red Moroccan leather belt and not a penny in prize money. Thirty years on and a hundred years ago the Open was still being played over the humps and hillocks of Prestwick (though it now shared the privilege with St Andrews and Musselburgh), and victory on this occasion went to the great Amateur golfer John Ball, who, to the considerable annoyance of every Scotsman, was born south of Hadrian's Wall. In last year's Open, held just a short drive away from Prestwick at Troon, American Mark Calcavecchia defeated an international field in front of a worldwide audience which ran into hundreds of millions and claimed a first-prize cheque for £80,000.

From a Scotsman called Park to an American named Calcavecchia: 130 years of Open Championship history and many, many memorable moments. It has been mentioned how the Centenary Open and Arnold Palmer's first appearance in 1960 (incidentally also the year of Calcavecchia's birth) marked something of a watershed for the championship; this is not surprising, for wherever Arnie went, the eyes of the world invariably followed. A number of the highlights from the past thirty years of the Open are recalled in various places

in this book. But what of the first hundred years? Well, now is our chance to reach back in time, to brush away the cobwebs and stir one or two golfing ghosts.

Golf's first ever hole-in-one took place at the Open in 1868. Tom Morris Junior was the player who performed the feat, and he was just seventeen years old. He went on to win the Open that year, the youngest ever Champion, and succeeded in defending the title three times in succession. His third win included an opening round of 47, a remarkable one under fours for the twelve holes and a Prestwick course record. 'Young' Tom's round was fashioned with a three at the 1st hole, which in those days measured 578 yards and was a bogey six. To him then the first ace and the first albatross? Unfortunately we'll never know how great a golfer he could have become, for Young Tom died before his twenty-fifth birthday.

The era of the great Triumvirate stretched from 1894, the year the Open was first held in England, to 1914. In that twenty-year span John H. Taylor, Harry Vardon and James Braid won sixteen championships between them. Among those who interrupted their private annual party were the Frenchman Arnaud Massy at Hoylake in 1907 (the world had to wait 72 years for the next winner from the Continent) and, in 1912, the larger-than-life, pipe-smoking, long-hitting Ted Ray.

Deal in Kent was chosen to host the first Open after the Great War in 1920. George Duncan won, playing his last 36 holes in 17 strokes fewer than his first, and somewhere at the back of the field was a brash American named Walter Hagen, competing in his first Open Championship. Like Julius Caesar, who first landed at Deal in 55 B.C., the American had expected to conquer. Hagen came and saw, but returned home with his tail firmly between his legs. No matter; two years later he returned to Kent and won the Open at Sandwich, whereupon he duly handed his entire winnings straight to his caddy.

Gene Sarazen's first appearance in the Open came as a twenty-one-year-old at Troon in 1923. He had won the US Open the previous year, but like Hagen on his first visit he failed to qualify for the final rounds. Sarazen eventually won the Open at Princes in 1932, the only time the Championship was ever staged there. In America Sarazen will be remembered most for a single stroke at Augusta, the holed 4-wood at the 15th in the 1935 Masters tournament; but our greatest memory of Sarazen will be of him at Troon – not in 1923 but fifty years later, in 1973. On this occasion the single shot was with a 5-iron. The television cameras captured the ace, and Sarazen declared that he wanted a copy of the film to take with him to heaven, so that he could show Walter Hagen what a 71-year-old could still get up to.

Another golfer likely to be interested in Sarazen's video is Bobby Jones. If Hagen was the game's Caesar, Jones was its Alexander the Great. (A good team for the Sunningdale Foursomes, don't you think?) Jones retired in 1930 at the age of twenty-eight – by which time he had already won three Opens and ten other major championships – because, it is said, 'he had no more worlds to conquer'. In 1926 Jones won his first Open at Royal Lytham. Amid the scrubland to the left of the 17th fairway a plaque commemorates the spot from which Jones played a miraculous recovery stroke to snatch the championship from a disbelieving playing partner, Al Waltrous. 'There goes a hundred thousand bucks', Waltrous is said to have uttered.

The record score for the first 36 holes in an Open was set as long ago as 1934. Henry Cotton was the man who did it, with rounds of 67 and 65, and it set up the first of his three championship wins. Cotton's 65 ranks as one of the greatest of all Open achievements; Dunlop were so impressed they named their famous golf ball after it. Cotton's victory in 1937 at Carnoustie probably gave him greater satisfaction, for practically the whole of the American Ryder Cup side were in the field; however, his finest hour arguably came

in 1948 at Muirfield, his third win, which included a second-round 66 performed in the presence of an admiring King George VI.

Sam Snead won the first post-war Open, in 1946 at St Andrews. It is rather ironic that Snead, an American through and through, should win this championship but never a US Open. With the exception of Ben Hogan's magnificent triumph at Carnoustie, there were no other American winners between Snead in 1946 and Palmer in 1961; in fact very few regularly made the trip.

The temporary absence of the Americans may have been bad news for the Open but it was good news for the Australian Peter Thomson and the South African Bobby Locke, who shared eight of the ten Opens between 1949 and 1958. If their competition wasn't as strong as it perhaps might have been, Thomson and Locke were great champions nonetheless, and proved it far beyond the British Isles.

Just one more Open Champion to mention before Palmer's arrival at St Andrews: Gary Player, winner at Muirfield in 1959. As Palmer would often discover, to his cost, golf has never produced a greater competitor than Player. None of the South African's three Open wins was at St Andrews, but when the game's greatest championship begins on the Old Course in July of this year, Player will be trying as hard if not harder than anyone else in the field. Of course nobody seriously believes that a fifty-four-year-old could win the Open. Apart from Gary Player, that is.

THE 1989 OPEN CHAMPIONSHIP

On Thursday morning they were offering odds of 5–2 against an American winning the 1989 Open Championship. On Saturday evening, after three days of warm sunshine and interesting, if not exactly electrifying, golf, the leader board was saying two things: firstly that in all probability it was going to be a close finish and secondly that American golfers were occupying eight of the top eleven positions. Apart from Olazabal and Feherty, the opera-loving Ulsterman, the much vaunted European challenge was proving about as threatening as the weather.

Forty-one players broke par on the first day of the championship, a record for the Open, and a reflection of the mild conditions that prevailed throughout the week. In 1988 Severiano Ballesteros held a two-shot lead after the first day's play. In 1989 the name at the top of the pile was one Wayne Stephens. Talk about chalk and cheese. Since turning professional, Channel Islander Stephens, still only 28, had visited the European Tour Qualifying School seven times. The name Stephens, however, stayed near the top of the leader board throughout the second day, but by the close of play another Wayne had taken over poll position: Australian Wayne Grady, who a month earlier had captured his first victory on the US Tour. A good player, Grady, but not many of us could picture his name being engraved on the trophy immediately following those of Lyle, Norman, Faldo and Ballesteros. The best score on the Friday was a record – equalling 65 by Payne Stewart, which gave him a two-round total of 137 and second place with Tom Watson, two behind Grady.

The third day was much like the second, with Grady (69), Watson (68) and Stewart (69) retaining their leading positions. The big Cs, Couples and Calcavecchia, two of America's longest hitters, both had 68s, and together with Feherty they occupied fourth place. Greg Norman had looked dangerous

Tom Watson still dreams of a sixth Open title

after collecting three early birdies but slipped to a back nine of 38 and finished seven behind Grady.

That Saturday evening in Troon it wouldn't have been possible to find anyone offering as much as 5–2 against Watson. Tom is one of Troon's favourite sons, having won his fourth championship here in 1982. But the omens didn't point to a sixth Watson win. The last time he had played in the final two-ball of the championship was in 1984 at St Andrews, and Watson has never been the same man since. That day too he was paired with an Australian whom few fancied to win.

By the time Watson and Grady teed off, Greg Norman had already scored six birdies, but nobody else, it seemed, was making any real progress. The two leaders started well enough, Grady with three birdies in the first six holes and Watson with two, but after that they could only manage a couple more

53

Norman – 'as he rose like a rocket, he fell like a stick'

'The world is my oyster' – Calcavecchia on the 18th

between them. 'The desire is still there but my game has been like having a tool box with only a hammer and a screwdriver in it,' said Watson. Four birdies by Calcavecchia on the back nine were the spanners in the works and Watson finished two adrift. Calcavecchia's final-hole birdie caught Norman, who had finished 13 under after a brilliant 64. Coming to the 17th, Grady knew that he could still be champion if only he could par the last two holes. If only.

The first three-man, four-hole play-off was over Troon's 1st, 2nd, 17th and 18th holes, and Norman began where he had left off, birdieing both the 1st and 2nd (11 birdies now

in 20 holes). Calcavecchia matched Norman's 3 at the 2nd, but Grady could 'only' play par golf. Then Norman dropped a shot at the 17th, despite hitting what Calcavecchia described as 'the best-looking 3-iron I ever saw'.

Like the 18th at Augusta earlier in the year, Norman will wish to forget the final hole at Troon, but Calcavecchia will never want to forget it, and he will surely never hit a finer shot than his 5-iron out of the rough that finished six feet from the pin.

Palmer, Weiskopf, Watson and now Calcavecchia. Once again the Gods of Troon had smiled on an American.

THE 1989 OPEN
FINAL SCORES

Mark Calcavecchia, the '89 Open Champion

*M. Calcavecchia	71	68	68	68	275	£80,000
G. Norman	69	70	72	64	275	55,000
W. Grady	68	67	69	71	275	55,000
T. Watson	69	68	68	72	277	40,000
J. Mudd	73	67	68	70	278	30,000
D. Feherty	71	67	69	72	279	26,000
F. Couples	68	71	68	72	279	26,000
E. Romero	68	70	75	67	280	21,000
P. Azinger	68	73	67	72	280	21,000
P. Stewart	72	65	69	74	280	21,000
M. McNulty	75	70	70	66	281	17,000
N. Faldo	71	71	70	69	281	17,000
H. Clark	72	68	72	70	282	13,000
P. Walton	69	74	69	70	282	13,000
C. Stadler	73	69	69	71	282	13,000
R. Chapman	76	68	67	71	282	13,000
M. James	69	70	71	72	282	13,000
S. Pate	69	70	70	73	282	13,000
D. Cooper	69	70	76	68	283	8,575
D. Pooley	73	70	69	71	283	8,575
T. Kite	70	74	67	72	283	8,575
L. Mize	71	74	66	72	283	8,575
D. Love III	72	70	73	69	284	6,733
V. Singh	71	73	73	69	284	6,733
J.M. Olazabal	68	72	69	75	284	6,733

* Winner in play-off.

THE OPEN
PAST WINNERS

1860	Willie Park
1861	Tom Morris, Sr
1862	Tom Morris, Sr
1863	Willie Park
1864	Tom Morris, Sr
1865	Andrew Strath
1866	Willie Park
1867	Tom Morris, Sr
1868	Tom Morris, Jr
1869	Tom Morris, Jr
1870	Tom Morris, Jr
1871	No Championship Played
1872	Tom Morris, Jr
1873	Tom Kidd
1874	Mungo Park
1875	Willie Park
1876	Bob Martin
1877	Jamie Anderson
1878	Jamie Anderson
1879	Jamie Anderson
1880	Robert Ferguson
1881	Robert Ferguson
1882	Robert Ferguson
1883	*Willie Fernie
1884	Jack Simpson
1885	Bob Martin
1886	David Brown
1887	Willie Park, Jr
1888	Jack Burns
1889	*Willie Park, Jr
1890	John Ball
1891	Hugh Kirkaldy
1892	Harold H. Hilton
1893	William Auchterlonie
1894	John H. Taylor
1895	John H. Taylor
1896	*Harry Vardon
1897	Harold H. Hilton
1898	Harry Vardon
1899	Harry Vardon
1900	John H. Taylor
1901	James Braid
1902	Alexander Herd
1903	Harry Vardon
1904	Jack White
1905	James Braid
1906	James Braid
1907	Arnaud Massy
1908	James Braid
1909	John H. Taylor

1910	James Braid	1970	*Jack Nicklaus
1911	Harry Vardon	1971	Lee Trevino
1912	Edward Ray	1972	Lee Trevino
1913	John H. Taylor	1973	Tom Weiskopf
1914	Harry Vardon	1974	Gary Player
1915-19	No Championships Played	1975	*Tom Watson
1920	George Duncan	1976	Johnny Miller
1921	*Jock Hutchison	1977	Tom Watson
1922	Walter Hagen	1978	Jack Nicklaus
1923	Arthur G. Havers	1979	Seve Ballesteros
1924	Walter Hagen	1980	Tom Watson
1925	James M. Barnes	1981	Bill Rogers
1926	Robert T. Jones, Jr	1982	Tom Watson
1927	Robert T. Jones, Jr	1983	Tom Watson
1928	Walter Hagen	1984	Seve Ballesteros
1929	Walter Hagen	1985	Sandy Lyle
1930	Robert T. Jones, Jr	1986	Greg Norman
1931	Tommy D. Armour	1987	Nick Faldo
1932	Gene Sarazen	1988	Seve Ballesteros
1933	*Denny Shute		
1934	Henry Cotton		

* Winner in play-off.

1935	Alfred Perry
1936	Alfred Padgham
1937	Henry Cotton
1938	R.A. Whitcombe
1939	Richard Burton
1940-45	No Championships Played
1946	Sam Snead
1947	Fred Daly
1948	Henry Cotton
1949	*Bobby Locke
1950	Bobby Locke
1951	Max Faulkner
1952	Bobby Locke
1953	Ben Hogan
1954	Peter Thomson
1955	Peter Thomson
1956	Peter Thomson
1957	Bobby Locke
1958	*Peter Thomson
1959	Gary Player
1960	Kel Nagle
1961	Arnold Palmer
1962	Arnold Palmer
1963	*Bob Charles
1964	Tony Lema
1965	Peter Thomson
1966	Jack Nicklaus
1967	Roberto DeVicenzo
1968	Gary Player
1969	Tony Jacklin

Sandy Lyle, Champion in '85

COMMENTARY:

In the Name of Destiny

'Destino'. Severiano Ballesteros, in his formative years, used to talk a great deal about destiny. He believed he was destined to win the Open Championship in 1979 – how else could a young man spend his afternoon in the car parking lot and still become Open Champion? He believed he was destined to become the youngest ever winner of the US Masters the following April at Augusta – even when he saw his 10-shot lead whittled down to only 2 strokes during the final 9 holes.

Greg Norman has never wanted to believe in destiny and yet it would seem that he more than any other golfer has called heads when it has been tails; in major championships he has been dealt more cruel cards than any other golfer. Surely Mark Calcavecchia was destined to win the 118th Open Championship? Having played 3 strokes to reach the 11th green he stood over a 40-foot putt believing that he was well and truly out of contention. 'I'll give it a go,' he thought. 'You never know.'

At that instant Greg Norman, accompanied by a massive gallery, was striding triumphantly down the final fairways nearing the end of his magnificent round. He had birdied the 1st, 2nd, 3rd, 4th, 5th, 6th, 11th, 12th and 16th holes, and the eyes of the golfing world were upon him, transfixed.

Mark Calcavecchia holed that 40-foot putt on the 11th green, and then from deep, tangling rough chipped straight into the hole from fully 30 yards at the 12th for a birdie 3. That putt and that outrageous chip altered the course of the Open Championship and determined that the famous claret jug would be heading across the Atlantic for the first time in six years.

As sorry as we might feel for Greg Norman and his fellow countryman Wayne Grady, who played the championship of his life, let us not belittle Mark Calcavecchia's achievement. For it takes great skill and courage as well as luck to win an Open Championship and it was he, not Greg Norman, who recorded most birdies that week at Troon (23). Calcavecchia also became the first American golfer since Bill Rogers in 1981 to hold both the British and Australian Open Championships at the same time. He plays an aggressive, exciting game, a type of golf not too dissimilar from Norman's. He tees the ball up and he lets rip – or, as one commentator put it, 'he tries to knock the socks off the ball.' More often than not he succeeds. If anybody seems destined to be a major force in the world of golf during the nineties, it is Calcavecchia.

And what of the Great White Shark? Maybe Greg Norman's luck will do an about-turn in the new decade: perhaps he will start holing outrageous pitch shots from improbable positions? The 1990 Open Championship at St Andrews would seem as good a place as any to start. You never know.

THE USPGA

Just as April leads us to Augusta and the US Masters tournament, so the month of August traditionally guides us to the season's final major championship, the USPGA ... to the least revered of the Big Four? This, it would seem, is the general consensus, although Americans Bob Tway and Payne Stewart would probably post dissenting opinions, and the view is unlikely to be of any consolation to the likes of Greg Norman and Mike Reid.

John Hopkins, golf correspondent of the *Sunday Times*, has his own theories as to how this situation came about. In his article he introduces us to the legendary Walter Hagen, 'Sir Walter', as he was affectionately known, golf's greatest showman, who dominated the USPGA during the 1920s when the championship was a match-play event.

The charismatic Hagen was the swashbuckling, cavalier golfer of his day. Since the PGA became a stroke-play tournament some thirty years ago, two players have been similarly described – Arnold Palmer and Severiano Ballesteros. Neither (at least, in Seve's case, to this date) has won the PGA Championship. 'Ah,' you say, 'but if it were head-to-head match-play . . .'

Bob Tway holes a bunker shot to win the '86 PGA Championship

THE USPGA

John Hopkins, *Sunday Times*

The championship of the American Professional Golfers' Association (the USPGA) is the least known, least regarded and least important of the four major championships that make up the modern 'grand slam'. Less famous than the US Masters, less prestigious than the US Open, less historic than the Open, it is nevertheless a championship of merit, and all the leading players want to add it to their haul of titles.

Why is the USPGA regarded as the runt of the litter? Speaking personally, I blame Ben Hogan.

In 1953 Hogan won the US Masters, the US Open at Oakmont and the Open at Carnoustie and thereby made history, because no one had won these three titles in one year. He had the chance to set a record that might never be broken. If he had gone on and won the USPGA Championship as well, he would have won the modern slam, the contemporary equivalent of Bobby Jones's fantastic sweep of the Opens and Amateur Championships of the US and Britain in 1930.

In 1953 the USPGA was held at Oakland Hills, outside Detroit, Michigan. It ought to have appealed to Hogan, for it was where he had won the 1951 US Open with what he later described as the best round of his life, a 67.

At this time the USPGA was decided not by stroke-play but by match-play, a form of golf that Hogan never really liked; moreover he believed that his legs hadn't fully recovered from the effects of a serious car accident a few years earlier and weren't strong enough to carry him around Oakland Hills for 36 holes each day. Any remaining enthusiasm Hogan might have had for this event disappeared when he discovered that it clashed with the Open at Carnoustie. So he gave the USPGA a miss and thereby stunted the growth of a major championship that had been in existence since the First World War.

In the early fifties American television looked at the USPGA with a view to transmitting it but decided its format made it too risky. Too many big names could be knocked out too soon; too many matches could finish out of range of the cameras. In 1958 the USPGA became a stroke-play event. At that moment, the officials of the USPGA forfeited the one characteristic that singled out their championship from every other.

Still, it remains the fourth major championship of the year and victory in it is much sought after. Majors are what matter most to the game's leading players, because they know it is by them that they will be judged. And this is where the USPGA, faults and all, has the advantage over all but the three other major championships.

No matter how much the Players Championship wants to become the game's fifth major championship, it cannot happen overnight. Tradition determines the differences between a major championship and other events. Tradition can't be bought, like a sack of potatoes. It grows. The USPGA has it; the Players' Championship does not. 'What's the difference between the British Open and the Players Championship?' Sandy Lyle was asked after winning the latter in 1987. 'About 120 years,' replied Lyle.

If you can tell the merit of a golfer by the quality of the courses on which he has won championships, then you can tell the worth of a championship by its winners. There are few weaknesses about the USPGA in this respect. Just about every great American player has won since the championship began in 1916.

Hogan, Gene Sarazen, Byron Nelson, Sam Snead, Tommy Armour, Jack Nicklaus, Lee Trevino. If you want exceptions to prove the general rule, then take Arnold Palmer, who went close in 1960, and Tom Watson, who lost a play-off in 1978.

At the time when the greatest name in golf was Walter Hagen, he won the USPGA so often he set a new standard. Frank Hannigan, a past executive director of the United States Golf Association, and a keen golf historian, makes an interesting claim on behalf of 'Sir Walter': 'Without the Slam to consider, of course, the story of American golf would swerve in another direction,' he has written. 'What would now be the enduring standard of excellence? My vote goes to Walter Hagen's performance in the PGA Championship during the 1920s.' Hagen, a showman from top to toe and a master tactician, relished the cut and thrust of match-play. He was never the most elegant or accurate of players, but he was unrivalled in the gentle art of tactics. It was Hagen, remember, who used to turn up at tournaments and ask in a loud voice: 'OK, fellas, who's going to come second?'

He won the championship in 1921, did not defend it in 1922, lost it to his old rival Gene Sarazen in 1923, and then won it four years in a row, from 1924 to 1927. He became so used to winning the PGA, he once said, that he had forgotten where he had put the trophy.

In the stroke-play era no one has dominated quite like Hagen, although Nicklaus has taken as many titles, winning his five championships between 1963 and 1980. For a while Nicklaus was a factor in the 1989 championship at Kemper Lakes near Chicago. On the opening day, both he and Palmer had 68s and Watson a 67. Three men who between them had won 33 grand slam tournaments were at the head of the field. It was like watching All Our Yesterdays.

THE 1989 USPGA CHAMPIONSHIP

Arnold Palmer took 31 for his first nine holes

The 71st USPGA Championship, staged at Kemper Lakes Golf Club near Chicago, presented the last opportunity to win a major championship during the eighties. Tom Watson had already won several, but for him it meant more than most. He needs the PGA Championship to complete his set and become only the fifth golfer ever to have won all four majors; and, not to make too fine a point of it, his time is running out.

Arnold Palmer's time ran out long ago. This was his 32nd successive PGA Championship, but in true Arnie fashion he gave it all he'd got. On the first day Palmer had five birdies in a row from the 4th; he was out in 31, and but for his dropped shots at the 17th

Reid: 'The tragedy'

and 18th he would have been joint leader at the end of the opening day.

Watson finished only one stroke off that early pace, the 66s set by Mike Reid and Leonard Thompson, and he was joined by Tom Kite. Nicklaus, like Palmer, had a 68, and this score was matched by Ian Woosnam.

On Day Two Reid, known on the US Tour as 'Radar' because of his exceptional accuracy from the tee, posted a 67, and at the end of a storm-interrupted Friday, his total of 133 was good enough to lead the championship at the half-way stage by two strokes. Thompson finished on 135, as did Craig Stadler, whose 64 would prove to be the lowest round of the week. Watson was just one further back on 136, while Woosnam continued to lead the European contingent on 138. By now Reid was in the groove, and his third-round 70 put him further ahead. Watson, Thompson and Stadler all faded, and although Reid's main challengers were crowding, they were not exactly threatening. If a big name was going to win the 1989 USPGA Championship he would have to produce some fourth-day fireworks – or Reid would have to crumble. Ballesteros (who had scored a third-round 66), Strange, and Woosnam were five shots behind Reid going into the final round, and they were grouped together. Not surprisingly they took a large crowd with them.

After seven holes the 'big three' were within two shots of Reid, each having made two birdies. But only Strange could sustain his challenge, and then Reid produced two birdies of his own.

Meanwhile Payne Stewart, who had set off six behind Reid and had turned in a modest 36, suddenly found some fireworks. Dressed in the orange, blue and white of the Chicago Bears football team, he looked the part. Stewart chipped in at the 14th, almost holed his second at the 15th and then sank an 18-footer for a third birdie at 16. At the difficult 17th he managed his par, and then, after a fine 9-iron second to the 18th, sank his putt from 10 feet.

Then Reid crumbled. On the 16th tee the man who had led the tournament all week was still two shots ahead of the field, but one

Stewart: 'The triumph'

THE 1989 USPGA
FINAL SCORES

Payne Stewart, the '89 USPGA Champion

of those strokes disappeared when he found water from the tee. Still, two pars would do it. The rest, as they say, is history: from the edge of the 17th green, Reid took four more shots, including three putts from under 15 feet; he nearly birdied the 18th, but it just wasn't to be.

It wasn't to be for Reid, and it wasn't to be for Watson. Stewart won his first major, Strange and Andy Bean tied Reid for second place, while Woosnam finished a creditable joint sixth. You can be sure that two men didn't get any sleep that night.

P. Stewart	74	66	69	67	276	$200,000
A. Bean	70	67	74	66	277	83,333
C. Strange	70	68	70	69	277	83,333
M. Reid	66	67	70	74	277	83,333
D. Rummells	68	69	69	72	278	45,000
I. Woosnam	68	70	70	71	279	40,000
C. Stadler	71	64	72	73	280	36,250
S. Hoch	69	69	69	73	280	36,250
N. Faldo	70	73	69	69	281	30,000
E. Fiori	70	67	75	69	281	30,000
T. Watson	67	69	74	71	281	30,000
G. Norman	74	71	67	70	282	21,900
M. Sullivan	76	66	67	73	282	21,900
J. Gallagher, Jr	73	69	68	72	282	21,900
M. Wiebe	71	70	69	72	282	21,900
S. Ballesteros	72	70	66	74	282	21,900
B. Gardner	72	71	70	70	283	15,000
I. Aoki	72	71	65	75	283	15,000
C. Perry	67	70	70	76	283	15,000
L. Mize	73	71	68	71	283	15,000
E. McCallister	71	72	70	70	283	15,000
D. Love III	73	69	72	69	283	15,000
B. Crenshaw	68	72	72	71	283	15,000

USPGA CHAMPIONSHIP
PAST WINNERS

1916	James M. Barnes
1917-18	No championships played
1919	James M. Barnes
1920	Jock Hutchison
1921	Walter Hagen
1922	Gene Sarazen
1923	Gene Sarazen
1924	Walter Hagen
1925	Walter Hagen
1926	Walter Hagen
1927	Walter Hagen
1928	Leo Diegel
1929	Leo Diegel
1930	Tommy Armour
1931	Tom Creavy
1932	Olin Dutra
1933	Gene Sarazen
1934	Paul Runyan
1935	Johnny Revolta
1936	Denny Shute
1937	Denny Shute
1938	Paul Runyan
1939	Henry Picard
1940	Byron Nelson
1941	Vic Ghezzi
1942	Sam Snead
1943	No championship played
1944	Bob Hamilton
1945	Byron Nelson
1946	Ben Hogan
1947	Jim Ferrier
1948	Ben Hogan
1949	Sam Snead
1950	Chandler Harper
1951	Sam Snead
1952	Jim Turnesa
1953	Walter Burkemo
1954	Chick Harbert
1955	Doug Ford
1956	Jack Burke
1957	Lionel Hebert
1958	Dow Finsterwald
1959	Bob Rosburg
1960	Jay Hebert
1961	*Jerry Barber
1962	Gary Player
1963	Jack Nicklaus
1964	Bobby Nichols
1965	Dave Marr
1966	Al Geiberger

1967	*Don January
1968	Julius Boros
1969	Ray Floyd
1970	Dave Stockton
1971	Jack Nicklaus
1972	Gary Player
1973	Jack Nicklaus
1974	Lee Trevino
1975	Jack Nicklaus
1976	Dave Stockton
1977	*Lanny Wadkins
1978	*John Mahaffey
1979	*David Graham
1980	Jack Nicklaus
1981	Larry Nelson
1982	Raymond Floyd
1983	Hal Sutton
1984	Lee Trevino
1985	Hubert Green
1986	Bob Tway
1987	*Larry Nelson
1988	Jeff Sluman

* Winner in play-off.

Lee Trevino, Champion in '84

COMMENTARY:

Triumph and Tragedy

Payne Stewart, golf's own Bobby Dazzler, smiled, looked into the cameras and gave the huge trophy a giant bear hug – one of the Chicago variety. In some hidden, quiet corner of the locker room that could be neither hidden nor quiet enough sat Mike Reid, desperately wishing the world would swallow him up. The triumph and the tragedy.

For Payne Stewart, the triumph was long overdue. Inside those extraordinary outfits, which, depending on your point of view, made him look either 'sartorially elegant' or 'a prize clown', there is a supremely talented golfer. Stewart's golf swing is the best sort – simple – and somewhat similar to that of double US Open Champion Hale Irwin, although a little more relaxed. A very consistent performer on the US Tour, Stewart had hitherto had a habit of finishing second, as he indeed did in Sandy Lyle's Open. In major championships Stewart had always been thereabouts; now he is most definitely there.

Will Stewart win many more major championships? If he can accelerate through the field as he did so brilliantly at Kemper Lakes, then surely he will, for he is likely to be in similar challenging positions on several future occasions; but there remains a question-mark over his nerve when coming down the final fairway in a head-to-head situation.

Stewart's play-off record reads 0–5 and since his PGA win he has been unable to rise to the occasion – both in the Ryder Cup and in the Nabisco Championships – but at the end of last summer he probably hadn't yet come down from the clouds. Assuming that he now has, the golfing world had better watch out.

The Marquis de Sade would have felt sorry for Mike Reid. It is said that after his debacle Jack Nicklaus approached him in the locker room and told him he had never felt more sorry for a fellow professional.

In recent years Jack must have felt quite a bit for his good friend Greg Norman. But at least Norman has won a major and will, more likely than not, win a few more in his time; Reid may never come so close again. Moreover, Norman didn't lose the '89 Open, nor did he exactly throw away the PGA of '86 or the Masters of '87; rather he was denied by other players producing the shots of their lives.

Like Ed Sneed, who 'dribbled away' the Masters ten years ago, Reid's thoughts will centre solely on his own errors. And what makes Reid such a tragic figure is that it happened not once in 1989 but twice. In addition to that huge trophy that he'll be thinking should be standing on his mantelpiece, a green blazer should be hanging in his wardrobe.

3

THE WORLD OF GOLF

'Go placidly amid the heather and gorse and remember what peace there may be on the fairway'

(Golfers' Desiderata)

EUROPE
THE RYDER CUP
THE UNITED STATES
JAPAN
AUSTRALASIA
THE REST OF THE WORLD
AMATEUR GOLF
SENIOR GOLF

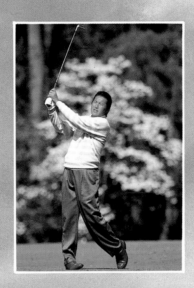

EUROPE

The Spaniard, the German and the Scottish
golf links

GOLF IN EUROPE

From early beginnings to major rumblings

Dutch golfers will occasionally try and tell you that our Royal and Ancient pastime was in fact invented in Holland during the later middle ages. Het Kolven they called it, apparently some bizarre sport more akin to modern-day ice hockey than anything else. The Scots consider this to be heresy – or at its best double-dutch gibbletruckey. Anyway it matters not: are we not all Europeans now, 'sharing one common home'?

What we would today recognize as golf certainly had its origins on the East Coast of Scotland. As early as the mid fifteenth century we know that it had so caught the people's imagination, together with medieval football, that it had begun to interfere with the nation's archery practice. In a bold attempt to try and prevent losing further battles to the Sassenachs, the Scottish parliament passed an act stating that 'the fute-ball and golf be utterly cryit down and nocht usit'. (Incidentally the Spanish word for crossbowmen is 'ballesteros'.)

While the game prospered in Scotland, and then spread into England (James I and his courtiers are said to have first thrashed a ball across London's Blackheath common in 1608), it appears that the game somehow lost its way in Europe and never really took a hold . . . until the last few years, that is. A dozen or so years ago, in most parts of Europe anyhow, a man spotted carrying a set of golf clubs was looked upon only a little less suspiciously than a man spotted carrying a set of golf clubs was looked upon only a little less suspiciously than a man with three heads. What a difference as we enter the 1990s! Golf is fast becoming 'the European game'. In some countries it is still a rich person's game, but that is changing, and golf courses are rapidly being constructed in every foreign field. In fact the biggest worry is that they cannot be built fast enough.

Without doubt some of the finest courses in the world are being built in France, a nation which already boasts the finest lady golfer in Europe. There again, more people are visiting Spanish courses, and few would disagree that Spain has produced the world's leading player of the eighties and that in Ballesteros and Olazabal it has golf's king and crown prince. As for Germany, it has already produced a Masters champion, Bernhard Langer, while several Swedish players have been knocking at the door of Ryder Cup selection for some years. Not that we in Britain and Ireland are doing too badly either!

The fact is, the health of the game has never been better across the whole of Europe. The European tours get longer and stronger each year; some three-quarters of professional events are now staged on the Continent and geographically the tours extend from Scandinavia to northern Africa. What with the Ryder, Walker and Curtis Cups all residing in Europe, and a flourishing professional and amateur scene, what is there left to conquer? Silly question to put on paper at a time when the Berlin Wall has just begun tumbling down.

THE 1989 EUROPEAN SEASON

It was not all that many years ago that professional golf in Europe did not get under way until the Masters tournament at Augusta had been and gone. Nowadays, thanks to the great and continuing successes of the PGA European Tour, the European season tees off in February; and by the time the Masters had been played last year Mark James had already twice mounted the winners' rostrum.

James went on to achieve a third success on the tour, winning the English Open at the Belfry, but 1989 was to be Rafferty's year. Like James he won three times, including the climactic curtain closer, the Volvo Masters at Valderrama, where he edged out Faldo, and more importantly Olazabal, to secure the Volvo Order of Merit crown. In the space of a few weeks Rafferty defeated Tom Kite, the US leading money winner, Curtis Strange, double US Open Champion, Sandy Lyle, former Masters and Open champion, and Mark Calcavecchia, the current Open champion, all in head-to-head confrontations.

The latter win took place during the Ryder Cup in September, where the general consensus was that a tie was the fairest result, especially after a final day of unparalleled golfing drama. Faldo's uncharacteristic 'splash down' at the 18th (one of five that day) when he had a chance to win the cup outright was just about the only low point in his extraordinary year. He followed his glorious win at Augusta with three wins on the regular tour and then claimed his first World Matchplay Championship after a titanic battle with his Ryder Cup partner, Ian Woosnam.

Although the Ryder Cup stayed in Europe, 1989 saw the departure across the Atlantic of both the Open Championship and the Dunhill Cup. A year ago who would have thought that a Nebraskan, Mark Calcavecchia, would have his hand on both trophies?

Ronan Rafferty, Europe's leading money winner in 1989

What of 1988's Champion Golfer? The fact that Ballesteros took three European titles yet still had a disappointing year says just about everything for his current standing in the game. Seve's great European rival, Bernhard Langer, proved once again that there can be life after the yips, winning both in Spain and in his native Germany, while the most popular victory of the year was undoubtedly Andrew Murray's remarkable triumph over spondylitis in the European Open. Cheers of joy at the Belfry, tears of joy at Walton Heath. 1989 will be a difficult act to follow.

23-26 February
TENERIFE OPEN *Golf del Sur, Tenerife*

Jose Maria Olazabal	69	68	68	70	275	£33,330
David Gilford	72	70	69	67	278	17,360
Jose Maria Canizares	70	66	70	72	278	17,360
Michael King	74	70	69	67	280	7,867
Philip Walton	70	70	68	72	280	7,867
Juan Quiros	70	73	69	68	280	7,867
Johan Rystrom	72	72	68	68	280	7,867
Jose Rivero	70	72	68	71	281	4,290
Mark Roe	68	69	69	75	281	4,290
Des Smyth	66	75	68	72	281	4,290
Roger Chapman	74	70	67	70	281	4,290

9-12 March
Renault OPEN DE BALEARES *Santa Ponsa, Majorca*

Ove Sellberg	68	71	69	71	279	£37,500
Mark McNulty	69	70	71	71	281	16,773
Jose Maria Olazabal	71	75	68	67	281	16,773
Philip Parkin	71	71	69	70	281	16,773
Denis Durnian	71	72	69	70	282	6,523
Jamie Howell	68	74	70	70	282	6,523
Bill Malley	69	70	70	73	282	6,523
Brett Ogle	70	70	71	71	282	6,523
Juan Quiros	71	70	71	70	282	6,523
Ronan Rafferty	72	69	69	72	282	6,523

16-19 March
Massimo Dutti CATALAN OPEN *Club de Pals, Barcelona*

Mark Roe	69	70	69	71	279	£33,330
Gordon Brand, Jnr	73	67	70	70	280	14,906
Colin Montgomerie	73	68	72	67	280	14,906
Jose Maria Olazabal	70	71	68	71	280	14,906
Denis Durnian	73	68	71	69	281	8,470
Howard Clark	72	68	70	72	282	6,000
Peter O'Malley	72	69	69	72	282	6,000
Grant Turner	73	66	70	73	282	6,000

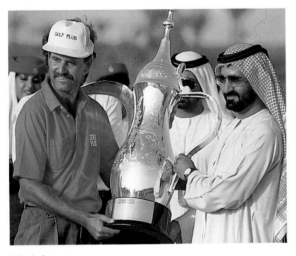

Mark James

2-5 March
Karl Litten DESERT CLASSIC *Dubai, UAE*

*Mark James	69	68	72	68	277	£41,660
Peter O'Malley	71	68	68	70	277	27,760
Paul Broadhurst	72	66	70	72	280	15,650
Brett Ogle	77	69	67	69	282	12,500
Magnus Persson	67	72	72	72	283	10,600
Emmanuel Dussart	71	71	72	70	284	6,620
Barry Lane	71	73	73	67	284	6,620
Mike Miller	72	74	67	71	284	6,620
Jim Rutledge	73	70	70	71	284	6,620
Sam Torrance	70	71	71	72	284	6,620

24-27 March
AGF OPEN *La Grande Motte, France*

Mark James	69	67	69	72	277	£22,909
Mark Mouland	72	73	70	65	280	15,266
Bryan Norton	70	70	70	71	281	8,604
Vijay Singh	73	68	73	68	282	5,408
Ronald Stelten	65	68	72	77	282	5,408
Sam Torrance	68	67	73	74	282	5,408
Grant Turner	73	73	65	71	282	5,408
Jamie Howell	70	75	70	68	283	3,257
Andrew Sherborne	72	70	70	71	283	3,257

* Winner in play-off.

1989 VOLVO TOUR RESULTS

Vijay Singh

European Airways JERSEY OPEN *La Moye, Jersey*

*Christy O'Connor, Jnr	73	70	66	72	281	£24,490
Denis Durnian	70	71	67	73	281	16,315
Mats Lanner	71	69	70	72	282	8,275
Paul Broadhurst	73	69	71	69	282	8,275
Des Smyth	74	69	71	69	283	4,552
Colin Montgomerie	69	75	68	71	283	4,552
Bernard Gallacher	71	70	70	72	283	4,552
Sam Torrance	72	70	69	72	283	4,552
Ronan Rafferty	74	69	68	72	283	4,552

* Winner in play-off.

13-16 April
Credit Lyonnais CANNES OPEN *Mougins, France*

Paul Broadhurst	65	70	72	207	£34,851
Jimmy Heggarty	69	72	67	208	15,588
Brett Ogle	71	68	69	208	15,588
Peter Senior	70	66	72	208	15,588
Ronan Rafferty	72	67	70	209	8,829
Jean Van De Velde	71	69	70	210	5,845
Tony Charnley	71	68	71	210	5,845
Mark McNulty	71	70	69	210	5,845
Derrick Cooper	73	64	73	210	5,845

20-23 April
Cepsa MADRID OPEN *Puerta de Hierro, Madrid*

Severiano Ballesteros	67	67	69	69	272	£37,500
Howard Clark	65	68	70	70	273	25,000
Philip Walton	70	67	70	68	275	14,070
Mats Lanner	70	70	68	68	276	11,250
Derrick Cooper	67	72	67	71	277	9,500
Tony Charnley	70	69	70	69	278	7,850
Rodger Davis	69	72	70	68	279	6,150
Magnus Persson	64	70	75	70	279	6,150

30 March-2 April
VOLVO OPEN *Is Molas, Sardinia*

Vijay Singh	72	68	68	68	276	£33,330
Peter Fowler	71	69	71	68	279	22,200
Gordon J. Brand	69	72	70	72	283	11,260
Bill Longmuir	71	69	72	71	283	11,260
Charles Bolling, Jnr	68	72	71	73	284	7,735
Christy O'Connor, Jnr	70	72	69	73	284	7,735
Massimo Mannelli	73	72	71	69	285	4,870
Peter O'Malley	72	70	68	75	285	4,870
Ronan Rafferty	72	68	71	74	285	4,870
David Williams	73	72	72	68	285	4,870

27-30 April
Peugeot SPANISH OPEN *El Saler, Valencia*

Bernhard Langer	70	72	67	72	281	£41,660
Jose Maria Canizares	72	72	70	70	284	21,705
Paul Carrigill	70	69	72	73	284	21,705
Jose Maria Olazabal	70	72	70	73	285	12,500
Mats Lanner	71	72	71	72	286	10,600
Gordon Brand, Jnr	71	73	69	74	287	8,125
Barry Lane	72	69	75	71	287	8,125
David Feherty	70	70	74	74	288	6,250

1989 VOLVO TOUR RESULTS

Seve Ballesteros

4-7 May
Epson GRAND PRIX *St Pierre G & CC, Chepstow*

QUARTER FINALS
Severiano Ballesteros (Sp) beat Mark
   Mouland (Wal)   2 holes
Mike Harwood (Aus) beat Ian Woosnam
   (Wal)   1 hole
Des Smyth (Ire) beat Jose Maria Olazabal
   (Sp)   1 hole
Denis Durnian (Eng) beat Ken Brown (Scot) 3 & 2
      All Quarter Final Losers won £9,900

SEMI FINALS
Severiano Ballesteros (Sp) beat Mike
   Harwood (Aus)   6 & 5
Denis Durnian (Eng) beat Des Smyth (Ire)   4 & 3

3RD & 4TH PLACE PLAY-OFF
Des Smyth (Ire) beat Mike Harwood (Aus)   1 hole
(£18,370)   (£14,750)

FINAL
Severiano Ballesteros (Sp) beat Denis
            Durnian (Eng)   4 & 3
(£50,000)   (£32,000)

11-14 May
Volvo BELGIAN OPEN *Royal Waterloo, Brussels*

Gordon J. Brand	67	69	68	69	273	£33,330
Kevin Dickens	70	67	67	73	277	22,200
Mark Davis	68	73	70	67	278	12,520
Jesper Parnevik	74	70	67	68	279	10,000
Richard Boxall	69	70	66	75	280	6,190
Marc Farry	69	69	71	71	280	6,190
Ronan Rafferty	70	73	67	70	280	6,190
Malcolm Mackenzie	70	72	71	67	280	6,190
Derrick Cooper	71	71	71	67	280	6,190

18-21 May
Lancia ITALIAN OPEN *Monticello, Italy*

Ronan Rafferty	71	69	68	65	273	£42,589
Sam Torrance	69	70	65	70	274	28,371
Magnus Persson	66	72	69	68	275	15,995
Robert Lee	66	73	69	69	277	12,772
Paul Carman	70	69	67	72	278	9,885
Andrew Sherborne	72	70	65	71	278	9,885
David Feherty	65	72	69	73	279	5,915
Severiano Ballesteros	71	69	68	71	279	5,915
Luis Carbonetti	76	68	67	68	279	5,915
Frank Nobilo	71	70	71	67	279	5,915
Neil Hansen	71	72	71	65	279	5,915

26-29 May
Volvo PGA CHAMPIONSHIP *Wentworth*

Nick Faldo	67	69	69	67	272	£58,330
Ian Woosnam	67	72	68	67	274	38,860
Craig Parry	68	68	69	71	276	21,910
Severiano Ballesteros	73	74	65	66	278	14,860
Mark McNulty	70	69	69	70	278	14,860
Christy O'Connor, Jnr	71	68	74	65	278	14,860
Denis Durnian	73	68	69	69	279	10,500
Vijay Singh	71	70	71	68	280	7,863
Mark James	71	75	68	66	280	7,863
Gordon J. Brand	74	72	65	69	280	7,863
Jeff Hawkes	75	70	66	70	281	5,860
Jose Maria Olazabal	72	74	69	66	281	5,860
Gavin Levenson	70	69	69	73	281	5,860
Neil Hansen	69	70	72	70	281	5,860
Ronan Rafferty	72	69	71	70	282	5,140

1989 VOLVO TOUR RESULTS

Nick Faldo

1-4 June
Dunhill BRITISH MASTERS *Woburn*

Nick Faldo	71	65	65	66	267	£50,000
Ronan Rafferty	70	65	67	69	271	33,300
Christy O'Connor, Jnr	69	66	73	68	276	15,493
Ove Sellberg	71	66	70	69	276	15,493
Mike Harwood	69	70	66	71	276	15,493
Ian Woosnam	71	70	70	66	277	9,000
Rick Hartmann	70	69	71	67	277	9,000
Mike Smith	71	69	66	71	277	9,000

8-11 June
Wang FOUR STARS NATIONAL PRO-CELEBRITY *Moor Park*

*Craig Parry	67	71	66	69	273	£32,000
Ian Woosnam	67	72	68	66	273	21,900
David Gilford	71	69	65	69	274	11,150
Mike Harwood	66	72	67	69	274	11,150
Barry Lane	72	68	68	68	276	7,650
Gordon Brand, Jnr	72	67	72	65	276	7,650
Jerry Anderson	70	69	69	69	277	5,800
Brian Marchbank	73	69	67	69	278	3,818
Peter Senior	72	67	68	71	278	3,818
Bob Shearer	69	72	65	72	278	3,818
Jeff Hawkes	71	70	66	71	278	3,818
Ross McFarlane	68	74	67	69	278	3,818

* Winner in play-off.

15-18 June
NM ENGLISH OPEN *The Belfry*

Mark James	72	70	69	68	279	£41,660
Eamonn Darcy	70	71	67	72	280	18,636
Craig Parry	66	74	73	67	280	18,636
Sam Torrance	66	73	70	71	280	18,636
Bryan Norton	74	70	67	71	282	9,675
John Bland	69	70	70	73	282	9,675
Martin Poxon	69	72	69	73	283	6,450
Peter Teravainen	71	75	69	68	283	6,450
Christy O'Connor, Jnr	71	73	68	71	283	6,450

22-25 June
Carrolls IRISH OPEN *Portmarnock*

*Ian Woosnam	70	67	71	70	278	£43,782
Philip Walton	68	69	69	72	278	29,159
Brett Ogle	69	69	74	70	282	13,566
Ronan Rafferty	67	71	72	72	282	13,566
Mark McNulty	71	67	71	73	282	13,566
Sam Torrance	71	70	72	70	283	7,381
Jose Maria Olazabal	69	70	73	71	283	7,381
Mark Davis	73	71	66	73	283	7,381
Peter McWhinney	70	68	73	72	283	7,381

* Winner in play-off.

29 June-2 July
Peugeot FRENCH OPEN *Chantilly, Paris*

Nick Faldo	70	70	64	69	273	£52,233
Hugh Baiocchi	69	67	68	70	274	23,359
Mark Roe	69	68	67	70	274	23,359
Bernhard Langer	70	67	71	66	274	23,359
Mark James	70	70	66	69	275	10,368
Ian Woosnam	67	70	69	69	275	10,368
Mike Harwood	68	68	69	70	275	10,368
Philip Parkin	71	68	72	64	275	10,368

1989 VOLVO TOUR RESULTS

5-8 July
Torras MONTE CARLO OPEN *Mont Agel, Monte Carlo*

Mark McNulty	68	64	64	65	261	£48,285
Jeff Hawkes	64	72	67	64	267	25,147
Jose Maria Canizares	68	66	65	68	267	25,147
Peter Senior	66	66	67	69	268	14,485
Robert Lee	68	70	69	64	271	11,202
Peter Mitchell	65	68	67	71	271	11,202
Peter Fowler	66	72	70	64	272	7,967
Luis Carbonetti	68	66	71	67	272	7,967

12-15 July
Bell's SCOTTISH OPEN *Gleneagles*

Michael Allen	73	66	70	63	272	£50,000
Jose Maria Olazabal	67	70	68	69	274	26,040
Ian Woosnam	65	70	71	68	274	26,040
Ronan Rafferty	69	67	70	70	276	13,850
David Feherty	71	67	69	69	276	13,850
Mark McNulty	69	71	67	70	277	9,750
Eduardo Romero	72	66	70	69	277	9,750
Roger Chapman	69	70	70	69	278	7,110
Larry Rinker	73	66	68	71	278	7,110

20-23 July
OPEN CHAMPIONSHIP *Royal Troon*

See pp. 50-57.

27-30 July
KLM DUTCH OPEN *Kennemer*

*Jose Maria Olazabal	67	66	68	76	277	£45,830
Roger Chapman	70	67	71	69	277	23,875
Ronan Rafferty	72	66	66	73	277	23,875
Jesper Parnevik	69	67	72	70	278	13,750
Gordon Brand, Jnr	65	68	74	72	279	11,665
Sam Torrance	69	70	72	69	280	8,937
Craig Parry	69	65	70	76	280	8,937
Des Smyth	71	68	70	72	281	6,180
Miguel Angel Martin	68	71	71	71	281	6,180
David Feherty	72	69	68	72	281	6,180

* Winner in play-off.

Michael Allen

27-30 July
Volvo SENIORS OPEN *Turnberry*

See p. 136.

3-6 August
SCANDINAVIAN ENTERPRISE OPEN *Drottningholm*

Ronan Rafferty	70	69	64	65	268	£55,810
Michael Allen	67	71	67	65	270	37,180
Peter Senior	64	70	73	67	274	20,970
Gordon Brand, Jnr	70	70	66	69	275	15,475
Vijay Singh	69	70	67	69	275	15,475
Brett Ogle	68	70	70	68	276	10,887
Derrick Cooper	70	70	69	67	276	10,887
David Whelan	68	73	72	64	277	7,526
Mark Mouland	70	71	67	69	277	7,526
Jerry Haas	71	68	68	70	277	7,526

1989 VOLVO TOUR RESULTS

Gordon Brand Jnr

10-13 August
BENSON AND HEDGES INTERNATIONAL *Fulford, York*

Gordon Brand, Jnr	64	72	72	64	272	£50,000
Derrick Cooper	67	66	68	72	273	33,300
Malcolm Mackenzie	66	68	71	69	274	18,780
Jose Maria Canizares	65	72	70	69	276	15,000
Craig Parry	68	72	67	70	277	9,925
Howard Clark	69	67	69	72	277	9,925
Ian Mosey	69	67	69	72	277	9,925
John Bland	67	68	70	72	277	9,925
Peter Fowler	69	71	70	68	278	6,360
Bradley Hughes	62	71	71	74	278	6,360
Des Smyth	67	73	69	70	279	5,520
Philip Harrison	71	69	70	70	280	4,747
Jose Rivero	69	72	68	71	280	4,747
Gary Player	69	67	73	71	280	4,747
Eamonn Darcy	67	72	71	70	280	4,747

16-19 August
MURPHY'S CUP *St Pierre G&CC, Chepstow*

Hugh Baiocchi	35	40	39	42	156	£33,000
Jeff Hawkes	36	39	37	42	154	17,500
John Bland	38	37	39	40	154	17,500
Mark McNulty	38	38	37	39	152	9,200
Sandy Stephen	37	38	37	39	151	7,500
Calvin Peete	35	42	35	37	149	5,800
Carl Mason	38	38	36	37	149	5,800

17-20 August
PLM OPEN *Bokskogens, Sweden*

Mike Harwood	66	70	67	68	271	£50,000
Peter Senior	68	67	65	72	272	33,300
Sam Torrance	71	67	65	70	273	18,780
Mats Lanner	70	68	69	67	274	13,850
Bernhard Langer	68	66	69	71	274	13,850
Ronan Rafferty	69	69	66	72	276	9,750
Philip Walton	67	72	66	71	276	9,750
Ove Sellberg	69	73	65	70	277	7,110
Leif Hederstrom	71	66	70	70	277	7,110

24-27 August
GERMAN OPEN *Frankfurt*

*Craig Parry	66	70	66	64	266	£54,222
Mark James	65	66	65	70	266	36,126
Michael Allen	68	66	64	69	267	20,374
Mike Harwood	65	65	68	70	268	16,273
Jose Maria Canizares	66	72	62	69	269	10,772
Jerry Haas	66	69	64	70	269	10,772
Gordon Brand, Jnr	71	66	67	65	269	10,772
Bernhard Langer	68	69	67	65	269	10,772

* Winner in play-off.

31 August-3 September
Ebel EUROPEAN MASTERS *Crans-sur-Sierre, Switzerland*

Severiano Ballesteros	65	68	66	67	266	£69,024
Craig Parry	66	69	66	67	268	45,988
Stephen Bennett	65	67	66	71	269	25,935
Jose Rivero	66	64	67	73	270	19,141
Paolo Quirici	72	67	66	65	270	19,141
Barry Lane	67	65	67	72	271	14,500
Colin Montgomerie	68	66	67	71	272	12,429
Gavin Levenson	68	66	71	68	273	9,308
Mats Lanner	65	72	65	71	273	9,308
Jose Maria Olazabal	69	70	69	65	273	9,308

1989 VOLVO TOUR RESULTS

Andrew Murray

7-10 September
Panasonic EUROPEAN OPEN *Walton Heath*

Andrew Murray	66	68	71	72	277	£58,330
Frank Nobilo	70	69	69	70	278	38,860
Sam Torrance	70	71	69	70	280	21,910
Craig Parry	73	72	70	66	281	16,165
Ian Woosnam	71	68	70	72	281	16,165
Russell Claydon	70	68	71	74	283	11,375
Ross Drummond	70	69	71	73	283	11,375
Sandy Lyle	69	74	71	70	284	7,863
Rodger Davis	69	73	72	70	284	7,863
David Feherty	72	71	71	70	284	7,863
Mark James	70	73	75	67	285	6,230
Scott Hoch	69	69	77	70	285	6,230

14-17 September
LANCÔME TROPHY *St Nom-la-Bretèche, Versailles*

Eduardo Romero	69	65	66	66	266	£68,330
Bernhard Langer	68	68	66	65	267	35,585
Jose Maria Olazabal	67	70	65	65	267	35,585
Peter Fowler	66	64	68	70	268	20,600
David Feherty	68	69	67	65	269	17,400
Vijay Singh	70	71	66	67	274	12,320
Howard Clark	69	74	67	64	274	12,320
Craig Parry	68	69	68	69	274	12,320

22-24 September
Johnnie Walker RYDER CUP *The Belfry*

See pp. 90-97.

25-26 September
EQUITY & LAW CHALLENGE *Royal Mid-Surrey, Richmond*

Brett Ogle	25 points	£22,570
Colin Montgomerie	21 points	11,285
David Feherty	20 points	7,335
Richard Boxall	20 points	4,850
Peter Senior	19 points	3,665

27-30 September
MOTOROLA CLASSIC *Burnham and Berrow*

David Llewellyn	64	69	72	67	272	£10,500
David Williams	70	68	67	71	276	7,100
Russell Weir	70	67	71	69	277	5,100
Paul Carrigill	71	71	71	65	278	4,100
Darren Prosser	71	69	69	70	279	3,450
Ronald Stelten	70	69	72	69	280	2,700
Brian Barnes	73	66	68	73	280	2,700
Steven Richardson	71	70	69	71	281	2,100

28 September-1 October
UAP UNDER 25s EUROPEAN OPEN *Le Prieuré, Paris*

Stephen Hamill	70	73	68	71	282	£12,973
Steven Bottomley	69	73	72	69	283	8,652
Miguel Angel Jimenez	66	77	73	69	285	4,866
Andrew Cotton	74	73	72	67	286	3,892
Neal Briggs	71	73	74	70	288	3,017
Jonathan Lomas	73	75	71	69	288	3,017

1989 VOLVO TOUR RESULTS

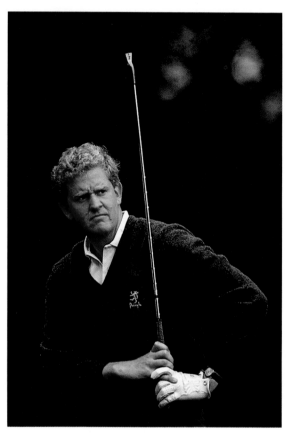

Colin Montgomerie

28 September-1 October
DUNHILL CUP *St Andrews*

See p. 79.

5-8 October
GERMAN MASTERS *Stuttgart*

Bernhard Langer	67	71	70	68	276	£55,302
Payne Stewart	69	67	70	71	277	28,813
Jose Maria Olazabal	73	66	69	69	277	28,813
Brett Ogle	73	68	71	68	280	15,336
Fred Couples	69	72	73	66	280	15,336
Derrick Cooper	70	72	71	68	281	11,618
Stephen Bennett	72	70	70	70	282	8,564
Bernard Gallacher	73	71	70	68	282	8,564
Nick Faldo	69	66	74	73	282	8,564

12-15 October
BMW INTERNATIONAL OPEN *Munich Nord*

David Feherty	62	66	68	73	269	£45,820
Fred Couples	68	69	67	70	274	30,540
Philip Walton	67	70	68	70	275	17,210
Eamonn Darcy	70	69	70	67	276	13,750
Mark Mouland	70	70	68	69	277	10,645
Mike Harwood	70	71	66	70	277	10,645
Gordon J. Brand	68	68	70	72	278	7,500
Tom Purtzer	69	69	69	71	278	7,500

12-15 October
Suntory WORLD MATCH-PLAY *Wentworth*

See p. 80.

19-22 October
PORTUGUESE OPEN TPC *Quinta do Lago*

Colin Montgomerie	67	65	69	63	264	£45,825
Mike Smith	70	69	66	70	275	20,498
Manuel Moreno	71	69	69	66	275	20,498
Rodger Davis	66	72	69	68	275	20,498
Manuel Pinero	68	70	72	66	276	10,640
Christy O'Connor, Jnr	69	68	71	68	276	10,640
Sandy Stephen	71	69	68	69	277	6,095
David Feherty	70	71	67	69	277	6,095
Gordon J. Brand	70	71	67	69	277	6,095
Peter Senior	73	65	71	68	277	6,095
Antonio Garrido	69	71	67	70	277	6,095
Peter Fowler	69	68	73	67	277	6,095

26-29 October
VOLVO MASTERS *Valderrama, Sotogrande, Spain*

Ronan Rafferty	72	69	70	71	282	£66,660
Nick Faldo	74	68	72	69	283	44,425
Jose Maria Olazabal	69	70	74	74	287	25,040
Sandy Lyle	70	76	69	74	289	20,000
Peter Fowler	75	72	69	74	290	14,316
Mark James	77	70	71	72	290	14,316
Howard Clark	73	70	74	73	290	14,316
Craig Parry	73	68	75	75	291	10,000
Vicente Fernandez	75	73	73	71	292	8,106
Eduardo Romero	73	73	74	72	292	8,106
Ove Sellberg	75	74	73	70	292	8,106

THE DUNHILL CUP

28 September – 1 October St Andrews

First round

Argentina	2½	–	½	Wales
USA	2	–	1	Korea
Sweden	2	–	1	Spain
Ireland	2	–	1	Taipei (China)
Scotland	2	–	1	New Zealand
Japan	2	–	1	Italy
France	2	–	1	Australia
England	2	–	1	Canada

Second round

Japan	3	–	1	France
USA	3	–	0	Argentina
Ireland	3	–	0	Sweden
England	2	–	1	Scotland

Semi finals

USA	*2*	–	*1*	*Ireland*
Calcavecchia	69	–	71	Walton
Kite	71	–	71	O'Connor
(Kite won play-off)				
Strange	72	–	71	Rafferty
Japan	*2*	–	*1*	*England*
N. Ozaki	70	–	72	Durnian
Suzuki	66	–	70	Clark
Meshiai	73	–	71	James

Play-off for 3rd and 4th places

England	*2*	–	*1*	*Ireland*
Durnian	72	–	71	Walton
Clark	72	–	75	Rafferty
James	69	–	76	O'Connor

FINAL

USA	*3½*	–	*2½*	*Japan*
Calcavecchia	67	–	68	Meshiai
Kite	68	–	68	N. Ozaki
Strange	72	–	75	Suzuki
Calcavecchia	66	–	68	Meshiai
Kite	74	–	71	Suzuki
Strange	71	–	69	N. Ozaki

USA receive £61,977 each; Japan receive £30,988 each

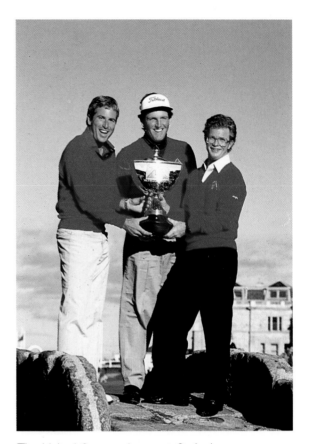

The United States, winners at St Andrews

THE SUNTORY WORLD MATCHPLAY CHAMPIONSHIP

12 – 15 October Wentworth

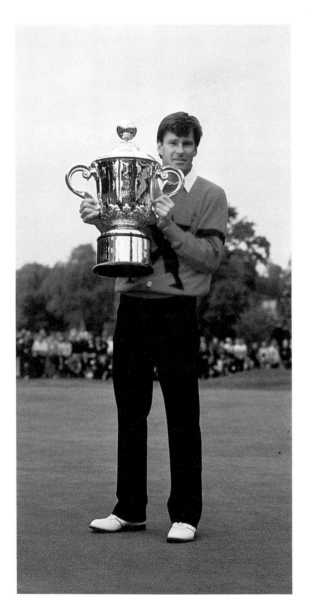

First round
R. RAFFERTY beat M. REID 3 and 2
J.-M. OLAZABAL beat S. HOCH 4 and 2
C. BECK beat A. OMACHI 8 and 6
D. FROST beat I. BAKER-FINCH 4 and 3
    First-round losers received £12,500

Second round
R. RAFFERTY beat S. LYLE 1 hole
I WOOSNAM beat J.-M. OLAZABAL 3 and 2
S. BALLESTEROS beat C. BECK 9 and 8
N. FALDO beat D. FROST at 38th
    Second-round losers received £17,500

Semi-finals
I. WOOSNAM beat R. RAFFERTY 2 and 1
N. FALDO beat S. BALLESTEROS 6 and 5

Play-off for 3rd and 4th places
S. BALLESTEROS beat R. RAFFERTY 5 and 3
    S. Ballesteros won £30,000; R. Rafferty received £20,000

FINAL
N. FALDO beat I. WOOSNAM 1 hole
    N. Faldo won £100,000; I. Woosnam received £60,000

Faldo – third British winner in succession

1989 PGA EUROPEAN TOUR WINNERS SUMMARY

February	TENERIFE OPEN	J.M. Olazabal	(Sp)
March	DESERT CLASSIC	M. James	(Eng)
	RENAULT OPEN DE BALEARES	O. Sellberg	(Sw)
	CATALAN OPEN	M. Roe	(Eng)
	AGF OPEN	M. James	(Eng)
	VOLVO OPEN	V. Singh	(Fj)
April	JERSEY OPEN	C. O'Connor	(Ire)
	CREDIT LYONNAIS CANNES OPEN	P. Broadhurst	(Eng)
	CEPSA MADRID OPEN	S. Ballesteros	(Sp)
	PEUGEOT SPANISH OPEN	B. Langer	(WG)
May	EPSON GRAND PRIX	S. Ballesteros	(Sp)
	VOLVO BELGIAN OPEN	G.J. Brand	(Eng)
	LANCIA ITALIAN OPEN	R. Rafferty	(NIre)
	VOLVO PGA CHAMPIONSHIP	N. Faldo	(Eng)
June	DUNHILL BRITISH MASTERS	N. Faldo	(Eng)
	WANG FOUR STARS PRO-CELEBRITY	C. Parry	(Aus)
	NM ENGLISH OPEN	M. James	(Eng)
	CARROLLS IRISH OPEN	I. Woosnam	(Wal)
	PEUGEOT FRENCH OPEN	N. Faldo	(Eng)
July	MONTE CARLO OPEN	M. McNulty	(Zimb)
	BELL'S SCOTTISH OPEN	M. Allen	(US)
	OPEN CHAMPIONSHIP	M. Calcavecchia	(US)
	KLM DUTCH OPEN	J.M. Olazabal	(Sp)
	*VOLVO SENIORS BRITISH OPEN	B. Charles	(NZ)
August	SCANDINAVIAN ENTERPRISE OPEN	R. Rafferty	(NIre)
	BENSON & HEDGES INTERNATIONAL	G. Brand Jnr	(Sco)
	*MURPHY'S CUP	H. Baiocchi	(SA)
	PLM OPEN	M. Harwood	(Aus)
	GERMAN OPEN	C. Parry	(Aus)
	EBEL EUROPEAN MASTERS – SWISS OPEN	S. Ballesteros	(Sp)
September	PANASONIC EUROPEAN OPEN	A. Murray	(Eng)
	LANCOME TROPHY	E. Romero	(Arg)
	*28th JOHNNIE WALKER RYDER CUP	Tied (14-14)	
	*EQUITY & LAW CHALLENGE	B. Ogle	(Aus)
	*MOTOROLA CLASSIC	D. Llewellyn	(Wal)
	*DUNHILL CUP	United States	
	*UAP UNDER 25's EUROPEAN OPEN	S. Hamill	(Ire)
October	GERMAN MASTERS	B. Langer	(WG)
	*SUNTORY WORLD MATCHPLAY	N. Faldo	(Eng)
	BMW INTERNATIONAL OPEN	D. Feherty	(NIre)
	PORTUGUESE OPEN TPC	C. Montgomerie	(Sco)
	VOLVO MASTERS	R. Rafferty	(NIre)

* PGA European Tour Approved Special Event

1989 PGA EUROPEAN TOUR

VOLVO ORDER OF MERIT: TOP 100

1	R. Rafferty (N. Ireland)	£400,311	51	C. Mason (England)	£52,904
2	J.-M. Olazabal (Spain)	336,239	52	D. Gilford (England)	52,337
3	C. Parry (Australia)	277,321	53	S. Lyle (Scotland)	49,408
4	N. Faldo (England)	251,552	54	J. Bland (SA)	44,818
5	M. James (England)	245,916	55	P. Parkin (Wales)	44,201
6	I. Woosnam (Wales)	210,100	56	P. O'Malley (Australia)	43,914
7	B. Langer (W Germany)	205,194	57	J. Hass (US)	43,841
8	S. Ballesteros (Spain)	202,762	58	P. Mitchell (England)	43,387
9	M. McNulty (Zimbabwe)	179,693	59	P. Carrigill (England)	42,588
10	D. Feherty (N Ireland)	178,167	60	V. Fernandez (Arg)	42,577
11	S. Torrance (Scotland)	170,650	61	J. van de Velde (France)	41,076
12	G. Brand Jnr (Scotland)	168,890	62	G. Turner (England)	40,757
13	E. Romero (Arg)	168,558	63	M. Poxon (England)	39,488
14	M. Harwood (Australia)	165,059	64	A. Sherbourne (England)	39,356
15	M. Allen (US)	157,644	65	H. Baiocchi (SA)	39,277
16	P. Senior (Australia)	143,954	66	L. Carbonetti (Arg)	38,624
17	P. Walton (Ireland)	135,195	67	E. Dussart (France)	38,282
18	J. M. Canizares (Spain)	133,289	68	P. Teravainen (US)	36,915
19	D. Cooper (England)	123,776	69	B. Longmuir (Scotland)	36,792
20	H. Clark (England)	123,566	70	B. Norton (US)	36,427
21	C. O'Connor Jnr (Ireland)	122,797	71	K. Brown (Scotland)	36,338
22	P. Fowler (Australia)	119,237	72	M. Pinero (Spain)	36,250
23	D. Durnian (England)	113,191	73	N. Hansen (England)	35,104
24	V. Singh (Fiji)	109,612	74	M. Moreno (Spain)	34,484
25	C. Montgomerie (Scotland)	109,084	75	G. Levenson (SA)	34,438
26	M. Roe (England)	107,647	76	M. Angel Martin (Spain)	34,434
27	B. Ogle (Australia)	106,002	77	K. Dickens (England)	34,332
28	A. Murray (England)	101,612	78	K. Waters (England)	34,057
29	O. Sellberg (Sweden)	101,575	79	R. Hartmann (US)	33,695
30	G.J. Brand (England)	98,914	80	A. Binaghi (It)	32,632
31	R. Chapman (England)	95,698	81	J. Rystrom (Sweden)	32,285
32	M. Lanner (Sweden)	95,330	82	J. Heggarty (N Ireland)	31,161
33	B. Lane (England)	87,144	83	M. Clayton (Australia)	29,855
34	J. Rivero (Spain)	85,981	84	B. Marchbank (Scotland)	29,833
35	E. Darcy (Ireland)	85,041	85	M. Angel Jimenez (Spain)	29,348
36	F. Nobilo (NZ)	79,325	86	R. Lee (England)	29,147
37	D. Smyth (Ireland)	79,313	87	R. Drummond (Scotland)	28,585
38	M. Persson (Sweden)	75,087	88	B. Malley (US)	28,250
39	M. Mouland (Wales)	74,829	89	B. Gallacher (Scotland)	28,258
40	R. Boxall (England)	71,093	90	T. Johnstone (Zimbabwe)	27,666
41	S. Bennett (England)	70,553	91	D. Jones (N Ireland)	27,149
42	P. Broadhurst (England)	67,103	92	D.A. Russell (England)	25,563
43	J. Hawkes (SA)	64,850	93	O. Moore (Australia)	25,425
44	R. Davis (Australia)	63,396	94	A. Garrido (Spain)	25,226
45	M. Davis (England)	61,362	95	J. Howell (US)	23,880
46	M. Smith (US)	60,457	96	R. McFarlane (England)	23,699
47	A. Charnley (England)	57,417	97	P. Curry (England)	23,544
48	M. Mackenzie (England)	57,238	98	S. McAllister (Scotland)	23,403
49	D. Williams (England)	55,773	99	J. Quiros (Spain)	23,230
50	J. Parnevik (Sweden)	55,537	100	M. Farry (France)	23,130

THE WPG EUROPEAN TOUR 1989

Marie Laure de Lorenzi

There is a charismatic superstar stalking the fairways of the Women's European Tour, a female Ballesteros, one might say. This is not a reference to big-hitting Laura Davies, US Open Champion in 1987, but to someone who, like Severiano, hails from the Continent – not Spain this time but France.

It is said that Marie Laure de Lorenzi has everything. Certainly she is a perfect ambassador for the women's game in Europe, and her successes on the fairways these past couple of years have been little short of breathtaking. Following her seven tour wins in 1988, Marie Laure began her 1989 campaign with finishes of 2nd–1st–1st–1st–2nd. A wrist injury limited her to just 12 events, but ten top-five finishes were sufficient for her once again to head the Woolmark Order of Merit table.

But enough of French flair: there is much else to admire on the still fledgling Women's European Tour. It is true that the 1989 season took a while to get off the ground; certain sponsors, it seems, were somewhat hesitant about putting their money where their mouths had earlier been, and in those dark days of 1989 there can have been few people who wanted to trade places with Tour Director Joe Flanagan. Hold your breath long enough, though, and hiccups have a habit of ceasing: the 1989 season closed on a highly optimistic note.

Aside from Marie Laure's great performances the highlights of the year included the three victories of Alison Nicholas, notably perhaps her win in the German Open, where she compiled an impressive 269 total; Australian Denise Hutton's late-season double; American Jane Geddes's victory in the Weetabix British Open, and the ever-consistent Kitrina Douglas's play-off victory over Marie Laure to capture the European Masters title.

The men's European tour prides itself on its international flavour, yet if anything the women's tour is even more cosmopolitan in its make-up. But with a roll of '89 champions that includes the likes of Anna Oxenstierna-Rhodin and Xonia Wunsch-Ruiz, how can the chaps compete?

1989 WPG EUROPEAN TOUR RESULTS

13-16 April
ROME CLASSIC *Olgiata, Italy*

Sofia Gronberg	70	71	69	210	£9,750
Marie Laure de Lorenzi	71	72	68	211	6,600
Gillian Stewart	75	65	72	212	4,550
Laurette Maritz	76	69	68	213	3,133
Florence Descampe	71	73	69	213	3,133
Tania Abitbol	72	75	70	217	2,112
Maureen Garner	75	72	70	217	2,112
Kitrina Douglas	71	70	77	218	1,460
Debbie Dowling	70	69	79	218	1,460
Dale Reid	72	71	75	218	1,460

26-29 April
FORD CLASSIC *Woburn, Bucks*

Marie Laure de Lorenzi	67	74	73	72	286	£7,500
Gillian Stewart	73	74	76	71	294	5,075
Sofia Gronberg	74	79	74	71	298	3,100
Mickey Walker	73	75	76	74	298	3,100
Barbara Helbig	76	76	76	71	299	1,790
Karen Lunn	73	78	79	69	299	1,790
Janet Soulsby	73	74	75	77	299	1,790
Alison Nicholas	77	74	77	72	300	1,185
Suzanne Strudwick	78	79	70	73	300	1,185

Alison Nicholas

25-28 May
HENNESSY CUP *St Germain, France*

Marie Laure de Lorenzi	68	66	72	73	279	£12,000
Corinne Dibnah	67	71	70	73	281	6,860
Jody Rosenthal	70	71	70	70	281	6,860
Laura Davies	69	68	70	75	282	4,320
Laurette Maritz	71	72	74	70	287	3,392
Alicia Dibbs	71	72	72	73	288	2,800
Corinne Soules	71	71	74	73	289	2,064
Florence Descampe	75	71	71	72	289	2,064
Lori Garbacz	75	72	69	73	289	2,064

1-4 June
BMW CLASSIC *Hubbelrath, W. Germany*

Marie Laure de Lorenzi	70	72	68	67	277	£10,500
Dennise Hutton	69	69	70	70	278	7,105
Corinne Dibnah	70	70	68	72	280	4,900
Corinne Soules	67	69	74	72	282	3,780
Susan Moon	67	72	71	73	283	2,968
Florence Descampe	68	75	67	74	284	2,450
Marie Wennersten-From	69	72	71	73	285	2,100
Suzanne Strudwick	71	73	75	67	286	1,750

15-18 June
FRENCH OPEN *Fourqueux, Paris*

*Suzanne Strudwick	70	69	74	72	285	£9,000
Marie Laure de Lorenzi	78	73	64	70	285	6,090
Debbie Petrizzi	72	73	73	72	290	4,200
Sue Nyhus	73	73	74	71	291	3,240
Rica Comstock	73	74	74	71	292	2,148
Claire Duffy	74	72	72	74	292	2,148
Laurette Maritz	69	76	75	72	292	2,148
Catherine Panton	75	75	72	71	293	1,348
Dale Reid	76	71	71	75	293	1,348
Maria Navarro Corbachio	71	76	71	75	293	1,348
Caroline Bourtayre	77	69	74	73	293	Amateur

* Winner in play-off.

1989 WPG EUROPEAN TOUR RESULTS

Jane Geddes

29 June-2 July
ST MORITZ CLASSIC *St Moritz, Switzerland*

*Kitrina Douglas	74	71	71	70	286	£10,500
Suzanne Strudwick	74	68	75	69	286	7,105
Nicole Lowien	75	72	69	72	288	4,900
Dennise Hutton	74	71	75	69	289	2,824
Laurette Maritz	73	71	71	74	289	2,824
Catherine Panton	71	75	74	69	289	2,824
Kris Hanson	73	71	74	71	289	2,824
Diane Barnard	71	72	75	72	290	1,442
Marie Laure de Lorenzi	76	72	76	66	290	1,442
Marie Wennersten-From	70	75	73	72	290	1,442
Florence Descampe	72	69	73	76	290	1,442
Melissa McNamara	72	72	75	71	290	1,442

* Winner in play-off.

6-9 July
TEC PLAYERS' CHAMPIONSHIP *Tytherington, Cheshire*

Anna Oxenstierna-Rhodin	75	74	66	71	286	£11,250
Laurette Maritz	69	73	73	73	288	7,610
Mickey Walker	73	72	74	72	291	5,250

Jane Connachan	73	76	73	70	292	3,285
Sofia Gronberg	74	78	70	70	292	3,285
Susan Moon	74	75	74	69	292	3,285
Peggy Conley	73	77	75	69	294	1,737
Corinne Dibnah	72	73	74	75	294	1,737
Kitrina Douglas	74	73	75	72	294	1,737
Maureen Garner	74	74	73	73	294	1,737
Suzanne Strudwick	76	70	75	73	294	1,737

13-16 July
BLOOR HOMES CLASSIC *Eastleigh, Hants*

*Debbie Dowling	69	65	65	62	261	£9,000
Rae Hast	67	67	64	63	261	4,510
Catherine Panton	66	65	63	67	261	4,510
Melissa McNamara	64	66	65	66	261	4,510
Diane Barnard	67	66	67	62	262	1,986
Peggy Conley	67	64	68	63	262	1,986
Anna Oxenstierna-Rhodin	66	66	67	63	262	1,986
Diane Pavich	66	65	66	65	262	1,986

* Winner in play-off.

27-30 July
Lufthansa GERMAN OPEN *Worthsee, Munich*

Alison Nicholas	67	69	68	65	269	£12,000
Patricia Gonzalez	68	71	66	69	274	8,120
Suzanne Strudwick	69	68	71	71	279	4,960
Patti Rizzo	67	68	71	73	279	4,960
Diane Barnard	70	70	70	70	280	3,096
Marie Laure de Lorenzi	70	70	69	71	280	3,096
Laurette Maritz	69	72	70	70	281	1,948
Florence Descampe	70	69	71	71	281	1,948
Martha Nause	75	69	68	69	281	1,948
Helen Alfredsson	70	66	74	71	281	1,948

3-6 August
Weetabix BRITISH OPEN *Ferndown, Dorset*

Jane Geddes	67	67	72	68	274	£18,000
Florence Descampe	73	66	70	67	276	12,340
Marie Laure de Lorenzi	68	71	67	72	278	8,880
Patti Rizzo	71	69	68	71	279	6,480
Muffin Spencer-Devlin	72	69	67	71	279	6,480
Peggy Conley	70	67	76	67	280	4,860
Xonia Wunsch-Ruiz	69	73	72	67	281	4,140
Kitrina Douglas	71	70	71	70	282	3,540
Alicia Dibos	67	75	72	69	283	3,060
Ray Bell	71	68	74	72	285	2,480
Maria Figueras-Dotti	69	71	72	73	285	2,480
Helen Alfredsson	73	70	69	73	285	2,480
Laurette Maritz	67	74	71	74	286	2,160
Laura Davies	76	71	69	71	287	1,924
Rae Hast	73	71	73	70	287	1,924
Alison Nicholas	71	69	71	76	287	1,924
Melissa McNamara	73	70	72	72	287	1,924
Cindy Scholefield	75	72	71	69	287	1,924

1989 WPG EUROPEAN TOUR RESULTS

Kitrina Douglas

17-20 August
DANISH OPEN *Rungsted, Copenhagen*

*Tania Abitbol	69	69	73	74	285	£9,750
Marie Laure de Lorenzi	75	70	68	72	285	6,660
Alison Nicholas	74	71	73	69	287	4,550
Suzanne Strudwick	75	67	77	70	289	3,520
Peggy Conley	69	69	74	80	292	2,151
Kitrina Douglas	75	73	70	74	292	2,151
Sofia Gronberg	75	73	73	71	292	2,151
Gillian Stewart	72	72	73	75	292	2,151
Dennise Hutton	73	71	76	73	293	1,317
Dale Reid	72	72	72	73	293	1,317
Corinne Soules	75	74	74	70	293	1,317

* Winner in play-off.

24-27 August
GISLAVED OPEN *Isaberg, Sweden*

Alison Nicholas	73	72	69	74	288	£9,750
Liselotte Neumann	77	68	74	71	290	6,600
Maxine Burton	77	75	71	69	292	4,030
Peggy Conley	73	73	71	75	292	4,030
Jane Connachan	73	72	74	75	294	2,515
Dennise Hutton	77	70	72	75	294	2,515
Federica Dassu	74	72	71	78	295	1,505
Debbie Dowling	73	75	73	74	295	1,505
Maureen Garner	80	69	73	73	295	1,505
Xonia Wunsch-Ruiz	76	72	72	75	295	1,505
Cindy Scholefield	76	73	72	74	295	1,505

31 August-3 September
VARIETY CLUB CELEBRITY CLASSIC *Calcot Park*

Corinne Dibnah	68	70	70	71	279	£6,500
Peggy Conley	68	71	72	70	281	4,400
Sally Prosser	71	76	71	65	283	3,400
Jane Connachan	70	72	74	70	286	2,166
Alison Nicholas	71	72	73	70	286	2,166
Sonja Van Wyk	72	71	75	68	286	2,166
Dale Reid	73	71	75	68	287	1,350
Kitrina Douglas	75	69	74	70	288	1,012
Dennise Hutton	72	66	76	74	288	1,012

7-10 September
Godiva **EUROPEAN MASTERS** *Bercuit, Belgium*

*Kitrina Douglas	69	75	73	70	287	£16,500
Marie Laure de Lorenzi	69	72	76	70	287	11,125
Helene Andersson	72	72	75	70	289	7,700
Laurette Maritz	75	72	73	71	291	5,302
Alison Nicholas	73	74	74	70	291	5,302
Karine Espinasse	75	73	74	70	292	3,850
Jane Connachan	76	71	74	73	294	3,300
Caroline Griffiths	76	75	75	69	295	2,471
Suzanne Strudwick	78	75	71	71	295	2,471
Florence Descampe	74	75	71	75	295	2,471
Laura Davies	75	76	74	71	296	2,024

* Winner in play-off.

14-17 September
Expedier **EUROPEAN OPEN** *Kingswood, Surrey*

Jane Connachan	65	73	70	71	279	£10,500
Gillian Stewart	75	69	71	67	282	7,105
Karen Lunn	73	76	71	65	285	4,340
Sonja Van Wyk	70	73	75	67	285	4,340
Maureen Garner	69	75	71	71	286	2,968
Jane Howard	75	73	71	68	287	2,100
Corinne Soules	72	72	75	68	287	2,100
Karen Davies	72	69	73	73	287	2,100
Peggy Conley	69	72	75	72	288	1,418
Claire Duffy	71	74	71	72	288	1,418
Anne Jones	69	76	72	71	288	1,418

1989 WPG EUROPEAN TOUR RESULTS

Laura Davies

28 September-1 October
ITALIAN OPEN *Carimate, Milan*

Xonia Wunsch-Ruiz	68	70	72	68	278	£12,000
Jane Connachan	67	69	73	71	280	8,120
Trish Johnson	67	71	71	74	283	5,600
Susan Moon	71	67	73	73	284	3,856
Alicia Dibos	70	70	74	70	284	3,856
Regine Lautens	70	70	72	73	285	2,600
Alison Nicholas	71	73	69	72	285	2,600
Suzanne Strudwick	68	72	73	73	286	2,000

12-15 October
LAING CHARITY CLASSIC *Stoke Poges, Bucks*

Laura Davies	72	64	72	68	276	£9,000
Jane Connachan	73	68	70	68	279	4,018
Corinne Dibnah	71	68	73	67	279	4,018
Susan Moon	67	70	72	70	279	4,018
Dale Reid	69	70	72	68	279	4,018
Peggy Conley	70	72	72	66	280	2,100
Cindy Scholefield	70	70	70	71	281	1,800
Federica Dassu	73	70	70	69	282	1,500

18-22 October
WOOLMARK MATCHPLAY *Vallromanas, Barcelona*

Quarter-Finals

H. Alfredson beat M.L. De Lorenzi	3 and 2
D. Hutton beat T. Abitbol	5 and 4
A. Jones beat K. Douglas	2 and 1
M. Garner beat K. Espinasse	2 and 1
All quarter-final losers won £2,400	

Semi-Finals

D. Hutton beat H. Alfredson	20th
M. Garner beat A. Jones	7 and 6
Semi-final losers won £5,000	

Final

D. Hutton beat M. Garner	2 holes
(£12,000) (£8,000)	

26-29 October
AGF BIARRITZ OPEN *Biarritz, France*

*Dennise Hutton	68	73	66	67	274	£9,000
Peggy Conley	70	64	70	70	274	6,090
Alison Nicholas	69	71	70	67	277	3,720
Helen Alfredsson	64	72	74	67	277	3,720
Sandrine Mendiburu	69	70	72	66	277	Amateur
Corinne Socles	70	70	70	68	278	2,544
Diane Barnard	71	68	73	67	279	1,800
Caroline Griffiths	71	71	68	69	279	1,800
Sally Prosser	71	72	68	68	279	1,800

* Winner in play-off.

1-3 November
QUALITAIR CLASSIC *La Manga, Spain*

Alison Nicholas	69	74	70	213	£7,500
Peggy Conley	69	76	70	215	4,287
Sofia Gronberg	70	76	69	215	4,287
Caroline Griffiths	74	72	70	216	2,410
Dale Reid	77	69	70	216	2,410
Regine Lautens	74	74	69	217	1,500
Florence Descampe	74	73	70	217	1,500
Tina Yarwood	74	71	72	217	1,500

9-12 November
BENSON AND HEDGES MIXED TEAM TROPHY
Aloha GC, Marbella, Spain

Miguel Angel Jimenez Xonia Wunsch-Ruiz	70	68	71	72	281	£23,400
Carl Mason Gillian Stewart	67	69	71	76	283	17,500
Gordon J. Brand Florence Descampe	69	71	72	72	284	13,400
Andrew Sherborne Kitrina Douglas	74	70	74	68	286	7,380
Ian Mosey Patricia Gonzalez	72	70	73	71	286	7,380
David Jones Cathy Panton	71	72	71	72	286	7,380
Jose Maria Canizares Tania Abitbol	72	73	68	73	286	7,380
Manuel Pinero Marta Figueras Dotti	72	70	70	74	286	7,380

1989 WPG EUROPEAN TOUR WINNERS SUMMARY

ROME CLASSIC	S. Gronberg	(Swe)
FORD CLASSIC	M. L. de Lorenzi	(Fr)
HENNESSY CUP	M. L. de Lorenzi	(Fr)
BMW CLASSIC	M. L. de Lorenzi	(Fr)
FRENCH OPEN	S. Strudwick	(GB)
ST MORITZ CLASSIC	K. Douglas	(GB)
TEC PLAYERS' CHAMPIONSHIP	A. Oxenstierna	(Swe)
BLOOR HOMES CLASSIC	D. Dowling	(GB)
GERMAN OPEN	A. Nicholas	(GB)
BRITISH OPEN	J. Geddes	(USA)
DANISH OPEN	T. Abitbol	(Sp)
GISLAVED OPEN	A. Nicholas	(GB)
VARIETY CLUB CELEBRITY CLASSIC	C. Dibnah	(Aus)
EUROPEAN MASTERS	K. Douglas	(GB)
EUROPEAN OPEN	J. Connachan	(GB)
ITALIAN OPEN	X. Wunsch-Ruiz	(Sp)
LAING CHARITY CLASSIC	L. Davies	(GB)
WOOLMARK MATCH PLAY	D. Hutton	(Aus)
BIARRITZ OPEN	D. Hutton	(Aus)
QUALITAIR CLASSIC	A. Nicholas	(GB)

WOOLMARK ORDER OF MERIT: TOP 50

1	M. L. de Lorenzi	£77,534	26	R. Hast	17,055
2	A. Nicholas	56,526	27	A. Jones	15,038
3	K. Douglas	48,534	28	P. Gonzalez	15,010
4	S. Strudwick	41,966	29	R. Lautes	15,002
5	D. Hutton	41,541	30	K. Espinasse	14,343
6	J. Connachan	38,227	31	K. Lunn	13,697
7	P. Conley	36,876	32	C. Scholefield	12,963
8	C. Dibnah	35,622	33	J. Soulsby	12,854
9	L. Maritz	33,978	34	F. Dassu	12,622
10	G. Stewart	31,700	35	S. Van Wyk	12,504
11	F. Descampe	31,003	36	T. Johnson	11,681
12	S. Gronberg	27,230	37	M. Walker	11,613
13	X. Wunsch-Ruiz	27,190	38	D. Petrizzi	11,547
14	M. Garner	26,923	39	C. Griffiths	11,066
15	S. Moon	25,904	40	M. McNamara	10,820
16	D. Dowling	24,977	41	K. Davies	10,557
17	T. Abitbol	23,275	42	S. Shapcott	9,773
18	D. Reid	21,782	43	R. Comstock	9,576
19	L. Davies	21,608	44	D. Pavich	9,576
20	H. Alfredsson	20,355	45	S. Prosser	9,010
21	C. Panton	19,919	46	B. Helbig	8,843
22	A. Dibos	19,725	47	M. Burton	8,693
23	C. Goules	19,500	48	J. Howard	8,619
24	D. Barnard	18,157	49	C. Duffy	8,503
25	A. Oxenstierna	18,032	50	H. Andersson	7,973

Twelve good men and true versus twelve good men and true – Europe v. USA, 1989

FOR THE RECORD

United States 21, Great Britain/Europe 5, Ties 2

1927 Worcester CC, Worcester, Mass. US 9½, Britain 2½
1929 Moortown, England Britain 7, US 5
1931 Scioto CC, Columbus, Ohio US 9, Britain 3
1933 Southport & Ainsdale, England Britain 6½, US 5½
1935 Ridgewood CC, Ridgewood, NJ US 9, Britain 3
1937 Southport & Ainsdale, England US 8, Britain 4

RYDER CUP NOT CONTESTED
DURING WORLD WAR II

1947 Portland Golf Club, Portland, Ore. US 11, Britain 1
1949 Ganton GC, Scarborough, England US 7, Britain 5
1951 Pinehurst CC, Pinehurst, NC US 9½, Britain 2½
1953 Wentworth, England US 6½, Britain 5½
1955 Thunderbird Ranch & CC, Palm Springs, Ca. US 8, Britain 4
1957 Lindrick GC, Yorkshire, England Britain 7½, US 4½
1959 Eldorado CC, Palm Desert, Ca. US 8½, Britain 3½
1961 Royal Lytham & St Anne's GC, St Anne's-on-the-Sea, England US 14½, Britain 9½

1963 East Lake CC, Atlanta, Ga. US 23, Britain 9
1965 Royal Birkdale GC, Southport, England US 19½, Britain 12½
1967 Champions GC, Houston, Tex. US 23½, Britain 8½
1969 Royal Birkdale GC, Southport, England US 16, Britain 16 (TIE)
1971 Old Warson CC, St Louis, Mo. US 18½, Britain 13½
1973 Muirfield, Scotland US 18, Britain 13
1975 Laurel Valley GC, Ligonier, Pa. US 21, Britain 11
1977 Royal Lytham & St Anne's GC, St Annes-on-the-Sea, England US 12½, Britain 7½
1979 The Greenbrier, White Sulphur Springs, W. Va. US 17, Europe 11
1981 Walton Heath GC, Surrey, England US 18½, Europe 9½
1983 PGA National GC, Palm Beach Gdns, Fla. US 14½, Europe 13½
1985 The Belfry, Sutton Coldfield, England Europe 16½, US 11½
1987 Muirfield Village, Ohio Europe 15, US 13
1989 The Belfry, Sutton Coldfield, England Europe 14, US 14 (TIE)

THE 28TH RYDER CUP

EUROPE	MATCHES	USA	MATCHES
Foursomes: Morning			
N. Faldo & I. Woosnam	½	C. Strange & T. Kite	½
H. Clark & M. James	0	L. Wadkins & P. Stewart (1 hole)	1
S. Ballesteros & J. Olazabal	½	T. Watson & C. Beck	½
B. Langer & R. Rafferty	0	M. Calcavecchia & K. Green (2 & 1)	1
Fourballs: Afternoon			
S. Torrance & G. Brand Jnr (1 hole)	1	C. Strange & P. Azinger	0
H. Clark & M. James (3 & 2)	1	F. Couples & L. Wadkins	0
N. Faldo & I. Woosnam (2 holes)	1	M. Calcavecchia & M. McCumber	0
S. Ballesteros & J. Olazabal (6 & 5)	1	T. Watson & M. O'Meara	0
Foursomes: Morning			
N. Faldo & I. Woosnam (3 & 2)	1	L. Wadkins & P. Stewart	0
G. Brand Jnr & S. Torrance	0	C. Beck & P. Azinger (4 & 3)	1
C. O'Connor & R. Rafferty	0	M. Calcavecchia & K. Green (3 & 2)	1
S. Ballesteros & J. Olazabal (1 hole)	1	T. Kite & C. Strange	0
Fourballs: Afternoon			
N. Faldo & I. Woosnam	0	C. Beck & P. Azinger (2 & 1)	1
B. Langer & J.M. Canizares	0	T. Kite & M. McCumber (2 & 1)	1
H. Clark & M. James (1 hole)	1	P. Stewart & C. Strange	0
S. Ballesteros & J. Olazabal (4 & 2)	1	M. Calcavecchia & K. Green	0
Single:			
S. Ballesteros	0	P. Azinger (1 hole)	1
B. Langer	0	C. Beck (3 & 1)	1
J. Olazabal (1 hole)	1	P. Stewart	0
R. Rafferty (1 hole)	1	M. Calcavecchia	0
H. Clark	0	T. Kite (8 & 7)	1
M. James (3 & 2)	1	M. O'Meara	0
C. O'Connor (1 hole)	1	F. Couples	0
J. M. Canizares (1 hole)	1	K. Green	0
G. Brand Jnr	0	M. McCumber (1 hole)	1
S. Torrance	0	T. Watson (3 & 1)	1
N. Faldo	0	L. Wadkins (1 hole)	1
I. Woosnam	0	C. Strange (2 holes)	1

EUROPE 14   USA 14

THE GREATEST MATCH

If, as many of us would like to think, golf really is 'the greatest game', then the Ryder Cup is surely 'the greatest match'. But this is very much a recent phenomenon.

Back in the 1920s, the time when Samuel Ryder first conceived his idea of a bi-annual 'us versus them' match, golf was enjoying a so-called 'Golden Age'. The Americans, led by Walter Hagen and Gene Sarazen – not to mention Bobby Jones, who as an amateur never played in the Ryder Cup – majestically strode the fairways; while in Abe Mitchell, Archie Compston and George Duncan, Britain and Ireland also had a few fellows who could play a bit.

As the greater general public remained blissfully unaware, the early matches were shared two games each. Then the rot set in. The Americans' own golden era continued with Nelson, Hogan and Snead, then Palmer, Nicklaus and Watson leading powerful sides towards crushing victories over the British and Irish with a monotonous regularity. A great match? Granted one or two famous upsets, the contest had become far too one-sided. The Cup had lost its appeal.

Then, as the decade of the eighties dawned, four things happened. Firstly, European golfers, who had demonstrated their abundant skills on the rapidly expanding European Tour, were brought into the British and Irish team. Secondly, those European golfers included in their number one Severiano Ballesteros and one Bernhard Langer, who by the mid-1980s were to be recognized as the two best golfers in the world. Thirdly, the global successes of Ballesteros and Langer would soon be matched by two 'home-grown' players, Sandy Lyle and Nick Faldo; Europe now had a collection of world-class players. And then finally there was the appointment of Tony Jacklin, who was destined to prove himself a most inspirational captain and leader. Now there really were the makings of a match.

A great match? The quality of golf that would be displayed in the ensuing contests would ensure that; but the greatest match? Well, in what other game today is such a level of sportsmanship on show to so many by so few? Ask the 200 million who watched the last contest. The Ryder Cup is undoubtedly the symbol of golf's new Golden Age.

Spanish Masters – Ballesteros and Olazabal

THE 28TH RYDER CUP

Sponsored by Johnnie Walker

22-24 September 1989 at The Belfry

On paper the twenty-eighth Ryder Cup looked like it was going to be a desperately close thing. The Europeans had every reason to feel confident, for they had a winning side and they had a settled side. Only Ronan Rafferty hadn't played in the Cup before and he would later head the European Order of Merit. They had Faldo, the most consistent golfer in the world in 1989, and they had Ballesteros.

Maybe the visitors were lacking a 'team', but in Strange, Calcavecchia and Stewart, they had three of the year's four Major winners and they had ample experience in Messrs Watson, Kite and Wadkins. It was widely reported that the US side were under Presidential instructions not to return home without the Cup. They were hyped-up; even the placid Watson declared that they were 'going to kick some butts', while the anything but placid Wadkins 'wanted the Cup back in the worst way'.

The long-awaited Friday morning came and the Europeans immediately got off to a slow start, while the visitors did a bit of butt-kicking. Europe's two strong pairings, Ballesteros and Olazabal and Faldo and Woosnam, both managed to halve their matches, but the other two pairings lost and the Americans lunched 3–1 ahead. Ironically the home side seemed to benefit most, as any over-confidence quickly vanished and, in an amazing about-turn, the afternoon brought a European whitewash; Ballesteros and Olazabal leading the way with a 6 and 5 trouncing of Watson and O'Meara. Talk about a day of two halves! At 2 o'clock it had been 1–3, by 6 o'clock it was 5–3.

On the Saturday morning the Europeans clung onto their two-point advantage. The Spanish once again proved too strong for America's top pairing, Kite and Strange, while Woosnam and Faldo, aided by a run of 8 threes in 9 holes, overwhelmed Wadkins and Stewart 3 and 2.

If major championships don't get going until the final 9 holes on Sunday, so Ryder Cups would appear to step up a gear on Saturday afternoon. Who will ever forget the scenes two years ago at Muirfield Village when Langer and Lyle hit those two stunning shots to the 18th green in the gathering gloom to win their match and set up victory for the following day? This time it was the turn of Clark and James to turn around a 1-down with 3 to play deficit against Stewart and Strange and so win a vital match. Had they lost, the final day would have started 8–8, yet thanks to their heroics it began 9–7 to Europe. The Spaniards remained undefeated, but Woosnam and Faldo finally succumbed to some brilliant golf.

John Hopkins put it beautifully in the *Sunday Times* when he described Faldo and

A painful ending – Stewart was one of five who went fishing on the final day

95

Woosnam as having the air of 'boxers who travel around the country ready to take on all-comers but who in the afternoon ran into an American tempest that had been brewing.' The tempest came in the form of Paul Azinger and Chip Beck, who were 11 under par for the seventeen holes they played in defeating the British pair. So the scene was set for a thrilling final day: 9–7 to Europe and with twelve singles matches to come.

Jacklin was determined that Europe should maintain their momentum; the best way to do this, he felt, would be to send Ballesteros out first. The Americans selected Saturday's hero, Azinger, to face him. It was a brilliant match which swung first one way then the other. On the 18th tee Azinger stood one up but hit his tee shot into the water. Surely Ballesteros, safely on the edge of the fairway, would square the match? Watching the ripples on the huge lake in front of the green seconds later was like witnessing the sinking of the Spanish Armada. Azinger had won the prize scalp, and within minutes Langer too had been defeated. When Tom Kite finished off Clark 8 and 7, Europe found themselves up in only one match, and defeat was staring them in the face. It was at that moment that America demonstrated to the world why she is known as the most generous nation on earth.

First US PGA Champion Stewart and then Open Champion Calcavecchia drove into the water from the 18th tee to lose their matches to Europe's young lions, Olazabal and Rafferty. Those two wins were significant and when James capped an excellent week by defeating O'Meara 3 and 2, Europe were back in the hunt. Yet the afternoon would belong to two grey-haired veterans, Europe's old boys O'Connor and Canizares, the Irishman and the Spaniard. The two memories we will always have will be of O'Connor's drilled 2-iron to within two feet of the flag at the 18th, and at the same hole Canizares holing a short putt then running across the green like a two-year-old into the outstretched arms of his team-mates.

But it wasn't quite all over, as Tom Kite prophetically and pointedly told the watching world. Europe had retained the Cup but America could still force a draw in the match. America's hopes rested on Wadkins and Strange, and they faced Europe's prize fighters. A vindictive person might think it a fitting ending had Faldo made Wadkins swallow his words by winning the trophy in the penultimate match; instead he became the third Major winner of the year to see his ball get swallowed by the lake on the 18th. The fourth 'Mr Major', Curtis Strange, however, seemed determined to prove to the world that America really does have a super-star. One down with four to play against Woosnam, he birdied the 15th, 16th and 17th holes, and then, with enormous pressure on his shoulders (not to mention Woosnam some fifty yards further up the fairway), he hit his second to the 18th almost stone dead. It was a magnificent shot to end a magnificent match; a tied match at 14–14, although, as everybody agreed, the game of golf had in fact shaded it on points.

Christy O'Connor Jnr: 'Who said God was a Mexican?'

96

THE GOOD, THE BAD AND THE EXTRAORDINARY

As in many walks of life, America seems to have been dealt an over-generous portion of all things good and all things bad to do with golf.

By common consent the three greatest golfers who have ever lived – Bobby Jones, Ben Hogan and Jack Nicklaus – were all American. By common consent the two most beautiful courses on earth – Augusta and Cypress Point – are both found in the United States. And again by common consent the greatest golfing challenge – Pine Valley – yes, it's in America. But look on the flip-side: more Americans prefer to tune into the annual Skins Game in November than watch the Masters in April. If you think golf can at times be tediously slow this side of the Atlantic, a feature on many American courses are the large signs warning players: 'Remember golf is a four-and-a-half-hour game'. And though American golf courses are by and large far better manicured and conditioned than ours, many of the best ones tend to be much of a muchness – water, water everywhere – there is nothing like the variety of courses we have in Europe, especially in Britain.

For Americans the magical dollar reigns supreme. This is why the Skins Game is so popular, and it explains why in 1989 the reigning US Amateur champion decided to turn professional and enter the Chattanooga Classic in preference to defending a title won five times by the immortal Jones.

Then again, perhaps because we European golfers have never had it so good, we have grown too eager to denigrate a nation that has given golf so much. The USA is the modern 'Home of Golf': more players and more courses than anywhere else. American golfers were victorious in twenty-nine of the forty major championships during the eighties; and if golf is so wonderful in Europe, why does Greg Norman choose to play practically all his golf on the US Tour, and why do European golfers get so frustrated at not being able to join him more often?

Compared with Scotland, golf is still a relatively young game in North America. The continent's first golf club was in fact established in Montreal, Canada, now Royal Montreal, in 1873. The oldest in the United States was founded at Yonkers on Long Island. The year was 1888, and less than fifty years on, the country's first 'superstar', and golf's greatest showman, Walter Hagen, was telling the world how he had earned a million dollars from the game – and spent a million dollars.

After Hagen came Jones and Sarazen and then Nelson, Snead and Hogan, followed by Palmer, Nicklaus, Trevino and Watson. America's relentless domination of the game was emphasized not only in the major championships and the World Cup but also in the biannual slaughter otherwise known as the Ryder Cup. Thankfully there is now a balance of power on the fairways, which can only be good for the development of golf worldwide. Complacent Europeans, however, would do well to remind themselves occasionally that the present state of affairs is but a recent phenomenon and that Uncle Sam never enjoyed playing second fiddle to anyone.

THE 1989 USPGA TOUR

It is probably just as well that Payne Stewart won his first major championship in 1989, the USPGA at Kemper Lakes in August, otherwise he would probably be forever haunted by nightmares about the three putts he took on the final green at Hilton Head in the Nabisco Championship. Two putts would have given him a 65 that day, a cheque for $450,000 and his third tournament win of the year. He would have also finished the season as the leading money winner (and with that a cash bonus of close on $200,000), and he might have secured the USPGA Tour's Player of the Year Award. As it was, all these titles went to Tom Kite, who defeated Stewart in a sudden-death play-off. One could say that they were playing for high stakes.

Tom Kite is himself no stranger to the art of missing out. 1989 was a brilliant year for Kite; in addition to winning the Nabisco Championship and all the accompanying paraphernalia, he won the Nestle Invitational and the Players Championship during successive weeks in March. Yet for all his successes he will have mixed feelings about 1989. He knows that he should have won the US Open in June and captured that elusive first major title. In years to come, Kite will open the record books and see against his name the scores of 67–69–69–78. No doubt he will choose not to linger at that particular page.

The US season began in January with the hitherto underrated Steve Jones winning the first two tournaments of the year. Mark Calcavecchia then won two of the next three; the first by seven strokes, the second by a single shot from Sandy Lyle. It was at about this time that Calcavecchia made his famous comment: 'Helping America win the Ryder Cup would mean more to me than winning a major championship.'

Tom Kite, leading money winner on the US Tour in 1989

Greg Norman ran into form a week too late to win the USPGA Championship, but his two tour titles and fourth place on the money list helped him to displace Ballesteros from the top of the Sony World Rankings. Sandy Lyle's impressive early season form fizzled out spectacularly and he ended the year in 43rd position on the money list, 17 places above Lanny Wadkins and 37 above Tom Watson, both of whom (unlike Lyle) played in the Ryder Cup.

1989 USPGA TOUR RESULTS

5-8 January
MONY TOURNAMENT OF CHAMPIONS
La Quinta, California

S. Jones	69	69	72	69	279	$135,000
D. Frost	72	70	72	68	282	67,000
J. Haas	75	67	72	68	282	67,000
G. Norman	71	72	72	68	283	37,000
C. Beck	69	70	74	71	284	31,000

12-16 January
BOB HOPE CHRYSLER CLASSIC *Palm Springs, California*

*S. Jones	76	68	67	63	69	343	$180,000
S. Lyle	70	68	68	68	69	343	88,000
P. Azinger	69	68	70	67	69	343	88,000
L. Wadkins	68	70	68	70	68	344	39,375
K. Knox	68	71	69	67	69	344	39,375
M. Calcavecchia	71	67	67	67	72	344	39,375
F. Couples	65	71	71	68	69	344	39,375

* Winner in play-off.

19-22 January
PHOENIX OPEN *Phoenix, Arizona*

M. Calcavecchia	66	68	65	64	263	$126,000
C. Beck	67	70	66	67	270	75,600
S. Hoch	64	70	69	68	271	36,400
B. Glasson	65	68	73	65	271	36,400
P. Azinger	68	68	68	67	271	36,400

26-29 January
AT&T PEBBLE BEACH NATIONAL PRO-AM *Pebble Beach, California*

M. O'Meara	66	68	73	70	277	$180,000
T. Kite	67	70	72	69	278	108,000
N. Price	66	74	67	73	280	52,000
S. Lyle	68	72	72	68	280	52,000
J. Carter	70	72	69	69	280	52,000

Mark Calcavecchia

2-5 February
NISSAN LOS ANGELES OPEN *Riviera, California*

M. Calcavecchia	68	66	70	68	272	$180,000
S. Lyle	68	66	68	71	273	108,000
H. Irwin	70	67	69	68	274	68,000
G. Sauers	67	70	72	67	276	41,333
S. Pate	67	71	68	70	276	41,333
P. Blackmar	68	72	67	69	276	41,333

9-12 February
HAWAIIAN OPEN *Waialae, Hawaii*

G. Sauers	65	67	65	197	$135,000
D. Ogrin	65	67	66	198	81,000
D. Rummells	70	65	64	199	51,000
J. Carter	64	66	70	200	36,000
D. Reese	69	69	64	202	28,500
C. Beck	69	64	69	202	28,500

1989 USPGA TOUR RESULTS

SHEARSON LEHMAN HUTTON OPEN *Torrey Pines, California*

G. Twiggs	68 70 64 69 271	$126,000
M. O'Meara	68 67 72 66 273	46,200
M. Wiebe	68 65 70 70 273	46,200
B. Faxon	67 69 69 68 273	46,200
S. Elkington	70 63 67 73 273	46,200

23-26 February
DORAL RYDER OPEN *Doral CC, Miami, Florida*

B. Glasson	71 65 67 72 275	$234,000
F. Couples	69 69 70 68 276	140,400
C. Strange	73 67 69 69 278	67,600
B. Lietzke	68 71 68 71 278	67,600
M. Calcavecchia	65 73 66 74 278	67,600

How many in this picture have won the Players Championship?

2-5 March
HONDA CLASSIC *Eagle Trace, Florida*

B. McCallister	70 67 65 64 266	$144,000
P. Stewart	68 65 70 67 270	86,400
S. Pate	70 67 64 70 271	46,400
C. Strange	68 71 67 65 271	46,400
D. Pohl	66 62 75 69 272	32,000

9-12 March
NESTLE INVITATIONAL *Bay Hill, Florida*

*T. Kite	68 72 67 71 278	$144,000
D. Love III	72 67 66 73 278	86,400
C. Strange	73 72 69 65 279	54,500
P. Stewart	76 69 65 70 280	33,067
D. Pooley	69 73 68 70 280	33,067
L. Roberts	66 73 69 72 280	33,067

* Winner in play-off.

16-19 March
THE PLAYERS CHAMPIONSHIP *Sawgrass, Florida*

T. Kite	69 70 69 71 279	$243,000
C. Beck	71 68 68 73 280	145,800
B. Lietzke	66 69 79 72 281	91,800
G. Norman	74 67 69 72 282	59,400
F. Couples	68 70 71 73 282	59,400

23-26 March
USF & G CLASSIC *English Turn, Louisiana*

T. Simpson	68	67	70	69	274	$135,000
G. Norman	68	68	68	72	276	66,000
H. Sutton	71	68	67	70	276	66,000
M. Hayes	72	71	67	68	278	36,000
B. Sander	68	71	70	70	279	26,344
P. Stewart	70	69	69	71	279	26,344
M. O'Meara	72	67	72	68	279	26,344
P.H. Horgan III	70	70	67	72	279	26,344

30 March-2 April
INDEPENDENT INSURANCE AGENT OPEN
The Woodlands, Texas

M. Sullivan	76	71	68	65	280	$144,000
C. Stadler	72	71	68	70	281	86,400
M. Reid	72	69	71	70	282	41,600
M. Donald	67	67	74	74	282	41,600
S. Ballesteros	69	69	72	72	282	41,600

6-9 April
THE MASTERS *Augusta, Georgia*

*N. Faldo	68	73	77	65	283	$200,000
S. Hoch	69	74	71	69	283	120,000
G. Norman	74	75	68	67	284	64,450
B. Crenshaw	71	72	70	71	284	64,450
S. Ballesteros	71	72	73	69	285	44,400
M. Reid	72	71	71	72	286	40,000

* Winner in play-off.

Scott Hoch

6-9 April
DEPOSIT GUARANTY CLASSIC *Hattiesburg, Mississippi*

*J. Booros	64	69	66	199	$36,000
M. Donald	68	65	66	199	21,600
R. Thompson	65	71	65	201	9,600
L. Ten Broeck	69	65	67	201	9,600
F. Funk	71	65	65	201	9,600
D. Peoples	68	68	65	201	9,600

* Winner in play-off.

13-16 April
MCI HERITAGE CLASSIC *Hilton Head Island, South Carolina*

P. Stewart	65	67	67	69	268	$144,000
K. Perry	65	67	70	71	273	86,400
B. Langer	69	70	67	71	277	46,400
F. Couples	71	72	69	65	277	46,400
L. Wadkins	72	69	70	67	278	29,200
C. Stadler	70	70	70	68	278	29,200
K. Knox	69	70	67	62	278	29,200

Ken Green

27-30 April
LAS VEGAS INVITATIONAL *Las Vegas, Nevada*

*S. Hoch	69	64	68	65	70	336	$225,000
R. Wrenn	69	66	66	69	66	336	135,000
C. Stadler	69	67	65	69	67	337	72,500
G. Morgan	70	63	73	64	67	337	72,500
M. Wiebe	71	67	66	68	66	338	43,906
D. Pohl	69	66	64	68	71	338	43,906
B. Bryant	67	68	69	70	64	338	43,906
R. Cochran	70	70	66	64	68	338	43,906

* Winner in play-off.

4-7 May
GTE BYRON NELSON CLASSIC *Las Colinas, Irving, Texas*

*J. Mudd	68	66	66	65	265	$180,000
L. Nelson	63	68	67	67	265	108,000
M. O'Meara	67	68	65	66	266	68,000
L. Roberts	65	68	66	68	267	48,000
W. Levi	62	67	68	71	268	36,500
C. Perry	65	65	70	68	268	36,500
L. Mize	67	67	63	71	268	36,500

* Winner in play-off.

11-14 May
MEMORIAL TOURNAMENT *Muirfield Village, Ohio*

B. Tway	71	69	68	69	277	$160,000
F. Zoeller	69	66	72	72	279	96,000
P. Stewart	70	73	73	65	281	60,440
B. Lietzke	73	70	69	71	283	40,835
M. Calcavecchia	72	68	73	70	283	40,835

18-21 May
COLONIAL NATIONAL INVITATION *Ft. Worth, Texas*

I. Baker-Finch	65	70	65	70	270	$180,000
D. Edwards	72	69	68	65	274	108,000
T. Simpson	71	71	66	68	276	58,000
D. Frost	70	66	71	69	276	58,000
C. Strange	74	71	66	66	277	36,500
N. Price	70	66	68	73	277	36,500
L. Hinkle	74	69	66	68	277	36,500

25-28 May
BELL SOUTH ATLANTA CLASSIC *Atlanta, Georgia*

*S. Simpson	72	68	71	67	278	$162,000
B. Tway	70	70	71	67	278	97,200
D. Love III	71	69	69	70	279	52,200
J. Blake	66	71	70	72	279	58,200
D. Peoples	70	71	70	69	280	34,200
D. Canipe	71	70	70	69	280	34,200

20-23 April
K-MART GREATER GREENSBORO OPEN
Forest Oaks CC, North Carolina

K. Green	73	66	66	72	277	$180,000
J. Huston	71	69	67	72	279	108,000
E. Fiori	70	71	73	67	281	68,000
D. Eichelberger	72	67	72	71	282	48,000
M. Sullivan	70	74	70	69	283	36,500
G. Norman	73	72	70	68	283	36,500
J. Booros	69	70	72	72	283	36,500

1989 USPGA TOUR RESULTS

1-4 June
KEMPER OPEN *Avenel, Potomac, Maryland*

T. Byrum	66	69	65	68	268	$162,000
J. Thorpe	70	69	67	67	273	67,200
T. Armour	68	70	64	71	273	67,200
B.R. Brown	69	67	70	67	273	67,200
G. Morgan	70	71	68	66	275	36,000

8-11 June
MANUFACTURERS HANOVER WESTCHESTER CLASSIC *Westchester, New York*

*W. Grady	69	65	71	72	277	$180,000
R. Black	69	71	69	68	277	108,000
T. Watson	71	69	70	68	278	58,000
C. Rose	72	69	67	70	278	58,000
J.C. Snead	67	68	70	74	279	35,125
T. Kite	70	67	72	70	279	35,125
B. Andrade	69	69	70	71	279	35,125
F. Couples	66	72	70	71	279	35,125

* Winner in play-off.

15-18 June
US OPEN *Oak Hill CC, Rochester, New York*

C. Strange	71	64	73	70	278	$200,000
I. Woosnam	70	68	73	68	279	67,823
M. McCumber	70	68	72	69	279	67,823
C. Beck	71	69	71	68	279	67,823
B. Claar	71	72	68	69	280	34,345
S. Simpson	67	70	69	75	281	28,221
M. Ozaki	70	71	68	72	281	28,221

22-25 June
CANADIAN OPEN *Glen Abbey, Ontario, Canada*

S. Jones	67	64	70	70	271	$162,000
M. Hulbert	71	66	72	64	273	67,200
C. Burroughs	69	66	64	74	273	67,200
M. Calcavecchia	67	69	68	69	273	67,200
J. Sindelar	69	72	65	68	274	32,850
M. McCumber	69	69	69	67	274	32,850
M. Brooks	67	73	68	66	274	32,850

29 June-2 July
BEATRICE WESTERN OPEN *Butler National, Illinois*

*M. McCumber	68	67	71	69	275	$180,000
P. Jacobsen	69	69	69	68	275	108,000
P. Azinger	67	68	72	69	276	68,000
J. Gallagher Jnr	71	72	70	66	279	48,000
L.T. Broeck	68	71	72	69	280	38,000
L. Trevino	73	71	67	69	280	38,000

* Winner in play-off.

Steve Jones

CANON GREATER HARTFORD OPEN
Hartford, Connecticut

P. Azinger	65	70	67	65	267	$180,000
W. Levi	69	68	64	67	268	108,000
D. Rummels	70	67	67	66	270	68,000
J. Carter	66	68	71	66	270	41,333
L. Trevino	70	64	70	67	271	41,333
M. Calcavecchia	67	68	67	69	271	41,333

13-16 July
ANHEUSER-BUSCH CLASSIC *Kingsmill, Virginia*

*M. Donald	67	66	70	65	268	$153,000
H. Sutton	64	71	65	68	268	74,800
T. Simpson	64	70	67	67	268	74,800
M. Hulbert	65	66	68	70	269	40,800
T. Byrum	70	70	64	66	270	34,000

* Winner in play-off.

20-23 July
HARDEE'S GOLF CLASSIC *Oakwood, Illinois*

C. Byrum	66	67	69	66	268	$126,000
B. Tennyson	69	69	67	64	269	61,600
B. Britton	70	65	69	65	269	61,600
B. Jaeckel	70	71	67	63	271	38,800
J. Gallagher Jnr	69	68	69	65	271	38,800

Paul Azinger

27-30 July
BUICK OPEN *Grand Blanc, Michigan*

L. Thompson	65	71	68	68	273	$180,000
B. Andrade	67	71	69	67	274	74,667
D. Tewell	69	66	70	69	274	74,667
P. Stewart	71	67	64	72	274	74,667
M. O'Meara	66	70	71	66	275	36,500
B. Eastwood	73	66	66	70	275	36,500
H. Sutton	67	68	68	72	275	36,500

10-13 August
PGA CHAMPIONSHIP *Kemper Lakes, Chicago, Illinois*

P. Stewart	74	66	69	67	276	$200,000
A. Bean	70	67	74	66	277	83,333
M. Reid	66	67	70	74	277	83,333
C. Strange	70	68	70	69	277	83,333
D. Rummells	68	69	69	72	278	45,000
I. Woosnam	68	70	70	71	279	40,000

3-6 August
FEDERAL EXPRESS ST JUDE CLASSIC *TPC at Southwind, Tennessee*

J. Mahaffey	70	71	66	65	272	$180,000
H. Green	70	69	73	63	275	66,000
B. Tway	66	72	68	69	275	66,000
B. Langer	67	69	68	71	275	66,000
B. Gilder	68	66	70	72	275	66,000

1989 USPGA TOUR RESULTS

17-20 August
THE INTERNATIONAL *Castle Rock, Colorado*

G. Norman	+ 13 points	$180,000
C. Rose	+ 11	108,000
C. Beck	+9	68,000
M. Lye	+8	44,000
B. Andrade	+8	44,000

24-27 August
NEC WORLD SERIES OF GOLF *Akron, Ohio*

*D. Frost	70	68	69	69	276	$180,000
B. Crenshaw	64	72	72	68	276	108,000
P. Stewart	72	67	68	71	278	68,000
G. Norman	73	65	70	71	279	48,000
L. Mize	73	66	70	71	280	38,000
M. Reid	68	71	70	71	280	38,000

24-27 August
CHATTANOOGA CLASSIC *Chattanooga, Tennessee*

S. Utley	69	66	64	64	263	$90,000
R. Stewart	71	63	67	63	264	54,000
R. Wadkins	67	67	65	66	265	29,000
D. Shirey Jnr	65	65	68	67	265	29,000
R. Zokol	68	67	65	66	266	17,562
J. Inman	66	68	67	65	266	17,562
B. Estes	69	65	66	66	266	17,562
R. Cochran	66	67	67	66	266	17,562

31 August-3 September
GREATER MILWAUKEE OPEN *Franklin, Wisconsin*

G. Norman	64	69	66	70	269	$144,000
A. Bean	70	69	67	66	272	86,400
M. Lye	67	66	62	68	273	46,400
A. Schultz	68	69	68	68	273	46,400
T. Purtzer	72	67	66	69	274	30,400
W. Levi	69	66	68	71	274	30,400

7-10 September
BC OPEN *Endicott, New York*

*M. Hulbert	69	66	68	65	268	$90,000
B. Estes	68	68	66	66	268	54,000
S. Elkington	68	72	67	62	269	34,000
F. Zoeller	69	67	66	69	271	22,000
D. Eichelberger	67	67	67	70	271	22,000

David Frost

14-17 September
BANK OF BOSTON CLASSIC *Pleasant Valley, Massachusetts*

B. McCallister	67	67	71	66	271	$126,000
B. Faxon	66	67	70	69	272	75,600
D. Pooley	66	65	72	70	273	36,400
C. Perry	68	69	70	66	273	36,400
M. Calcavecchia	67	68	69	69	273	36,400

21-24 September
SOUTHERN OPEN *Columbus, Georgia*

T. Schulz	66	66	68	66	266	$72,000
T. Simpson	66	73	65	63	267	35,200
J. Haas	68	67	64	68	267	35,200
B. Tway	69	69	65	67	270	16,533
L. Rinker	70	68	64	68	270	16,533
L. Ten Broeck	70	66	65	69	270	16,533

28 September-1 October
CENTEL CLASSIC *Tallahassee, Florida*

B. Britton	71	66	63	200	$135,000
R. Black	67	67	70	204	81,000
R. Hallberg	68	71	66	205	51,000
M. Reid	69	68	69	206	31,000
T. Pernice Jnr	68	65	73	206	31,000
B. Buttner	69	66	71	206	31,000

5-8 October
TEXAS OPEN *San Antonio, Texas*

D. Hammond	65	64	65	64	258	$108,000
P. Azinger	64	62	70	69	265	64,500
B. Lohr	66	64	66	71	267	31,200
D. Waldorf	67	63	66	71	267	31,200
M. Wiebe	62	68	70	67	267	31,200

19-22 October
WALT DISNEY WORLD/OLDSMOBILE CLASSIC *Lake Buena Vista, Florida*

T. Simpson	65	67	70	70	272	$144,000
D. Hammond	72	65	65	71	273	86,400
P. Azinger	65	70	71	68	274	41,600
K. Knox	70	65	71	68	274	41,600
F. Couples	70	65	69	70	274	41,600

26-29 October
NABISCO CHAMPIONSHIPS *Hilton Head Island, South Carolina*

*T. Kite	69	65	74	68	276	$450,000
P. Stewart	69	70	71	66	276	270,000
P. Azinger	71	73	67	67	278	146,250
W. Levi	71	72	63	72	278	146,250
D. Hammond	65	73	69	72	279	100,000

* Winner in play-off.

Payne Stewart

1989 USPGA TOUR WINNERS SUMMARY

MONY TOURNAMENT OF CHAMPIONS	S. Jones	(US)
BOB HOPE CHRYSLER CLASSIC	*S. Jones	(US)
PHOENIX OPEN	M. Calcavecchia	(US)
AT&T PEBBLE BEACH NATIONAL PRO-AM	M. O'Meara	(US)
NISSAN LOS ANGELES OPEN	M. Calcavecchia	(US)
HAWAIIAN OPEN	G. Sauers	(US)
SHEARSON LEHMAN HUTTON ANDY WILLIAMS OPEN	G. Twiggs	(US)
DORAL RYDER OPEN	B. Glasson	(US)
HONDA CLASSIC	B. McCallister	(US)
THE NESTLE INVITATIONAL	*T. Kite	(US)
THE PLAYERS' CHAMPIONSHIP	T. Kite	(US)
U.S.F.&G. CLASSIC	T. Simpson	(US)
INDEPENDENT INSURANCE AGENT OPEN	M. Sullivan	(US)
THE MASTERS	*N. Faldo	(GB)
DEPOSIT GUARANTY GOLF CLASSIC	*J. Booros	(US)
MCI HERITAGE CLASSIC	P. Stewart	(US)
K-MART GREATER GREENSBORO OPEN	K. Green	(US)
LAS VEGAS PRO-AM INVITATIONAL	*S. Hoch	(US)
G.T.E. BYRON NELSON GOLF CLASSIC	*J. Mudd	(US)
MEMORIAL TOURNAMENT	B. Tway	(US)
SOUTHWESTERN BELL COLONIAL	I. Baker-Finch	(Aus)
BELL SOUTH ATLANTA GOLF CLASSIC	*S. Simpson	(US)
KEMPER OPEN	T. Byrum	(US)
MANUFACTURERS' HANOVER WESTCHESTER CLASSIC	*W. Grady	(Aus)
US OPEN	C. Strange	(US)
CANADIAN OPEN	S. Jones	(US)
BEATRICE WESTERN OPEN	*M. McCumber	(US)
CANON GREATER HARTFORD OPEN	P. Azinger	(US)
ANHEUSER-BUSCH GOLF CLASSIC	*M. Donald	(US)
HARDEE'S GOLF CLASSIC	C. Byrum	(US)
BUICK OPEN	L. Thompson	(US)
FEDERAL EXPRESS ST JUDE CLASSIC	J. Mahaffey	(US)
P.G.A. CHAMPIONSHIP	P. Stewart	(US)
THE INTERNATIONAL	G. Norman	(Aus)
CHATTANOOGA CLASSIC	S. Utley	(US)
NEC WORLD SERIES OF GOLF	*D. Frost	(SA)
GREATER MILWAUKEE OPEN	G. Norman	(Aus)
B.C. OPEN	*M. Hulbert	(US)
BANK OF BOSTON CLASSIC	B. McCallister	(US)
SOUTHERN OPEN	T. Schultz	(US)
CENTEL CLASSIC	B. Britton	(US)
TEXAS OPEN	D. Hammond	(US)
WALT DISNEY WORLD/OLDSMOBILE CLASSIC	T. Simpson	(US)
NABISCO CHAMPIONSHIPS	*T. Kite	(US)

* Winner in play-off

1989 USPGA TOUR

TOP 100 MONEY LIST

1	Tom Kite	$1,395,278	51	Ronnie Black	264,988
2	Payne Stewart	1,201,301	52	Leonard Thompson	261,397
3	Paul Azinger	951,649	53	Ian Baker-Finch	253,309
4	Greg Norman	835,096	54	Jay Hass	248,834
5	Mark Calcavecchia	807,741	55	Robert Wrenn	243,638
6	Tim Simpson	761,597	56	Mark Lye	242,884
7	Curtis Strange	752,587	57	David Edwards	238,908
8	Steve Jones	745,578	58	Andy Bean	236,097
9	Chip Beck	694,087	59	David Ogrin	234,196
10	Scott Hoch	670,680	60	Lanny Wadkins	233,363
11	Fred Couples	653,944	61	Steve Elkington	231,062
12	David Frost	620,430	62	Kenny Knox	230,012
13	Mark O'Meara	615,804	63	Brad Faxon	222,076
14	Mark McCumber	546,587	64	Curt Byrum	221,702
15	Blaine McCallister	523,891	65	Fuzzy Zoeller	217,742
16	Wayne Levi	499,292	66	Don Pooley	214,662
17	Bob Tway	488,340	67	Chris Perry	206,932
18	Mike Hulbert	477,621	68	John Huston	203,207
19	Bill Glasson	474,511	69	Billy Andrade	202,242
20	Donnie Hammond	458,741	70	Kenny Perry	202,099
21	Ben Crenshaw	443,095	71	Jay Don Blake	200,499
22	Mike Donald	430,232	72	Joey Sindelar	196,092
23	Hal Sutton	422,703	73	Bernhard Langer	195,973
24	Dave Rummells	419,979	74	Dan Pohl	195,789
25	Craig Stadler	409,419	75	Dave Barr	190,480
26	Jodie Mudd	404,860	76	Brian Tennyson	189,345
27	Wayne Grady	402,364	77	Ed Fiori	188,637
28	Mike Reid	401,665	78	Bob Gilder	187,910
29	John Mahaffey	400,467	79	Larry Nelson	186,869
30	Ted Schulz	391,855	80	Tom Watson	185,398
31	Nick Faldo	327,981	81	Tommy Armour	185,018
32	Tom Byrum	320,939	82	Corey Pavin	177,084
33	Jim Carter	319,719	83	Doug Tewell	174,607
34	Bill Britton	307,978	84	Brad Bryant	174,393
35	Steve Pate	306,554	85	Billy Ray Brown	162,964
36	Bruce Lietzke	305,987	86	Hubert Green	161,190
37	Ken Green	304,754	87	James Hallett	155,658
38	Gene Sauers	303,669	88	Tom Purtzer	154,868
39	Gill Morgan	300,395	89	Jeff Sluman	154,507
40	Scott Simpson	298,920	90	Greg Twiggs	154,302
41	Mark Wiebe	296,269	91	Bobby Wadkins	152,184
42	Nick Price	296,170	92	Lon Hinkle	151,828
43	Sandy Lyle	292,293	93	Hale Irwin	150,977
44	Davis Love III	278,760	94	Duffy Waldorf	149,945
45	Larry Mize	278,388	95	Gary Hallberg	146,833
46	Loren Roberts	275,882	96	Lance Ten Broeck	146,568
47	Mike Sullivan	273,962	97	Ian Woosnam	146,323
48	Peter Jacobsen	267,241	98	Bob Lohr	144,242
49	Clarence Rose	267,141	99	Dan Forsman	141,174
50	Jim Gallagher Jnr	265,809	100	Phil Blackmar	140,949

UNITED STATES LADIES PGA TOUR

1989 TOURNAMENT WINNERS

The Jamaica Classic: Betsy King
Oldsmobile LPGA Classic: Dottie Mochrie
Hawaiian Open: Sherri Turner
Women's Kemper Open: Betsy King
Circle K LPGA Tucson: Lori Garbacz
Standard Register Turquoise Classic: Allison Finney
Nabisco Dinah Shore: Julie Inkster
Red Robin Kyocera Inamori Classic: Patti Rizzo
Al Star/Centinela Hospital Classic: Pat Bradley
USX Golf Classic: Betsy King
Sara Lee Classic: Kathy Postlewait
Crestar Classic: Julie Inkster
Chrysler-Plymouth Classic: Cindy Rarick
Mazda LPGA Championship: Nancy Lopez
LPGA Corning Classic: Ayako Okamoto
Rochester International: Patty Sheehan
Planters Pat Bradley International: Robin Hood
Lady Keystone Open: Laura Davies

McDonald's Championship: Betsy King
du Maurier Classic: Tammie Green
Jamie Farr Toledo Classic: Penny Hammel
US Women's Open: Betsy King
Boston Five Classic: Amy Alcott
Atlantic City LPGA Classic: Nancy Lopez
Greater Washington Open: Beth Daniel
Nestle World Championship: Betsy King
Ocean State Open: Tina Barrett
Rail Charity Classic: Beth Daniel
Cellular One-Ping Golf Championship: Muffin Spencer-Devlin
Safeco Classic: Beth Daniel
Nippon Travel-MBS Classic: Nancy Lopez
Konica San Jose Classic: Beth Daniel
Nichirei Ladies Cup US-Japan Team Championship: Colleen Walker
Mazda Japan Classic: Elaine Crosby

LPGA Money List

1	Betsy King	$654,132	16	Penny Hammel	176,836
2	Beth Daniel	504,851	17	Kathy Postlewait	168,192
3	Nancy Lopez	487,153	18	Amy Alcott	168,089
4	Pat Bradley	423,714	19	Dawn Coe	143,423
5	Patty Sheehan	253,605	20	Allison Finney	143,342
6	Ayako Okamoto	205,745	21	Martha Nause	138,639
7	Colleen Walker	204,666	22	Lori Garbacz	138,124
8	Tammie Green	204,143	23	Danielle Ammaccapane	135,109
9	Patti Rizzo	198,868	24	Hollis Stacy	134,460
10	Sherri Turner	198,353	25	Shirley Furlong	133,149
11	Cindy Rarick	196,611	26	Jody Rosenthal	132,982
12	Jane Geddes	186,485	27	Dottie Mochrie	130,830
13	Laura Davies	181,574	28	Elaine Crosby	126,899
14	Julie Inkster	180,848	29	Nancy Brown	123,837
15	Alice Ritzman	177,507	30	Liselotte Neumann	119,915

JAPAN

GOLF IN JAPAN

Having earlier laid some of the blame for the curse of slow play at the American golfer's door, it is fair to suggest that the Japanese player often presents an even closer resemblance to the golfing tortoise. Racism on the fairways is not intended; rather one should have considerable sympathy for the vast majority of those Japanese bitten by the bug. For a start, getting a game in Japan can be incredibly difficult. Only in the United States are there a greater number of golfers, in fact about twice as many, yet there are eight times as many courses. The cost of a round of golf in Japan is very high, while membership of a club can border on the astronomical. Little wonder that the Japanese travel overseas for their golf, and when they do so, little wonder that they are determined to make the most of the experience!

One hears stories of Japanese golfers regularly jetting to Australia, North America and even to Europe just for a 'quick eighteen holes' because they cannot get a round in Japan. And then there are those who cannot afford the air fare and spend their entire lives 'warming up' hitting millions of balls on enormous multitiered driving ranges. 'Invest in land,' Mark Twain advised his son. 'It's the one thing they're not making any more of.' More's the pity for the golf-crazy Japanese.

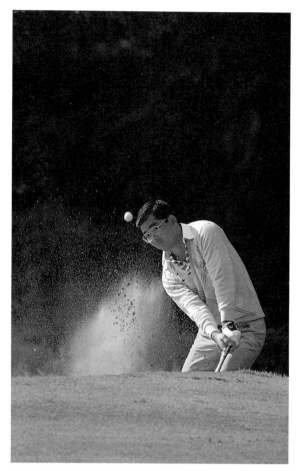

Tommy Nakajima

THE 1989 JAPAN PGA TOUR

Jumbo Ozaki, Japan Open winner, 1989

For several years commentators have been saying, 'It's only a matter of time before a Japanese golfer wins a major championship.' Japan's 'big three' of the seventies and eighties, Ozaki, Aoki and Nakajima, have all threatened to deliver at various times. Aoki, he of the extraordinary putting stroke, came closest in 1980 when he finished ahead of all but Jack Nicklaus in the US Open at Baltusrol. A decade on, could 1990 at last be the year of the big breakthrough?

Like a fine wine, Ozaki seems to improve with age. In 1989 he won six times on the Japanese tour, his victories including the Japan Open, Japan PGA Championship and the Japan PGA Matchplay. Ozaki rarely competes overseas, but in 1989 he finished only three strokes behind Curtis Strange in the US Open and was tied for the lead at one stage. Perhaps Ozaki's time will come soon: the world has already hailed a US Open and Masters champion named Fuzzy, so why should it not soon salute a champion called Jumbo?

Extending well beyond the European and USPGA tours, the Japanese tour attracts some very strong fields late in the season. Its international flavour is enhanced by the annual Four Tours tournament in November, an event won in 1989 by the USPGA Tour. By the end of the year tournament winners had included Jose-Maria Olazabal and Larry Mize, while no fewer than five Australians triumphed on the tour in 1989.

JAPAN PGA TOUR 1989

Tournament winners

Shizuoka Open Koichi Suzuki
Setonaiki Open Naomichi Ozaki
Pocarisweat Open Yoshikazu Yokoshima
Bridgestone Aso Open Craig Parry
Chunichi Crowns Greg Norman
Fuji Sankei Classic Masashi 'Jumbo' Ozaki
Japan PGA Matchplay Masashi 'Jumbo' Ozaki
Pepsi-Ube Tournament Akihito Yokoyama
Mitsubishi Galant Tateo 'Jet' Ozaki
Sendai Hoso Classic Masashi 'Jumbo' Ozaki
Sapporo Tokyu Graham Marsh
Yomiuri Sapporo Hajime Meshiai
Mizuno Open Akyoshi Omachi
Kanto (Eastern Japan) PGA Championship Saburo Fujiki
Kansai (Western Japan) PGA Championship Hajime Matsui
Hiroshima Open Masashi 'Jumbo' Ozaki

NCT Niigata Open Katsuyoshi Tomori
Japan PGA Championship Masashi 'Jumbo' Ozaki
Nikkei Cup Yoshimi Niizeki
Maruman Open Koichi Suzuki
KBC Augusta Teruo Sugihara
Suntory Open Larry Nelson
ANA Apporo Open Masashi 'Jumbo' Ozaki
Jun Classic Tateo 'Jet' Ozaki
Tokai Classic Isao Aoki
Japan Open Masashi 'Jumbo' Ozaki
Golf Digest Open Yoshikazu Yokoshima
Bridgestone Open Roger Mackay
Lark Cup Brian Jones
Taiheiyo Masters Jose Maria Olazabal
Dunlop Phoenix Larry Mize
Casio World Open Isao Aoki
Japan Series Hitachi Cup Akyoshi Omachi
Daikyo Open Nobuo Serizawa

1989 Japan PGA Tour Money List

1	'Jumbo' Ozaki	Y108,715,733
2	Naomichi Ozaki	76,690,766
3	Brian Jones	70,690,766
4	Isao Aoki	53,125,400
5	Graham Marsh	52,601,000
6	Nobuo Serizawa	50,697,499
7	Jet Ozaki	50,045,314
8	Yoshikazu Yokoshima	47,795,371
9	Tsuneyaki Nakajima	46,807,186
10	Akyoshi Omachi	45,793,100

£1 = Y242 *(approximately)*

'Inscrutable' Isao Aoki

JAPAN'S 'INTERNATIONAL' TOUR .

ASAHI GLASS FOUR TOURS WORLD CHAMPIONSHIP

Tokyo Yomiuri, 2-5 November

FIRST DAY
USPGA Tour halved with PGA European Tour 6-6
Aust./NZ. PGA Tour beat PGA Japan 8-4

SECOND DAY
USPGA Tour beat Aust./NZ. PGA Tour 10-2
PGA Japan lost to PGA European Tour 3-9

THIRD DAY
Aust./NZ. Tour lost to PGA European Tour 5-7
USPGA Tour beat PGA Japan 10-2

FINAL ROUND-ROBIN TABLE
USPGA Tour 26 points
PGA European Tour 22 points
Aust./NZ. Tour 15 points
PGA Japan 9 points

FOURTH DAY
Third/fourth place play-off
Aust./NZ. Tour lost to PGA Japan 3-9

FINAL .
PGA European Tour halved with USPGA Tour 6-6
(USA won 404 strokes to 410)
James (74) lost to Calcavecchia (68).
Rafferty (66) beat Green (70).
Brand Jnr (69) beat Stewart (70).
Langer (68) lost to Beck (62).
Woosnam (71) lost to Kite (65).
Olazabal (68) beat Strange (69).

LEADING INDIVIDUAL SCORES

C. Beck	69	69	65	62	265
G. Norman	68	71	64	65	268
C. Strange	65	68	68	69	270
R. Rafferty	69	66	69	66	270
T. Kite	70	69	69	65	273
B. Langer	70	69	66	68	273
M. Calcavecchia	72	67	67	68	274
N. Ozaki	68	72	67	67	274

VISA TAIHEIYO MASTERS

Taiheiyo, 9-12 November

J.M. Olazabal	66	70	67	203	Y16,200,000
N. Ozaki	70	66	70	206	7,560,000
I. Aoki	71	70	65	206	7,560,000
N. Serizawa	69	67	71	207	3,720,000
B. Lane	67	72	68	207	3,720,000
K. Green	71	65	71	207	3,720,000
G. Marsh	70	69	69	208	2,610,000
T.M. Chen	71	67	70	208	2,610,000
R. Kawagishi	69	67	72	208	2,610,000
J. Sluman	73	69	67	209	2,070,000
M. Ozaki	73	70	67	210	1,476,000

DUNLOP PHOENIX

Phoenix, 16-19 November

L. Mize	69	64	71	68	272	Y28,800,000
N. Ozaki	66	70	69	71	276	16,000,000
B. McCallister	68	69	72	69	278	10,880,000
T. Ozaki	72	66	71	70	279	7,680,000
M. Reid	71	69	70	70	280	6,080,000
J. Sluman	69	70	70	71	280	6,080,000
Y. Yokoshim	68	69	70	75	282	4,880,000
L. Nelson	73	67	72	70	282	4,880,000
A. Yokoyama	72	70	70	71	283	3,920,000
S. Ballesteros	73	68	69	73	283	3,920,000

CASIO WORLD OPEN

Ibusuki, 23-26 November

I. Aoki	70	70	65	69	274	Y18,000,000
L. Mize	67	71	67	70	275	10,000,000
G. Marsh	68	71	67	70	276	6,800,000
M. Calcavecchia	69	69	70	69	277	4,800,000
T.C. Chen	68	72	68	70	278	4,000,000
N. Ozaki	66	70	74	69	279	2,920,000
T. Nakamura	71	69	71	68	279	2,920,000
H. Green	68	67	69	75	279	2,920,000
B. McCallister	70	70	69	70	279	2,920,000
S. Simpson	74	68	68	69	279	2,920,000

Graham Marsh

AUSTRALASIA

Huntingdale, near Melbourne, home of the Australian Masters

GOLF IN AUSTRALASIA

It is hardly surprising that people on the other side of the world refer to the British as pommie so-and-so's. In 1973 Britain joined the Common Market and within six years there were European golfers playing in the Ryder Cup. I don't suppose it crossed the minds of the powers-that-be to consider inviting Commonwealth players to join the 'home' side to face the all-conquering Americans. How might we have fared with the addition of Von Nida, Thomson (five times an Open Champion), Nagle (Open Champion of 1960), Crampton and Charles (Open Champion of 1963) in the side during the fifties and sixties? Had Ryder Cup history taken such a course it is possible that Greg Norman and not Seve Ballesteros would have been Tony Jacklin's 'inspirational lieutenant' throughout the classic Ryder Cup encounters of the 1980s. It's an interesting thought.

During the past decade the growth of a strong professional tour in Australasia has been stifled by fierce competition in the early summer months (October and November) from the lucrative Japanese tour and from prestigious end-of-season events on the American and European tours and in January and February by the early starts of those same tours. Despite this the Australasian Tour has a number of attractive fixtures; moreover the quality of the courses over which these tournaments are staged is second to none.

Brett Ogle

Ian Baker-Finch

THE 1989 AUSTRALASIAN TOUR

Greg Norman's two tour wins early in 1989, including a fifth Australian Masters title, were somewhat eclipsed by a brilliant end-of-year hat-trick from fellow Queenslander Peter Senior. Senior spent much of 1989 on the European tour, where he had a fairly frustrating and winless year. But in November and December he found his form with a vengeance. Wielding his broom-handled putter like a magician with a wand, he first captured the Australian PGA Championship and then stormed to a seven-stroke victory in the Australian Open at Kingston Heath. Only five Australians have previously achieved the PGA–Open double. As if that were not enough, he celebrated Christmas early with a five-stroke win over Norman in the Johnnie Walker Classic at Royal Melbourne.

Senior's win in the Australian Open was particularly impressive because, in addition to Norman, his competition included Faldo, the Masters champion, Strange, the US Open champion, and Calcavecchia, the reigning British Open champion.

The Australian Masters was one of five victories that Norman achieved worldwide in 1989. At Huntingdale he was so nearly denied by the then English amateur player Russell Claydon. Only a late surge over the final nine holes by Norman decided the issue. Two months later at Augusta he came desperately close to securing a unique Australian–US Masters double.

Early in the year there were wins on the tour for Curtis Strange and Isao Aoki, and sharing Senior's end-of-year party were popular winners Rodger Davis and Nick Price.

Curtis Strange, an early winner in Australia

1989 AUSTRALASIAN TOUR WINNERS

Palm Meadows Cup	Curtis Strange
Coca-Cola International	Isao Aoki
Victorian PGA Championship	David Ecob
Victorian Open	Mike Clayton
Australian Matchplay	Ossie Moore
Australian Masters	Greg Norman
Australian TPC	Greg Norman
Nedland Masters	Louis Brown
Joondalup Classic	Brad King
Tasmanian Open	Ian Stanley
Air New Zealand/Shell Open	Don Bies
AMP New Zealand Open	Greg Turner
Australian PGA Championship	Peter Senior
New South Wales Open	Rodger Davis
West End Open	Nick Price
Australian Open	Peter Senior
Johnnie Walker Classic	Peter Senior
Queensland Open	Brett Ogle

Greg Norman's fifth Australian Masters win

Peter Senior, Australian Open winner, 1989

THE REST OF THE WORLD

GLOBAL GOLF

It must seem a cruel world to those who detest the game of golf. From its parochial beginnings on the East Coast of Scotland, some 500 years ago, golf has been taken to every corner of the globe. Not even the exotic islands of Tahiti and Bali have escaped. There is a golf club in the Arctic, the appropriately named 'Polar Bear Club', and at least one in the Himalayas, while the Americans have even taken golf to the surface of the Moon. The *Benson and Hedges Golf Year* intends to stay firmly on terra firma.

For a variety of reasons the majority of the world's leading players rarely compete away from their home circuits. In any sport it is always harder to win away from home. For this reason Gary Player's record (he long ago passed the 100 victories worldwide landmark) over the past thirty-five years is remarkable. It is also why Ben Hogan's greatest triumph came at Carnoustie in the 1953 Open, the only one he ever entered, and why Jack Nicklaus values his six Australian Open Championship wins so highly.

This section includes the 1989 results from some of the world's smaller tours and from the World Cup of Golf, the one tournament on the global calendar where the minnows can really get to rub shoulders with the mighty.

ASIAN TOUR

1989 Tournament winners

Philippine Open	Emlyn Aubrey
Hong Kong Open	Brian Claar
Thailand Open	Brian Claar
Pakistan Open	Frankie Minoza
Indian Open	Remi Bouchard
Singapore Open	Lu-Chien Soon
Indonesian Open	Kasiyadi
Malaysian Open	Jeff Maggert
Taiwan Open	Chien-Chun Lu
Korean Open	Hsi-Cheun Lu
Dunlop International	Terry Gale

SOUTH AFRICAN TOUR

1989 Tournament winners

Dewars White Label Trophy	John Bland
ICL International	Chris Williams
Lexington PGA Championship	Tony Johnstone
Palabora Classic	Stuart Smith
South African Open	Fred Wadsworth
AECI Classic	Jeff Hawkes
Swazi Sun Pro-Am	Jeff Hawkes
Trust Bank Tournament of Champions	Jay Townsend
South African Nissan Skins	Gary Player
Bloemfontein Classic	Des Terblanche
Minolta Copiers Matchplay	Fulton Allem
Wild Coast Skins	Scott Hoch
Sun City $1 Million Challenge	David Frost
South Africa Masters	Hugh Baiocchi

SAFARI TOUR

1989 Tournament winners

Zimbabwe Open	Vijay Singh
Zambia Open	Craig Maltman
Kenya Open	David Jones
Nigerian Open	Vijay Singh
Ivory Coast Open	Vijay Singh

THE WORLD CUP, LAS BRISAS, MARBELLA

16-19 NOVEMBER

The rain in Spain fell mainly at Las Brisas during the World Cup

LEADING FINAL SCORES

AUSTRALIA	**278**			
P. Fowler	66	71	137	
W. Grady	68	73	141	$120,000 each
SPAIN	**281**			
J.M. Olazabal	70	73	143	
J.M. Canizares	71	67	138	60,000 each
UNITED STATES	**287**			
P. Azinger	70	71	141	
M. McCumber	73	73	146	38,000 each
SWEDEN	**287**			
M. Lanner	69	73	142	
O. Sellberg	73	72	145	38,000 each
WALES	**288**			
P. Parkin	72	72	144	
M. Mouland	75	69	144	25,000 each
ARGENTINA	**290**			
M. Fernandez	71	69	140	
J. Coceres	77	73	150	17,500 each
NEW ZEALAND	**290**			
S. Owen	72	72	144	
G. Turner	73	73	146	17,500 each
DENMARK	**291**			
A. Sorensen	70	68	138	
S. Tinning	78	75	153	10,500 each
ENGLAND	**291**			
M. Roe	71	70	141	
D. Durnian	74	76	150	10,500 each
IRELAND	**294**			
D. Smyth	72	76	148	
C. O'Connor Jnr	73	73	146	8,000 each
SCOTLAND	**295**			
G. Brand Jnr	74	74	148	
S. Torrance	75	72	147	7,000 each
WEST GERMANY	**296**			
H.P. Thuel	72	73	145	
M. Gideon	76	75	151	5,000 each
FRANCE	**296**			
J. Van de Velde	73	75	148	
E. Dussart	75	73	148	5,000 each
ITALY	**296**			
M. Mannelli	74	74	148	
A. Bingahi	74	74	148	5,000 each

LEADING INDIVIDUAL SCORES

P. Fowler	66	71	137
A. Sorensen	70	68	138
J.M. Canizares	71	67	138
M. Fernandez	71	69	140
M. Roe	71	70	141
P. Azinger	70	71	141
W. Grady	68	73	141
M. Lanner	69	73	142
J.M. Olazabal	70	73	143

AMATEUR GOLF

Quite what the greatest of all amateur golfers, Bobby Jones, would have made of the scenes at Peachtree in his beloved Georgia last summer, it is difficult to imagine. Times have certainly changed, but one thing we can be sure of is that the American side would dearly have loved to have his like in their team to save them from losing the Walker Cup for the first time ever on home soil.

Although he never turned professional, Jones towered above his contemporaries, as he would surely have done in any era. His achievement in 1930 of winning the original Grand Slam – the Open, US Open, British Amateur and US Amateur – will surely never be equalled. Today any golfer who is suffi-

ciently talented to be considered a potential 'major' winner is unlikely to remain an amateur for long.

In the next few years we shall see if Russell Claydon has what it takes and can emulate Sandy Lyle and Nick Faldo, and – looking slightly further into the future – whether Helen Dobson, who at age 18 had such a brilliant year in 1989, can follow in Laura Davies's footsteps.

It being an even year, 1990 sees the staging of the Curtis Cup, with Britain and Ireland going for a hat-trick. With both the Walker and Curtis cups sitting on the British and Irish sideboard, surely the standard of our amateur game has rarely been higher.

The 1989 Walker Cup teams at Peachtree, Georgia

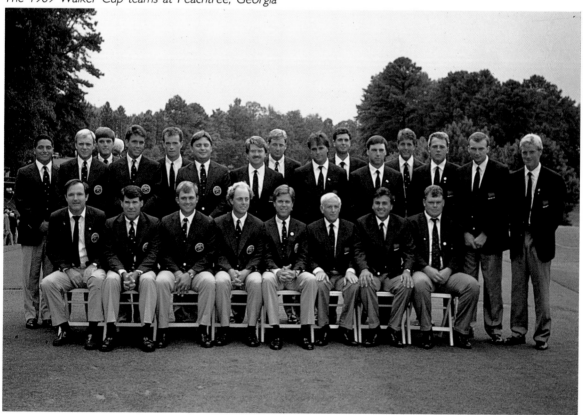

1989 THE WALKER CUP

Peachtree Golf Club, Atlanta, Georgia 16-17 August

HISTORY IN THE MAKING

'Milligan the Marvel' ... 'Milligan pulls Walker Cup out of the fire' ran the headlines last Friday, 18 August. It was, of course, the morning after the magnificent victory at Peachtree. If the Friday morning was a time for golfing hangovers, then the Thursday afternoon had so nearly been a time for golfing nightmares – at least on the British and Irish side.

Having outplayed a strong US side for a day and a half, the visitors went into the afternoon's eight singles matches with a seemingly unassailable 11 to 5 lead, requiring just one and a half points (or three halves, if you like) to gain a famous victory. At 4.30 pm that afternoon the scoreboards were telling an unbelievable story. The United States were up in all eight matches. One can imagine how quickly the news reached the American players and boosted their morale. That the visiting team eventually rallied to win the necessary three halves speaks volumes for the courage no less than the talent of the young British and Irish players. As the Irishman Eamonn Darcy will be forever remembered as the man who secured the first ever Ryder Cup win on American soil, so Scotsman Jim Milligan will be known as the player who created similar Walker Cup history. Darcy came back against a putterless Crenshaw; Milligan did it against Jay Sigel, the leading American amateur over the last two decades, and he did it despite being three down with seven to play, and two down with three to play. The shot that did it was a holed pitch from off the green at the 17th to square the match. Shades of Watson at Pebble Beach.

So, to all you collectors of golfing memorabilia, what price the 1989 double – O'Connor's 2-iron and Milligan's wedge?

Milligan does a Watson at the 17th

GREAT BRITAIN AND IRELAND   12½
UNITED STATES   11½

Great Britain and Ireland Team: C. Cassells; R. Claydon; S. Dodd; A. Hare; P. McEvoy; G. McGimpsey; J. Milligan; E. O'Connell; D. Prosser; N. Roderick

1989 AMATEUR CHAMPIONSHIP

Royal Birkdale 5-10 June

Second round

S. Bouvier beat J. Milligan 3 and 2
J. Payne beat D. Bathgate 2 and 1
R. Willison beat N. Williamson 5 and 4
B. Jackson beat M. Hastie 4 and 3
C. Cassells beat D. Basson at 19th
G. McGimpsey beat J. Robson at 22nd
J. Cook beat G. Walmsley at 19th
P. McEvoy beat G. Shaw 3 and 1
P. Nyman beat C. Dalrymple 2 and 1
C. Davison beat G. Vanier 2 and 1
R. Bardsley beat S. Wilkinson 4 and 3
S. Dodd beat K. Weeks 3 and 2
R. Karlsson beat T. Foster 2 holes
M. Smith beat D. Lee 2 and 1
A. Hare beat A. Coltart 4 and 3
S. McCraw beat G. Evans 3 and 2

Third round

J. Payne beat S. Bouvier 6 and 4
C. Cassells beat R. Willison 5 and 4
P. McEvoy beat J. Cook 1 hole
C. Davison beat P. Nyman 7 and 5
G. McGimpsey beat B. Jackson 1 hole
S. Dodd beat R. Bardsley 3 and 1
M. Smith beat R. Karlsson 2 and 1
S. McCraw beat A. Hare 4 and 3

Quarter-finals

C. Cassells beat J. Payne 1 hole
G. McGimpsey beat P. McEvoy 2 and 1
S. Dodd beat C. Davison 3 and 1
S. McCraw beat M. Smith at 19th

Semi-finals

C. Cassells beat G. McGimpsey 1 hole
S. Dodd beat S. McCraw 1 hole

Final

S. Dodd beat C. Cassells 5 and 3

Stephen Dodd, Amateur Champion, 1989

PAST CHAMPIONS

Post 1945

1946	J. Bruen
1947	W. Turnesa
1948	F. Stranahan
1949	S. McCready
1950	F. Stranahan
1951	R. Chapman
1952	E. Ward
1953	J. Carr
1954	D. Bachli
1955	J. Conrad
1956	J. Beharrell
1957	R. Reid-Jack
1958	J. Carr
1959	D. Beaman
1960	J. Carr
1961	M. Bonallack
1962	R. Davies
1963	M. Lunt
1964	G. Clark
1965	M. Bonallack
1966	R. Cole
1967	R. Dickson
1968	M. Bonallack
1969	M. Bonallack
1970	M. Bonallack
1971	S. Melnyk
1972	T. Homer
1973	R. Siderowf
1974	T. Homer
1975	M. Giles
1976	R. Siderowf
1977	P. McEvoy
1978	P. McEvoy
1979	J. Sigel
1980	D. Evans
1981	P. Ploujoux
1982	M. Thompson
1983	P. Parkin
1984	J. Olazabal
1985	G. McGimpsey
1986	D. Curry
1987	P. Mayo
1988	C. Hardin

Most Victories
John Ball (8) between
1888 and 1912

AMATEUR CHAMPIONS OF 1989

British Amateur S. Dodd
English Amateur S. Richardson
Scottish Amateur A. Thomson
Welsh Amateur S. Dodd
Irish Amateur P. McGinley
British Youths M. Smith
British Boys C. Watts
British Seniors C. Green
English Amateur Strokeplay R. Roderick
Scottish Amateur Strokeplay F. Illouz
Welsh Amateur Strokeplay V. Thomas
Irish Amateur Strokeplay P. McGinley
English Boys I. Garbutt
Scottish Boys M. King
Welsh Boys R. Johnson
European Team Championship England
**Silver Medal – Leading Amateur in the Open
   Championship** R. Claydon
British Ladies H. Dobson 6 & 5; **runner-up**
   E. Farquharson
English Ladies H. Dobson
Scottish Ladies S. Huggan
Welsh Ladies V. Thomas
Irish Ladies M. McKenna
British Girls M. McKinlay
British Ladies Strokeplay H. Dobson

US Amateur C. Patton bt D Green 3 & 1

Russell Claydon, leading Amateur in the Open

GLOBE AMATEUR ORDER OF MERIT

1989

1	S. Dodd (Brynhill)	2896	14	J. Carvill (Warrenpoint)	957
2	P. McEvoy (Copt Heath)	1868	15	J. Payne (Sandilands)	884
3	J. Milligan (Kilmarnock Barassie)	1643	16	J. Cook (Leamington & County)	835
4	C. Cassells (Murcar)	1528	17	C. Everett (Cambuslang)	825
5	G. McGimpsey (Bangor)	1455	18	P. McGinley (The Grange)	817
6	D. Clarke (Dungannon)	1328	19	S. Easingwood (Dunbar)	788
7	N. Anderson (Shandon Park)	1121	20	J. Peters (Southerndown)	782
8	D. Carrick (Douglas Park)	1104		M. Smith (Brockenhurst Manor)	782
9	E. O'Connell (Killarney)	1097	22	J. Metcalfe (Arcot Hall)	751
10	R. Eggo (L'Ancresse)	1061	23	G. Wolstenholme (Leicestershire)	713
11	A. Coltart (Thornhill)	1033	24	C. Davison (Eaglescliffe)	645
12	R. Willison (Ealing)	1007	25	I. MacNamara (Woodbrook)	641
13	A. Thomson (Ayr Belleisle)	965			

SENIOR GOLF

No disrespect whatsoever to the likes of Neil Coles and Christy O'Connor, but if the next Ryder Cup were to be staged as an over-fifties event, Great Britain and Ireland (with or without Europe) would, one suspects, have little more than the proverbial cat in Hell's chance of retaining the trophy. Just imagine our boys teeing up against Nicklaus, Palmer, Trevino, Casper *et al.* . . . and in their own backyard as well – a frightening thought!

During the eighties, senior golf has grown from strength to strength in America, and with Jack Nicklaus and Lee ('I've been counting the days') Trevino now having reached the magical age and ready to renew their past battles, there are those who believe that the US Senior Tour will produce more excitement and thrills than its junior counterpart. Messrs Strange and Stewart would doubtless challenge such a suggestion, but with 1990 also heralding a fairways reunion of the sixties' 'Big Three', Palmer, Player and Nicklaus, the attraction is clearly apparent.

Meanwhile at home the Volvo British Seniors Open continues to produce strong fields and worthy winners. 1989 saw the title remain in the Southern Hemisphere when the man in black, Gary Player, relinquished his title to the man with the famous putter, Bob Charles.

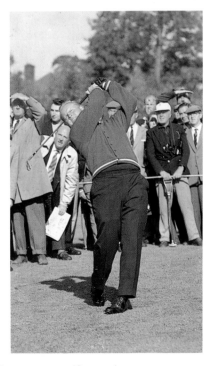

The 'Big Three' of the sixties – Palmer, Player and Nicklaus – now golfing seniors

VOLVO BRITISH SENIORS OPEN

Turnberry 27–30 July 1989

Great things happen at Turnberry: the Open of 1977 when Nicklaus and Watson turned the championship into an epic head-to-head confrontation and Greg Norman's 63 achieved in a strong wind en route to his winning the 1986 Open.

1988 and 1989 have seen two firsts at Turnberry. In 1988 Gary Player became the first golfer to win the British Open–British Seniors Open double. Last year Bob Charles equalled this feat, and as he is the only left-handed player ever to win either event, one wonders whether his particular double will ever be repeated. New Zealander Charles, who was pipped by Player for the US Seniors Title in 1988, won the Seniors Championship over Turnberry's Ailsa Course by an impressive seven shots and with an even more impressive total of 269. The winning margin was in fact the result of a last-day collapse by American Billy Casper, who had led the tournament throughout the first three rounds.

Like Nicklaus and Watson in 1977, both Charles and Casper scored third-round 65s, and playing together they had a remarkable better-ball score of 60. They say life begins at forty; for golfers, it seems, it can tee off a little later.

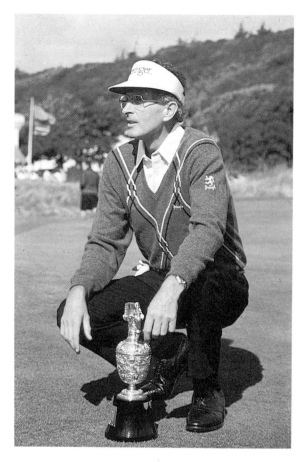

Bob Charles, British Seniors Champion, 1989

LEADING FINAL SCORES

Bob Charles (NZ)	70	68	65	66	269	£25,000	Anthony Grubb (Eng)	73	72	70	73	288	3,235
Bill Casper (USA)	67	69	65	75	276	16,400	Bert Yancey (USA)	75	68	71	75	289	2,716
Bryant Hiskey (USA)	71	71	65	72	279	9,150	Larry Mancour (USA)	72	68	73	76	289	2,716
Gary Player (SA)	74	68	69	71	282	6,750	Doug Dalziel (USA)	72	76	71	70	289	2,716
David Butler (Eng)	72	74	67	69	282	6,750	Ross Whitehead (Eng)	73	73	68	76	290	2,430
Neil Coles (Eng)	70	74	70	69	283	5,100	Jack O'Keefe (USA)	76	74	71	70	291	2,200
Christy O'Connor (Ire)	76	70	70	68	284	4,340	Art Silverstone (USA)	73	74	73	71	291	2,200
Arnold Palmer (USA)	74	72	70	70	286	3,610	Agim Bardha (Alb)	70	77	69	75	291	2,200

1989 US SENIORS TOUR WINNERS

Gary Player won senior golf's richest prize in 1989, the RJR Championship

MONY Tournament of Champions	Miller Barber
PGA Championship	Larry Mowry
GTE Suncoast Classic	Bob Charles
Aetna Challenge	Gene Littler
Vintage Chrysler Invitational	Miller Barber
MONY Arizona Classic	Bruce Crampton
Fuji Electric Grand Slam	Bob Charles
Murata Seniors Reunion	Don Bies
The TRADITON at Desert Mountain	Don Bies
Chrysler Cup	USA
Legends of Golf	Al Geiberger and Harold Henning
RJR At The Dominion	Larry Mowry
Bell Atlantic	Dave Hill
NYNEX/Golf Digest Commemorative	Bob Charles
Southwestern Bell Classic	Bobby Nichols
Doug Sanders Kingwood Celebrity	Homero Blancas
Mazda Senior TPC	Orville Moody
Northville Long Island Classic	Butch Baird
MONY Syracuse Senior Classic	Jim Dent
USGA Senior Open	Orville Moody
Digital Seniors Classic	Bob Charles
Greater Grand Rapids Open	John Paul Cain
Ameritech Senior Open	Bruce Crampton
Newport Cup	Jim Dent
Showdown Classic	Tom Shaw
Rancho Murieta Senior Gold Rush	Dave Hill
GTE Northwest Classic	Al Geiberger
Sunwest Bank/Charley Pride Classic	Bob Charles
RJR Bank One Classic	Rives McBee
GTE North Classic	Gary Player
Crestar Classic	Chi Chi Rodriguez
Fairfield Barnett Space Coast Classic	Bob Charles
The RJR Championship	Gary Player
Gatlin Brothers Southwest Classic	George Archer
Transamerica Championship	Billy Casper
General Tire Classic	Charles Coody
GTE Classic	Walter Zembriski
GTE Kaanapali Classic	Don Bies

4

WHEN THE PEN IS MIGHTIER
THAN THE PUTTER

'Man is only truly great when he acts from his passions'
(Disraeli)

GREATEST CHAMPIONSHIP MOMENTS
GREATEST 18 HOLES
GREATEST MISTAKES
GREATEST BRITISH LADY GOLFER
GREATEST GOLF RESORT
GREATEST GAME
GREATEST ROUNDS

GREATEST CHAMPIONSHIP MOMENTS

Colin Callander

Ben Hogan at Carnoustie, 1953

1953 was the year of two Coronations. One took place in London, the other in a small town on the east coast of Scotland. It was the year when Ben Hogan came to Britain to try to add the Open Championship to his already impressive collection of major titles. That week golf's history books were rewritten. Hogan at Carnoustie was one of the game's greatest championship moments.

1977 was the year of the Silver Jubilee and also the year that Jack Nicklaus sought revenge for his defeat by Tom Watson earlier that year in the Masters; the unforgettable High Noon at Turnberry.

Colin Callander, deputy editor of *Golf Monthly*, describes some of golf's many great championship moments and how, in his opinion, there was an occasion when even 1953 and 1977 were surpassed.

It was in the summer of 1953 that Ben Hogan made his historic trip across the Atlantic to compete in the Open Championship. In almost a fortnight in and around Carnoustie he was to mesmerize the locals with his technique and stun them with his will to succeed. The name Hogan is still voiced in reverential tones in the small Angus town. Over the years its inhabitants have welcomed almost all of the world's top golfers to their windswept course, but it is the man that was christened the 'Wee Ice Mon' who is still considered supreme.

Prior to 1953 Hogan had claimed all three of the major championships held in the USA. He had won the USPGA and the Masters twice and the US Open three times, but he had never considered it worthwhile to come to the oldest championship of them all. In the end it was only the persuasive powers of some of his American colleagues which made him realize that his record wouldn't be complete without an Open crown.

Even as we enter the 1990s memories of Hogan are still fresh in Carnoustie. A succession of the town's older golfers have passed on tales of his awesome accuracy and his successful struggle in practice to come to terms with the small British ball, which he had never encountered before. A whole generation of local schoolchildren has read how the campaign produced four rounds, each lower than the one before (73–71–70–68) to finish four shots clear of a demoralized field. The whole episode remains one of the most enduring highlights in a game which is blessed with a wealth of wonderful tales.

Right from its inception in 1860 the Open has produced more memorable moments than most sporting events. But the Open isn't alone in this. Thousands of words have been written on the highlights from the three American majors. The game of golf is fortunate in its rich lore just as it is in the characters who have graced its past.

Another man to emulate Hogan in winning the Open title at his first attempt was fellow American Tony Lema. A lover of the high life, 'Champagne Tony' reached the pinnacle of his career at the Open at St Andrews in 1964.

Lema's triumph was without doubt one of the most remarkable achievements in the history of the championship. He had never played in Europe before and had allowed a mere 36 hours to acquaint himself with the peculiarities of the Old Course. But over the four rounds of the Championship he showed rare judgment in coming to terms with the vast double-greens, which have baffled overseas visitors, and a superb touch for manufacturing shots which in America a golfer is seldom called on to master.

At the time it seemed certain that Lema would go on to win many more major titles. But that glorious prospect was lost in 1966 when he died in a private aircraft which crashed on landing at Lansing, Illinois. His wife, Betty, and a number of his closest friends also perished.

Bobby Jones was another golfer with a short but glorious career and a strong bond with the Home of Golf. He first came to Britain in 1921, when he lost in the fourth round of the Amateur Championship at Hoylake before travelling to St Andrews for the Open. Though he later grew to love the Old Course above all others, and was to be granted the freedom of the Burgh (the first American to be so honoured since Benjamin Franklin), his first trip to the Fife town could hardly have ended more inauspiciously. Infuriated by the subtleties of the Old Course, he tore up his card during the fourth round. Later he was to win both the Open (1927) and the Amateur (1930) over the same course, but his earlier indiscretion haunted him till his death in 1971.

In the space of seven years from 1923 until 1930, when he retired from competitive golf at the tender age of 28, Jones put together a record which remains unique. During that time he won 13 major titles (four US Opens, five US Amateurs, three Opens and one Amateur). He even achieved the Grand Slam by winning all four events in 1930. Bernard Darwin once suggested that Jones shared with Harry Vardon a relentless precision not given to a single other golfer.

But it wasn't just on the course that the world's best amateur golfer left his mark.

Jones's other major contribution to the game of golf was that he was instrumental in founding Augusta National GC and its hallowed Masters tournament. It started as a humble club invitational but was to develop into one of the most prestigious championships in the world. It has gained a special place in the hearts of all golfers and has produced more than its share of magical moments.

No single shot has ever achieved such lasting fame as the 4-wood which Gene Sarazen holed for an albatross on the 15th hole in the final round of the Masters in 1935. It enabled Sarazen to catch Craig Wood, who had seemed to have an unassailable lead in the clubhouse, and to beat him in the subsequent play-off. It was also instrumental in Sarazen becoming the first golfer to win all four of the modern major titles and was responsible for putting Augusta and the Masters on the map.

Sarazen's shot was later described, without an ounce of exaggeration, as 'a shot heard round the world'. Alongside Tom Watson's pitch on the 17th hole in the final round of the 1982 US Open at Pebble Beach and Bob Tway's holed bunker shot on the final hole of the 1986 USPGA Championship at Inverness it remains one of the most dramatic examples of a single shot transforming the outcome of a major championship.

In this category one would also place the miraculous pitch which Larry Mize holed on the second extra hole to win the Masters in 1987 and Lee Trevino's outrageous chip on the penultimate hole at the Open at Muirfield in 1972. In all these instances one shot decided the outcome of a tournament at a time when it seemed the trophy was destined to go to someone else.

Thus far in this trip down memory lane we have recounted some of the most memorable moments witnessed in the last 60 years of championship golf. Each warrants a revered place in the annals of the game, but none, I believe, can compare with two episodes which stand out even more.

A cursory glance at his record will convince even the most sceptical reader that Jack Nicklaus has achieved a unique place

Larry Mize

in the game of golf. But the records alone don't tell us all. A list of his achievements can never paint a true picture of his massive contribution. It is not enough to know that he has won 20 majors in three decades, or that in the majors he has come second 19 times and finished in the top ten on no fewer than 71 occasions. He has also been a central figure in some of the finest dramas ever seen on a golf course.

One such was the famous 'Duel in the Sun' in the 1977 Open at Turnberry, in which Nicklaus and Tom Watson fought such a spectacular contest that the third-place finisher was left languishing ten shots behind. On that occasion both Nicklaus and Watson seemed almost superhuman. For four rounds the leading protagonists fought head to head over the spectacular Ayrshire links. The issue was only decided when both birdied the final hole in front of thousands surrounding the green and a worldwide TV audience of millions. Such was the spectacle it was a shame that either had to lose. But it was Watson who triumphed when he holed his three-foot putt to complete a record score of 268.

For some, the 'Duel in the Sun' represents the finest chapter in the rich history of championship golf. It was one of those rare occasions when two of the world's best golfers both managed to surpass themselves at the same time. But to this mind at least it is pushed into second place by another drama which occurred some nine years later on the other side of the world.

When the same Jack Nicklaus arrived at Augusta National in 1986 to compete in the annual Masters tournament most commentators believed that he was no longer the force he once had been. He was 46. It was six years since he had captured a Major and 22 months since he had won a tournament at all. But he was about to produce arguably his finest performance.

In times to come, the 1986 Masters will be recalled as the championship in which the Bear turned the clock back. Stung by a comment in the US press that he was finished, he seemed to shed almost 20 years overnight.

Starting the final round four shots behind the leaders, Nicklaus romped round the formidable Augusta course in 65 to register his most spectacular triumph. During the final nine holes it was noisier at Augusta than at Piccadilly Circus in the rush-hour as his fans celebrated something which most thought they would never witness again.

With due respect to Hogan and the residents of Carnoustie, this was the crowning moment in the rich history of championship golf.

Nicklaus captures his sixth Masters title in 1986

GREATEST 18 HOLES

Derek Lawrenson

Is there a golf course in heaven? If so, what does the Pearly Gates Golf and Country Club look like? It is said that the golfing Englishman prays for a second Sunningdale; the Scotsman, for a replica of the Old Course at St Andrews, and the American for a celestial Cypress Point. But why not a good mixture of all three, with perhaps a dash of Augusta and Royal County Down thrown in for good measure?

Roving golf writer **Derek Lawrenson** has decided that he cannot wait until he gets to heaven. Instead he has conjured his own perfect 18 holes by way of an eventful and highly pleasurable dream. But then, judging by the conclusion to his dream, there must be some doubt as to whether St Peter would accept his application for membership anyway.

The sleep is a deep one and the dream so real you feel you are out there living it. You are playing your favourite 18 holes, but they are not scattered all over the globe, they have been gathered together for your delectation.

As far as golf goes, this is your ultimate dream. All you have to do is to conjure up the hole in your mind's eye and there it will be, waiting for you to play it, with no intrusive souls in front, no rain, and just the softest of summer breezes.

The rest of nature will present itself. Of course there will be oceans involved, for what golfer has never fallen in love with the sound of waves crashing against rocks as he putts? There will also be spectacular woodlands, for what golfer has not marvelled at the different species of trees, even as his ball heads for the most troublesome of them?

You decide quickly that your dream 18 holes will be like a proper golf course, albeit a golf course that only the Almighty could construct. Your first instinct was that there would be a surfeit of par threes, for the world is full of great short holes. In the end you restrict yourself to five, add four par fives and nine fours. Your par is 71, and in front of you lie approximately 6,650 yards of utopia. You start with a hearty breakfast, courtesy of The Berkshire, and wish yourself good luck.

You have no problem whatsoever choosing a starting hole. Although the rest of the holes in your dream course will not correspond precisely with their placing in their real homes, you find that many of them do so because that feels their true position. You feel, for example, the great starting holes could only be just that; if they were placed anywhere else in the round, they would be incongruous.

So you are on the first tee and to the left of you is the Atlantic, an ocean you will see much of during your round. Straight ahead is a six-mile-long beach with the fairway half right as you look. There is no other possible starting hole than the first at Machrihanish in Scotland.

No sooner has the first ocean zephyr raised your senses than you are on the second, the 4th at Valderrama in Spain. This is a long and winding par five that tapers to the narrowest of targets. While you pass along its length the beauty of the Spanish countryside consumes you, and all the while the waterfall that cuts into the right side of the green comes into ever-sharper focus.

You wonder at the fact that the owner could spend £1 million simply constructing this hazard, but it does bring a magnificent par five to a suitably dramatic conclusion. You decide that you would like to go back to the Atlantic next, to the 5th at Royal Portrush in Northern Ireland for your third hole. If the ocean was any closer to the green here, you think wellington boots would be needed rather than golf shoes. You would settle for a par four every time.

For your first par three you summon up the 17th at La Quinta, in Palm Springs, California. The green here truly is an oasis, the only safe ground in an area otherwise covered in desert rocks. The desert mountains are all around. You hit the green with your tee shot, which is not what happened in real life.

The fifth is the 5th at Sunningdale Old, arguably Britain's best inland course. Selecting just one hole here caused you problems but you settled on this medium-length par four where the accent is on the driver. And what a drive it is from that elevated tee!

And what a drive it is from your sixth, the par-five 15th at the vastly underrated Seefeld course in Austria! The Alps and Alpine woodland abound and the hole demands unerring accuracy. The view is equally breathtaking at the par-three seventh, which is the 7th at Pebble Beach in California. Robert Louis Stevenson once described this coastline as the 'finest meeting of land and sea in the world', and you remember once driving down to this course from San Francisco and agreeing with every word the author wrote. And this hole, surrounded on two sides by Atlantic breakers, captures the imagery perfectly.

You're in no mood to leave the sea now, and from your eighth, the Irish Sea is at your back. You are now standing on the famous 9th tee at Turnberry, a terrifying tee shot, but on this day one that holds no worries. The lighthouse stands fearlessly and so do you.

The ninth is similarly intimidating, the 9th at Royal County Down in Northern Ireland. Here you have a blind tee shot, your ball plunging into the fairway valley below. As you stand on the brow, you drink the view. The sea is there again, but so are the mountains. In the foreground is the lovely town of Newcastle and behind it the peerless mountains of Mourne which, as the poet said, really do sweep down to the sea.

After all that, you are feeling a little peckish and decide that a sausage sandwich from the old halfway hut at Wentworth would fit the bill perfectly.

And then it is off to the 10th at The Belfry. You had noted the lack of a great short par four and decide that now is the time. Even in your ultimate dream, however, you decide that to emulate Severiano Ballesteros's 310-yard tee shot to the green, all carry, is to stretch credulity a little too far.

Your eleventh is anything but short, the 17th at Muirfield. Pieces chipped from the hearts of Tony Jacklin (1972 Open) and Paul Azinger (1987) are to be found scattered on this par five, but better they rest on one of the great par fives than on a humdrum affair.

You decide your twelfth will be a par three and note how many great par threes are to be found in such a position on a course. You could choose Augusta's or Muirfield Village's, but eventually you settle on Royal Birkdale's, a treacherous hole if ever there was one, with accuracy with a long iron an absolute premium.

The 17th at the PGA West stadium course, La Quinta,
California

The 4th at Valderrama

The 17th at St Andrews

Augusta has to feature somewhere, of course, and you settle on its par-five 13th as your thirteenth. You hum to yourself how television does not really do it justice, failing to pick up the dramatic dog-leg sweep which must be mastered if the green is to be found in two blows.

You feel that Nicklaus's masterpiece at Muirfield Village must also be represented somewhere and you settle on its majestic short 12th as your fourteenth.

The fifteenth is the brutish par-four 15th at Carnoustie, while the sixteenth is a wolf in sheep's clothing. That is the par-three 17th at Cypress Point in California, a course so wonderful it was once referred to as the 'Sistine Chapel of Golf'.

But for your own seventeenth it has to be the Road Hole at the game's spiritual home, St Andrews, and the eighteenth has to be the finishing hole at Royal Lytham, a hole that invokes so many Open Championship memories; Tony Jacklin's arrow-straight drive en route to winning the 1969 Championship, Gary Player putting left-handed from up against the Clubhouse wall in 1974, and its two most recent championships, where the world has twice watched Ballesteros storm home in cavalier fashion.

And then it is over and it is off for lunch, a club sandwich on the lawns of Augusta. It was your round of a lifetime and you are wondering what life can there possibly be after it. You decide the only way to live after such an experience would be to spend the evening with Cherie Lunghi. But as you contemplate this heady prospect you are aware that someone is violently shaking you. It is your wife and when you are fully awake she throws reality all over you. 'Who's Cherie?' she says.

GREATEST MISTAKES

Chris Plumridge

'How on earth did he miss that one?' or 'Even I could have hit the green from that distance.'

We've all said it, and yet deep down we all know that we've missed shorter putts, and, when the chips are down, are rather prone to fluff wedge shots from the simplest of lies. Of course, it's no fun tweaking a three-footer which, if sunk, would have put us into the quarter-finals of the Withington Winter Knock-Out, but for most of us it's not going to materially affect our lives. Professional golfers inhabit a different world, where such mistakes can be disastrous.

Someone once said that the greatest chapter in the book of life is the chapter of accidents. Prolific golf writer **Chris Plumridge** guides us to the lengthy paragraph headed 'golfing mistakes'.

The moment early man first picked up a stick and took a swipe at a pebble he was, unwittingly, unleashing an enormous potential for disaster. Any time an object is launched into space by human endeavour, the chances are that the object, at some time or another, will create mayhem. In its simplest terms, golf is merely the launching of an object into space over an area specifically allotted for such an activity. Therefore, it would seem that the potential for disaster is somewhat limited and that golfers happily send the golf ball into the air with nary a thought to any of the consequences. Such naivety is touching and totally misplaced.

But how can a mere game and the disasters which emerge from it compare with the myriad disasters which daily fill the columns of our newspapers? Flood, drought, pestilence and famine are real disasters, surely not somebody missing a putt of three feet to take all the marbles? This opinion, although worthy, loses sight of the fact that golf is more than just a game and to a professional golfer it is a career, a livelihood, a roof over the family's head and three square meals a day on the table. Faced with such pressures it is hardly surprising that those who are the most skilled exponents suffer the most calamitous falls from grace. If an ordinary golfer takes 11 strokes to complete one hole, very few people outside his immediate circle of friends will hear about it. If Severiano Ballesteros takes 11 strokes to complete a hole (something he once did, incidentally), the world is very quickly informed.

How do such things happen? The answer lies in the dark recesses of the human psyche: those occasions when the brain and the body are working in diametric opposition and a kind of madness takes over. When this happens it is not a pretty sight. Golfers of a nervous disposition may wish to move on to something less harrowing before studying the following case histories.

What a stupid I am

Some ten million people watching the 1968 US Masters on television witnessed Roberto de Vicenzo gain a birdie three on the 17th hole in the final round. But one very important person didn't see the birdie, namely Tommy Aaron, who was playing with de Vicenzo and marking his card. Aaron put down a four on the Argentinian's card. At the completion of the round, de Vicenzo signed his card for what he thought was a 65 and was rushed off for a TV interview, as it was likely he would be the winner or at least tie with Bob Goalby for the title.

Suddenly it became apparent that a dreadful error had been perpetrated. By signing his card de Vicenzo had made his four at the 17th inviolate, and his total for the round, 66, had to stand. It made de Vicenzo's total 278 against Goalby's 277, and Goalby was the Masters champion. It was a hollow victory from which Goalby never recovered. On the other hand, de Vicenzo took this disaster on the chin and in his speech at the prize-giving remarked in his broken English: 'What a stupid I am.'

Agony at Augusta

In the 1979 US Masters at Augusta National, Ed Sneed had dominated the event and with three holes to play held a three-stroke lead. He three-putted the 16th, but no matter, one par and a bogey would see him home. On the 17th his second shot ran through the green and he took three more to get down. Now he was sweating. His second shot to the 18th came up short of the green, he chipped up to five feet, and then watched in agony as his putt for victory hung on the edge of the hole. His three closing bogeys meant he had tied on a score of 280 with Tom Watson and Fuzzy Zoeller, and it was Zoeller who claimed the title on the second hole of the first sudden-death play-off in Masters history.

And some have disaster thrust upon them

In the 1978 US Masters, Japan's Tsuneyuki Nakajima was making a creditable first appearance in the tournament. In the third round he came to the 13th hole handily placed for a decent cheque. From the tee he hooked his ball into the creek which meanders alongside the hole before crossing in front of the green. He dropped out under penalty and hit his third shot up the fairway. His pitch to the green fell into the creek but he felt he could play the ball. He played it quite well, but it bounced back off the bank and struck him on the foot, thereby adding two penalty strokes. He then handed the club back to his caddie, who dropped it in the water — two more penalty strokes added to the ledger. Finally Nakajima pitched over the green with his tenth shot, chipped and two-putted for a 13.

The Japanese are a philosophical nation, and Nakajima believed that the gods would compensate him for his woes on some future date. But the golfing gods are perverse and

Tommy Nakajima

in July of the same year, while playing in the Open at St Andrews, Nakajima was struck again, this time on the infamous Road Hole, St Andrews' 17th. Here he was on the front of the green in two shots, putted up the crest and watched in anguish as his ball turned sharp left into the Road Bunker. Four attempts later he returned to the green and walked off with a nine.

A catalogue of misses

The one area of the game where disaster is most clearly defined is on the putting green. Here there is no escape. It is the final act of the drama and it is this finality which creates the most pressure and therefore the most chilling demonstrations of self-destruction.

In the 1970 Open Championship at St Andrews, Doug Sanders came to the final hole needing a par four to win with a score of 282. His second shot was a little too strong and he faced a putt of some 30 feet down the slope to the hole. The first attempt came up two feet short. With the wind tugging at his trousers, Sanders lined up the putt and then at the last minute reached down to clear some microscopic debris from his line. At that moment one could sense that he would not hole the putt, and his nervous jab at the ball confirmed this assessment. The miss put him in a play-off with Jack Nicklaus, which Sanders lost by one stroke (72–73), having

holed a longer putt on the same green for a birdie three.

Sanders' miss stood as the shortest putt missed to win a major championship until the 1989 US Masters. Here the distinction was passed on to Scott Hoch, who missed an even shorter putt on the first extra hole of the sudden-death play-off with Nick Faldo. Hoch showed how nerves can affect the normal routine, for he also bent down *à la* Sanders to remove a wisp of something insignificant just prior to hitting the ball.

Shorter putts, much shorter, have been missed in the heat of competition. In the third round of the 1983 Open Championship at Royal Birkdale, Hale Irwin went to back-hand the ball into the hole on the 14th and missed it completely from about two inches. Inevitably, he finished one stroke behind the winner, Tom Watson. A similar occurrence happened in the Open of 1889 at Musselburgh when Andrew Kirkaldy tied with Willie Park and then lost the play-off. In the 1953 Ryder Cup match at Wentworth both Peter Alliss and Bernard Hunt missed short putts on the final green to allow the Americans to beat the British and Irish by one point. In 1985 the balance was redressed a little when America's Craig Stadler missed a putt of less than two feet on the last green of the second-day four-ball matches at the Belfry. The shock to the Americans was such that they never recovered and the Ryder Cup returned to this side of the Atlantic for the first time in 28 years.

Above right: Doug Sanders

Right: Craig Stadler

GREATEST BRITISH LADY GOLFER

Bill Johnson

So who was the greatest?

Bill Johnson follows attractive, talented women around Europe. Before his good lady wife sues us, it should be at once stated that he is one of those fortunate people charting the exploits of the Women's European Tour.

We felt he was admirably qualified to tackle our question. Having snared him, would he come off the fence? Could he? After all, it's one of those Rocky Marciano v. Muhammad Ali dilemmas, and how could we ask a weary golf writer to deliver the knock-out punch?

After months of humping a suitcase and type-writer around Europe – no, I'm not yet a member of the Tandy set – it was nice to be home again. The autumnal tints on the trees painted a marvellous colourful picture, and it was all so peaceful.

That was until the telephone began to ring. 'Bob Brand here. Could you let me have 1,200 or so words on "Who was the Greatest British Lady Golfer of all time"?' As I was accepting the assignment I knew, deep down, that I should be saying no. 'That is an almost impossible subject,' I protested. 'I know, but I am sure you'll cope,' replied Brand, confident that his victim had been well and truly hooked.

The words of Jack Nicklaus and the late Bobby Jones came flooding back. 'You can only beat those who are around at the same time as you, and you can't compare champions of different ages,' they agreed.

Bearing in mind that one can only examine the claims of those who dominated the scene in their own particular era, the first priority for consideration will be a victory in the Ladies' Championship (now known as the British Open Amateur Championship, to distinguish it from the British Open Championship which was inaugurated in 1976).

From the very outset Lady Margaret Scott wrote her name into the record books by winning the first British title in 1893 and retaining it for each of the next two years. Then came Dorothy Campbell from Edinburgh, who in the space of three years from 1909 won two British, two American and three Canadian titles, while Gladys Ravenscroft followed her British win in 1912 by taking the US title the following year.

So, in this particular era before the First World War it is fair to say that Dorothy Campbell, who also won the Scottish title three times, was the first of the great women amateur golfers, although the remarkable Cecil Leitch was already waiting in the wings.

In 1908, at the tender age of 17, Cecil Leitch had reached the semi-finals of the British Championship and she won the French

Cecil Leitch

title four years later. In 1914 the Silloth golfer won the English, British and French titles, and had World War I not intervened her record would surely have been even more formidable.

In all Cecil Leitch won four British, five French and two English championships between 1912 and 1926, but what makes her record all the more remarkable is that Joyce Wethered was embarking on her own triumphant march at about the same time.

It was in 1920 that Joyce Wethered won the first of five consecutive English championships, and she won the British crown four times between 1922 and 1929. Leitch and Wethered set new standards for Ladies' golf and between them amassed 20 major championship titles in a period covering 17 years. Surprisingly, on only three occasions did they meet in the final of a major event. In 1921 Miss Leitch beat Miss Wethered in the final of the British Ladies at Turnberry, a result Miss Wethered reversed the following year at Prince's. Miss Wethered's victory in the final of the 1920 English Championship at Sheringham gave her a slight edge.

During the early 1930s Enid Wilson carried on where Joyce Wethered and Cecil Leitch had left off. She took the English championship in 1928 and 1930, then at Portmarnock the following year won the first of three consecutive British championships.

This was just before Pam Barton gave notice of a rare talent when in 1934, at the age of 17, she won the French Championship at Le Touquet. Two years later Miss Barton won both the US and the British championships in the same year, the only player to pull off this remarkable double since Dorothy Campbell back in 1909.

She followed this great achievement by winning the British title again in 1939. Alas, we were never to find out what heights Miss Barton would scale. A Flight Officer in the WAAF, she was tragically killed in a plane crash at an RAF airfield in Kent in 1943.

New names emerged in the immediate postwar years with Jessie Valentine, winner of the British Championship in 1937, adding two more titles in 1955 and 1958. There was also

Enid Wilson

Philomena Garvey, losing finalist when the championship was resumed at Hunstanton in 1946.

Miss Garvey was to lose three more finals, but at Gleneagles in 1957 she beat Jessie Valentine to win an elusive title at last. Her run of 15 Irish championships between 1946 and 1970 was nothing less than remarkable.

Frances Smith (Bunty Stephens) and Elizabeth Price fought many titanic battles during the 1950s, and none more so than the 1955 final of the English Championship at Woodhall Spa, where Mrs Smith, assisted by a hole-in-one at the fifth, went out in 30 and at lunch was six up on Miss Price.

Now it was Miss Price's turn and she finally managed to square the match after 33 holes, only to watch Mrs Smith cruelly hole from some seven yards for a birdie at the 37th hole to settle the issue.

Between 1948 and 1955 Mrs Smith won two British, three English and the French championship. In Curtis Cup golf she played in the winning team at Muirfield in 1952, won the crucial game against Polly Riley by one hole at Prince's when Britain and Ireland triumphed again in 1956, and was unbeaten in five singles matches.

At the time I was fortunate to play golf occasionally with Mrs Smith, who modestly reckoned to be within birdie range from a 5-iron downwards – beyond any question, one of the all-time greats.

Life at the top is limited, and soon it was Marley Spearman, Elizabeth Chadwick, Ann Irvin and Belle Robertson. By now golf was burgeoning on the Continent, and Michelle Walker proved that golfing horizons were widening when she added the Spanish and Portuguese titles to the two British championships and the one English victory she had already claimed.

Not only is it impossible to compare champions of different eras but you have to take into account the changing pattern of the game, which now reaches the four corners of the earth.

In men's golf it is unlikely that anyone will remotely approach the record of Michael Bonallack, and a significant move in 1979 made it equally sure that the marvellous records I have discussed will remain intact. This was the year when women's professional golf arrived in Europe. As in men's golf, women now no longer undertake long amateur careers as they did in the previous 80 years and new names command the world stage even though they may have failed to capture a national title as an amateur.

There is no better example than Laura Davies, who at the age of 23 became the proud holder of the British Open Championship, to which, in less than twelve months, she added the US Women's Open title.

How do you balance these achievements against those of Joyce Wethered, Cecil Leitch and Frances Smith? You can't, as Jack Nicklaus and Bobby Jones insisted. One can say no more than that all were great champions whose achievements are in the record books for all to see and for all time.

Alison Nicholas and Laura Davies

GREATEST GOLF RESORT

David Smith

There is a golf resort in America – indeed there may be more than one – where golfers are transported around the course, and to and from the myriad accompanying amenities, by a chauffeur-driven powered buggy. This may not surprise the European golfer, but imagine your power-driven buggy having a frontage that completely replicates a Rolls Royce motor car – right down to the silver lady on the bonnet! It could only happen in America.

Golf resorts the other side of 'the pond' are something else. We asked **David Smith**, Editor of *Executive Golfer Magazine*, who has travelled the world sampling some of the very finest resorts, to name the one he thought worthy of the title 'the greatest'. Perhaps not surprisingly, he found his dream in California.

From coast to coast, and even further, to the Hawaiian Islands, the United States are blessed with numerous golfing resorts – many naturally claiming to be 'the best'. Opinions on which is indeed the best inevitably differ, as opinion is purely a reflection of one individual's taste. My selection – based on the guidelines of climate, comfort, cuisine, comprehensive facilities, and above all service and satisfaction guaranteed – would be the Desert Springs Resort and Spa in Palm Desert, California.

Located in the Coachella Valley of the southern Californian desert, which is known as the playground of the rich and where leisure is the lifestyle, Desert Springs Resort reigns supreme. In an area where luxury resorts abound, the quality and service it offers are unsurpassed; indeed, they have to be experienced to be believed.

Just a twenty-minute drive from Palm Springs Airport, Marriott's Desert Springs Resort and Spa almost overwhelms guests with sun-washed beauty, pampering them with a rare combination of luxurious accommodation, impeccable service, extensive amenities . . . and more.

Two 18-hole championship golf courses; 16 tennis courts; a fully equipped 27,000-square-foot spa; more than 51,000 square feet of meeting and exhibition space; three swimming pools, superb catering and dining in ten restaurants and lounges; acres of glistening freshwater lakes; fabulous shopping and entertainment; and still more!

From the moment you enter the breathtaking eight-storey atrium reception, you begin to realize what makes Desert Springs Resort unique. Lush tropical greenery drapes from the walkways above you, and palm trees rise from colourful clusters of fresh flowers. Tranquil pools of brilliant blue water flow softly into spectacular, multi-tier cascades, while through the expansive windows you can view the stunning setting of the golf courses overlooked by the San Bernardino and Santa Rosa mountains. In the midst of all this opulent splendour, a canopied boat passes from the outdoor lake to the indoor dock in this magnificent reception – climb aboard and be transported to the restaurants or the nightclub, or take a trip through the gardens enjoying the superb vistas.

Marriott has been chosen as the Official Hotel and Resort Company of the PGA Tour, Senior PGA and the PGA of America. It is easy to understand why, having experienced the accommodations, the exceptional facilities and the two excellent championship courses available at Desert Springs Resort.

Both courses were designed by Ted Robinson – 'king of waterscapes'. Yardages range from 6,760 yards to 5,490 yards on The Palms course and from 6,645 yards to 5,255 yards on The Valley course. With the choice of tees, you can make your games as challenging as you wish.

Beautifully maintained rolling fairways and lush greens twist, roll and curve around clumps of tall palms, shrubs, banks of flowers and 38 acres of gleaming blue lakes with their own special hazards.

The stair-stepped waterfall on the par-three 17th hole, for example, is typical of the picture-postcard beauty and the challenges that await. Two of the holes on The Palms course have been ranked among the 'Best 18 Holes in the Desert' by *Palm Springs Life*; and *Golf Digest* nominated The Valley course as one of the best new resort courses of 1988.

Year-round golf facilities include a fully equipped pro shop, an expansive practice range and two putting greens. Snack bars are located at the first and ninth tees – a phone-in service from the tee ensures that your refreshment is ready as you leave the green! Qualified professionals are available for private lessons, including video-taping your swing. Golf clinics are scheduled for novices or those who wish to fine-tune their game. As a special convenience, ardent 'can't wait' golfers can reserve tee times up to one week in advance of their arrival.

In addition to golf, there is a limitless assortment of outdoor activities awaiting guests at the Desert Springs Resort. The Californian desert's balmy and dry climate is ideal for exercise in comfort. For swimmers and sunbathers, the excellent swimming pools each have a secluded whirlpool, and enjoy stunning mountain views. Tennis enthusiasts have no trouble whatsoever in getting a game at the resort's Lawn & Tennis Club. It has sixteen hard-surface tennis courts, seven of which are floodlit. When you arrive, racquet in hand and wishing to play, the 'find-a-partner' service will guarantee you a game. If guests of a similar standard are not available, the Club will ring around to local residents to find you a partner, and should this also fail, they will give you free lessons with the professional, or, if you prefer, a session with the tennis-ball delivery machine. Their slogan could well be 'have racquet – will play'.

The measure of a great hotel is its responsiveness to its guests' needs, and in modern times, concern for health while conducting business or holidaying has become a top priority. In addition to sunshine, clean air and a luxurious environment, travellers also want on-site exercise facilities, trained professionals, and healthy calorie-controlled diets. Desert Springs can meet all these needs – the Spa features exercise facilities and programmes, spa treatments, spa cuisine and a full medical suite. The Spa's exercise facilities include an outdoor exercise pool; hydrotherapy and plunge pools; Swiss showers, sauna and steam room; exercise lawn; walking and jogging paths; men's and women's aerobics rooms and a 22-station gym. The Spa restaurant serves calorie-, sodium- and cholesterol-controlled dishes as well as standard gourmet cuisine.

Dining at Desert Springs Resort can be a simple affair or a gourmet experience. For dinner with a Japanese flair, the Mikado Restaurant features Teppan Yaki cooking, whilst the Sea Grille is a casual seafood restaurant complete with an oyster bar, featuring hot and cold appetizers and wood-burning stove for pizza and bread. For formal dining the 225-seat Lakeview Restaurant is open for breakfast, lunch and dinner, as is the Club

Room, the most casual of the restaurants. The Club Room is located in the golf pro shop area and incorporates a lounge where cocktails can be enjoyed in a relaxing atmosphere after a round of golf.

For dancing and live entertainment there are four lounges: the Costas Lounge, the Lakeview Lounge, the Mikado Lounge and the Atrium Lounge, which features different champagnes and cognacs by the glass.

Marriott's Desert Springs Resort and Spa is also a place to work – an entire wing, providing 51,000 square feet of space, has been dedicated exclusively to meeting and conference areas. The facilities available are unusually flexible – the two grand ballrooms are divisible into smaller rooms, allowing functions from as many as 7,200 people to as few as 20 (accommodated in separate boardrooms) to be held. All the facilities associated with first-class conference centres, such as state-of-the-art audiovisual and communications systems, are available, and there are 250 staff devoted exclusively to servicing and co-ordinating meetings and conferences.

A $3,000,000 prop room enables the resort to create any theme party required, on-site, and a palm-fringed beach has been constructed alongside one of the swimming pools to set the scene for beach parties etc. The combination of all the features at the conference centre will allow meeting-planners, with the help of a Marriott convention service co-ordinator, to be as creative as their imaginations allow.

Marriott's Desert Springs Resort and Spa is a truly great resort – and my brief description has covered only a little of what is available. However, perhaps the best indication of its greatness is how closely the 'satisfaction guaranteed' philosophy is adhered to. If for any reason you are dissatisfied with any aspect of your dining, accommodation, leisure or conference arrangements, Marriott's offer a no-charge guarantee. This policy is even extended to room service – if your dinner arrives at 7.46 pm and you were told it would be there for 7.45 pm, you are not charged. Can one say more!

The 18th green on The Palms course at Desert Springs

GREATEST GAME

Ron Wills

Last September millions of people witnessed the extraordinary climax to the Ryder Cup. People who normally would have switched channels were glued to their television sets: 'I don't often watch golf . . . but that was something else!'

Many of those millions will have been hooked – they'll have caught the golfing bug. Not so long ago it was all very different. **Ron Wills**, golf correspondent of the *Daily Mirror*, investigates the reasons behind golf's great switch from being the game of the privileged to the privileged game.

The good old days?

Golf is a sport that is rich in history, steeped in tradition and currently in the midst of an unprecedented, worldwide boom. Around four decades ago, however, only a relative handful of people were aware of that history and tradition; the boom hadn't even been conceived and golf was as baffling as the workings of the Stock Exchange to 95 per cent of the population.

Around 1950, some 90 years after the sport's history had got seriously underway with Willie Park's victory in the first Open Championship at Prestwick, even sporting enthusiasts were largely indifferent and bewildered by a game that used such odd words as 'eagle' and 'birdie' to indicate scoring.

To the vast majority, it was 'an old man's game' – worse, a game solely for rich old men, dominated by Colonel Blimp types, in plus-fours, and therefore of no interest to that same vast majority.

The nation's staple sporting diet was football, cricket and boxing, and in 1950, with Britain struggling to cope with post-war austerity, that was sufficient. The sporting chatter of the time was of the FA Cup triumphs of 'Wor' Jackie Milburn and Newcastle United, the swashbuckling cricket of Denis Compton, and the ring battles of the recently retired boxing legend Joe Louis, and his successors as world heavyweight champion, Ezzard Charles and Jersey Joe Walcott. The fact that the late Sir Henry Cotton, arguably Britain's greatest golfer, had won his third Open in 1948 barely rated a mention.

Forty years on, golf has blossomed into the sporting success story of the second half of the twentieth century.

Pose the question 'Why?', however, and you are inundated with a host of theories, most of which have a claim to be included in the answer.

The Affluent Society, which brought car ownership to most of the nation, is one reason. The motor car put the golf club, often situated in an isolated location and seldom on handy bus routes, within reach. It took the hassle out of the effort to get there, as opposed to strolling to the local football ground, historically situated in or near the town centre.

The car, however, is only a contributory factor. The two most important reasons behind golf's boom are television and, at least in Britain, the emergence of a home-grown sporting hero in Jacklin, and more significantly the financial rewards of his victories in the 1969 Open and 1970 US Open.

Television brought the dazzling colours of Augusta in April and Wentworth in the autumn into the country's living rooms, along with golf's intense competition, which – unlike so many other sports – is a combat without hostility. As John Shrewsbury, executive golf producer for the BBC, explains, 'Suddenly, people realized they were able to see a civilized sport with well-behaved players. It was refreshing to see performers who didn't complain to the referee and who were always well dressed.'

Shrewsbury also pointed out another big plus for golf when he said, 'The viewers can watch a footballer score a hat-trick at Wembley, a tennis-player win a championship at Wimbledon or a cricketer hit a century at Lords. They're all great to watch, but it ends there. In golf, however, it's different. They can see Nick Faldo win the Open and a week later they can play on the same course, and tell their friends how they scored a birdie at the hole where Faldo dropped a shot. But the viewers' hopes of playing football at Wembley, cricket at Lords or tennis at Wimbledon are virtually nil.'

Very true. The fact that the club golfer hit a career-best 4-iron at a 170 yards short hole, watched his ball dribble onto the front fringe and then holed a monster putt doesn't matter. He got his birdie while Faldo hit a 7-iron at the same hole, got a bad bounce into a bunker and took four. They are both playing the same game; but fans of tennis, football and cricket just couldn't live with their heroes in the same way. They don't play the same game.

Similarly, many golfers have enjoyed playing in pro-ams and later boast how, with the aid of their shots, they improved on the pro's score at seven holes. A four-game start on a tennis court would still leave most of us losing 6–4 to John McEnroe.

Ballesteros wins the 1979 Open

Sandy Lyle in 1985

The handicapping system is, in fact, one more factor in golf's ever-growing popularity, as is the knowledge that it is a sport that can provide a lifetime's involvement.

It was Sir Henry Cotton who once described it as a game for 'eight-year-olds to 80-year-olds', and, as Shrewsbury puts it, 'in what other sport can you improve while you are in your 50s? In practically every other activity you've got to be on the way down, or out of it totally, but a 51-year-old can still reduce his handicap at golf.'

But as with all sports, there must be heroes, the players who reach the peak of excellence, players who appeal to mass audiences, performers the media – television and newspapers – can spotlight and know that the public will be interested.

Football, a little short on heroes currently, had its 1966 winning World Cup team, cricket had Ian Botham, while Barry McGuigan and Frank Bruno were the boxers who could fill the halls.

Jacklin filled the role in golf and launched phase one of the boom in the 1970s; and phase two came in the 1980s when Severiano Ballesteros, Sandy Lyle and Nick Faldo took on the world's best and beat them in two successive Ryder Cup victories and a tied match to retain the trophy, providing the ultimate pinnacle.

As Shrewsbury says, 'Seve may be a Spaniard, but the fans regard him as an honorary Brit, and he is without question the most charismatic player in golf today. If we're covering an event he's playing in, we make sure he gets maximum exposure – and we don't get any complaints from the viewers.'

The growth of the sport, the success of British players – and Seve – have aided the boom in golfing equipment. Sales of golf clubs in the last ten years have grown by a remarkable 55 per cent, and there's no hint of a downward trend. The golf trade had a turnover of £85 million in 1987, and that figure is projected to top £100 million in 1990, around 60 per cent of that being spent on new clubs.

A recent market research study revealed a steady increase in golfing sales during the 1980s, an increase that became a giant leap following Europe's 1985 and 1987 Ryder Cup triumphs.

It's all a far cry from the days of the mashie niblick, the gutty ball, women in ankle-length skirts and gentlemen who resisted taking off their ties on the links in that far-off era of golf's infancy.

But even if today's golfers wear casual shirts and multi-coloured sweaters, one vital element of the sport remains: honesty and self-control.

Nick Faldo and Sandy Lyle may lose to one another and grit their teeth in fury for doing so, but, on the surface at least, they act like gentlemen, shake hands and say 'Well done'. The fact that the loser then goes home and kicks the cat doesn't matter. The image of the golfers as sporting gents has been maintained.

And as long as that is maintained, along with the golfer's honesty, for example calling himself if he grounds his club in a bunker, there is no reason why the golfing boom shouldn't go on and on.

It is that honesty, that self-control which lifts it above the tantrums of a John McEnroe, the punch-ups of soccer players and fans, and the stabbing finger of an English cricket captain accusing an umpire.

The public is tiring of such antics, which can, of course, only swell the growth and success of golf, a sport alone.

The greatest game.

GREATEST ROUNDS

Nick Edmund

The wise old oak tree watched attentively as the smart young man in the plus-fours putted out on the final green. It was Sunningdale, 1926, and Bobby Jones was completing his historic round of 66 in the Open Championship pre-qualifying event.

Jones's performance would be hailed as the greatest round of golf ever played. Using equipment vastly inferior to that employed by today's heroes, Jones went out in 33 strokes and came home in 33 strokes, and his round comprised 33 shots from tee to green and 33 putts. Had his normally faithful putter, 'Calamity Jane', risen to the occasion – Jones missed a number of shortish putts – his score would have been considerably lower.

Whether Jones's 66 was in truth 'the greatest round' is of course a matter of conjecture; however, for many years it has certainly been used as the bench-mark against which all other outstanding rounds and scores have been judged.

To me falls the pleasure of looking back over three decades and weighing up the credentials of some of the latter-day claimants to Jones's Sunningdale crown.

Let us begin by reaching back 30 years to 1960, to the start of a new decade, and in many ways of a new golfing era. It was the year Arnold Palmer revitalized the Open Championship by making the pilgrimage to St Andrews to play in the Centenary Open. Earlier that year Palmer had firmly established himself as the world's number-one player by storming through the field with a final-round 65 to win his first and only US Open Championship. (At St Andrews he came within a whisker of achieving the Open double.) That 65 was the finest round of an illustrious career and one which personified Palmer. It was highlighted by six birdies in the first seven holes and gave birth to the legendary 'Palmer charge'. It is also worth noting that it was achieved at Cherry Hills, one of the US Open's toughest venues. Of course there have been many rounds lower than Palmer's. The lowest score ever recorded in a US tournament is 59 by the 1966 USPGA Champion Al Geiberger, a score also returned by Gary Player in the 1974 Brazilian Open.

Johnny Miller, one of the dominant figures in world golf during the seventies, had a reputation for compiling spectacular scores, and twice in as many weeks in 1975 returned 61s; but neither Geiberger's and Player's 59s nor Miller's 61s were achieved in major championships, where the golfer is under much greater pressure. Miller, however, did score a brilliant 63 in the final round of the 1973 US Open at Oakmont, and although it was perhaps a slightly easier course than Cherry Hills – that week at least – it nevertheless stands as the lowest ever final round by the winner of a major championship. Three years later the mercurial Miller scored a final round 66 at Royal Birkdale to win the Open Championship by six strokes.

We have already mentioned Palmer's finest hour, and so it is appropriate that we should now examine the great performances of the other members of the sixties' 'big three', Gary Player and Jack Nicklaus. Although Player had many great major championship rounds during the sixties, he will probably best be

Arnold Palmer – on a charge

remembered in that decade for his extraordinary comeback against Tony Lema in the semi-final of the World Match-Play Championship at Wentworth in 1965. Played over 36 holes, Player found himself 7 down with 17 holes to play, yet somehow managed to snatch victory from an astonished Lema. Player's lowest round in the Majors came when he was 48 years old, a 63 in the second round of the 1984 USPGA Championship at Shoal Creek; but the one round that Player would rank above all others took place at Augusta in the 1978 Masters. Player started the final day 7 shots behind the reigning US Open Champion Hubert Green but came through to win his third Masters title with 7 birdies in the final 10 holes and a round of 64. As Miller's 63 stands as the lowest round to win the US Open, so Player's 64 is the lowest by a Masters champion – one shot fewer than the scores made by Nicklaus in 1986 and Faldo in 1989.

Jack Nicklaus has himself scored a 64 in the US Masters. It came in the third round of the 1965 tournament, an event Nicklaus won by a record 9 strokes from Player and Palmer, provoking the comment from Bobby Jones, 'Mr Nicklaus plays a game with which I am not familiar.' Nicklaus has also scored a 63 in the US Open, but again never in the final round; rather it came in the first round of his fourth championship triumph in 1980. Probably his two most memorable final rounds in the Majors were his 65 to win the 1967 US Open at Baltusrol and the magical 65 at Augusta 19 years later, which, like Player's 64 was fashioned by a brilliant back 9 of 30.

Perhaps the greatest golf that Nicklaus ever played occurred during the final two rounds of the Open Championship at Turnberry in 1977. Nicklaus scored 65–66, yet this still wasn't good enough to defeat Tom Watson, who, in a head-to-head duel, having started level, scored 65–65. That week Nicklaus fin-

Nicklaus congratulates Watson after the 'Duel in the Sun'

in one under par yet was still beaten.

British golf has been very fortunate in having two of the finest players of the eighties, Nick Faldo and Sandy Lyle. In passing, we have already mentioned Faldo's magnificent 65 at Augusta last year; he also produced some incredible golf later in the season to defeat Ian Woosnam in the World Matchplay final in October. Lyle, like Greg Norman, whom we shall come to, is known for his final-round charges, but unlike Faldo he hasn't yet produced a 65 to win a Major. Instead Lyle's claim to fame is that he is regarded as having played probably the greatest shot to an 18th green that ever won a Major – his 7-iron out of a bunker in the Masters of 1988. As we are looking at British golfers, perhaps we can cheat a little to include one famous event, the 'greatest round that never quite was', when Tony Jacklin, the defending champion in the Open at St Andrews in 1970, played the first nine holes in just 29 strokes before a storm forced play to be halted. On resumption Jacklin had lost the Midas touch and eventually completed his round in 67.

Two Europeans have indelibly left their mark on the history of golf in the eighties: Bernhard Langer and Severiano Ballesteros. Few would disagree that Langer's greatest round to date is his spectacular 62 in the final round of the Spanish Open in 1984. Again this was not a major championship, but what makes it such an awesome performance is that it took place at El Saler, widely acknowledged as one of the Continent's toughest challenges, and in far from ideal conditions. For these reasons Langer's 62 compares very favourably, for instance, with the more widely celebrated 62 by Curtis Strange at St Andrews.

More has been written about the legendary feats of Ballesteros in the 1980s than about any other golfer. He had ended the previous decade by winning the Open Championship at Royal Lytham aged 22 with an extraordinary round of golf – extraordinary because on the back nine holes his ball rarely landed on the fairway: it was largely a case of tee – to rough (even car park) – to green – to back of the

ished 10 ahead of Hubert Green in third place. Considering the pressure Tom Watson was up against, playing for two days alongside an inspired and hungry Golden Bear (out to avenge his Masters defeat by Watson earlier that year), it must rank as one of the greatest championship performances of all time. When Nicklaus birdied the twelfth hole in the final round, to move two strokes ahead, Peter Alliss commented, 'Who in the world can give Jack Nicklaus two shots over six holes and still beat him.' Nicklaus played the last six holes

Greg Norman shows off his Turnberry 63

Greg Norman has been the Johnny Miller of the eighties, the golfer most likely to 'shoot the lights out', the one golfer who could have out-charged a charging Palmer. Norman holds the course records at Turnberry and Troon; he has had a 63 at St Andrews, a 64 at Augusta and a 62 at Canada's tough Glen Abbey.

Norman's 63 at Turnberry during the 1986 Open Championship contained three dropped shots, including three putts on the 18th green. Two putts would have given him the first 62 ever recorded in a Major. Typically, Greg fired his first putt well past the hole – he was after a 61! Given that the conditions were very far from perfect, as they had been during the Nicklaus–Watson showdown nine years earlier – Norman's round was all the more remarkable. Had he holed his birdie putt on the final green there would probably have been no question as to which was the 'greatest round'. Imagine a 61 at Turnberry, in a stiff wind, with two dropped shots!

The Australian's most famous charge came in last year's Open at Troon. He began his round, as nobody had ever done before in an Open, with six straight birdies; but again it was a case of what might have been, as he dropped a stroke on the shortest hole on the course. A birdie 2 at the Postage Stamp instead of a 4, and again we would have witnessed a 62. A 62 on the last day of a major championship, by a player coming through the field to snatch victory from 7 strokes behind. The stuff that dreams are made of. And, alas, only dreams.

hole. Seve's greatest round in the eighties, or, as he described it, 'a round that happens once every twenty-five or fifty years', was his stunning final 65 to win the 1988 Open Championship, Royal Lytham again being the venue. During that round Ballesteros played the 6th to 11th holes with scores of: birdie – eagle – birdie – par – birdie – birdie; he came within inches of holing his second to the 16th and finished in style by almost chipping into the hole from the back of the 18th green in front of an ecstatic crowd.

Arguably we have left the finest until last.

5

GOLF COURSES OF GREAT BRITAIN AND IRELAND

'Concentrate your mind on the match until you are dormy.
Then look at the surrounding scenery and expatiate on its beauties.'

(A. J. Robertson)

ENGLAND
SCOTLAND
WALES
IRELAND

St Andrews

On first viewing St Andrews, American golfer Sam Snead was of the opinion that it 'looked like the kind of real estate you couldn't give away'. Some years earlier his fellow countryman Bobby Jones's first experience of the hallowed turf was to result in him tearing up his card and storming off the course. Both men went on to achieve great things at St Andrews. Snead was the first post-war Open Champion, winning at St Andrews in 1946, and Jones too won an Open at St Andrews in 1927. Indeed Jones became so attached to the Old Course that he was later to declare: 'The more I studied the Old Course the more I loved it, and the more I loved it, the more I studied it, so that I came to feel that it was for me the most favourable meeting ground possible for an important contest.'

Love it or hate it, St Andrews is the one place that anyone who has ever picked up and swung a rusty 3-iron will have wanted to visit at some time or other, if for no other reason than that it is, quite simply, 'the Home of Golf'.

Hard by the sea, the narrow stretch of humpy and hillocky, dune-strewn land over which the St Andrews courses have been laid exemplifies the type of golf course for which Britain and Ireland are most famous. This is the 'golfing links'.

Clearly nature did not possess a sense of golfing justice when ideal links land was distributed around our shores; Scotland has rather more than its fair share, both to the east (St Andrews, Carnoustie and Muirfield) and to the west (Turnberry, Troon and Prestwick), all able to tell wondrous Open Championship tales; and Ireland also has an enviable selection: in Portmarnock, Ballybunion, Royal Portrush and Royal County Down, it has four of the finest links courses in the world.

England and Wales, of course, have many a good golfing links themselves (and no little Open Championship history either) but many of the leading courses south of the border are found inland. Sunningdale, The Berkshire, Wentworth and Walton Heath, that illustrious Surrey-Berkshire quartet, immedi-

Sunningdale

ately spring to mind – places where World Matchplay Championships, PGAs and European Opens are won and lost. They represent heathland golf at its best – heather, pine, fir, silver birch and a dash of gorse in season. Such golf is not confined to southern England. That wonderful golfing oasis, Woodhall Spa in Lincolnshire, and the Notts Golf Club at Hollinwell also fall into that category.

If our islands are best known for their Open Championship courses, perhaps our greatest strength is the sheer variety of the terrain and accompanying landscape (or seascape) over which we can play golf. So far only links and heathland courses have been mentioned, but there is also moorland golf, two examples from opposite ends of the golfing map being the world-renowned Gleneagles in Perthshire and the Manor House Hotel course at Moretonhampstead on Dartmoor; parkland golf, as can be found at Little Aston near Birmingham and Moor Park near London, and also a plethora of spectacular clifftop courses, notably in the West Country,

Northern Norfolk, North Wales and on the Antrim coast of Northern Ireland. Finally the last fifteen years have seen the emergence of what might be termed anglicized American-type courses, from The Belfry to St Mellion to the East Sussex National.

'Golf,' Henry Longhurst once said, 'takes us to such beautiful places.' From Bamburgh Castle in Northumberland to Killarney in South-West Ireland, Britain and Ireland have more than sufficient beauty to partner variety. Whoever said Australia was the lucky country!

There are close to 2,000 golf courses in the British Isles and Ireland, the great majority of which are open to visitors, although most insist that the golfer has done a little more than swing his rusty 3-iron. The following pages comprise a directory of British and Irish courses, giving addresses, telephone numbers and course yardages. Space prevents the provision of additional information; however, our recommendation is that visitors should always contact the club before setting off.

ENGLAND

AVON

Bath G.C.
(0225) 63834
Sham Castle, North Road, Bath
(18) 6369 yards

Bristol and Clifton G.C.
(0272) 393474
Beggar Bush Lane, Failand, Bristol
(18) 6294 yards

Chipping Sodbury G.C.
(0454) 319042
Chipping Sodbury
(18) 6912 yards

Clevedon G.C.
(0272) 874057
Castle Road, Clevedon
(18) 5835 yards

Filton G.C.
(0272) 694169
Golf Course Lane, Filton, Bristol
(18) 6227 yards

Fosseway C.C.
(0761) 412214
Charlton Lane, Midsomer Norton
(9) 4148 yards

Henbury G.C.
(0272) 500044
Henbury Hill, Westbury-on-Trym, Bristol
(18) 6039 yards

Knowle G.C.
(0272) 770660
Brislington, Bristol
(18) 6016 yards

Lansdown G.C.
(0225) 22138
Lansdown, Bath
(18) 6267 yards

Long Ashton G.C.
(0272) 392316
Long Ashton, Bristol
(18) 6051 yards

Mangotsfield G.C.
(0272) 565501
Carsons Road, Mangotsfield
(18) 5337 yards

Mendip G.C.
(0749) 840570
Gurney Slade, Bath
(18) 5982 yards

Saltford G.C.
(0225) 873220
Manor Road, Saltford
(18) 6081 yards

Shirehampton Park G.C.
(0272) 822083
Parkhill, Shirehampton, Bristol
(18) 5943 yards

Tracy Park G. & C.C.
(027582) 2251
Bath Road, Wick
(18) 6613 yards
(9) 5200 yards

Weston-Super-Mare G.C.
(0934) 621360
Uphill Road, Weston-Super-Mare
(18) 6225 yards

Worlebury G.C.
(0934) 623214
Worlebury Hill Road, Weston-Super-Mare
(18) 5945 yards

BEDFORDSHIRE

Aspley Guise & Woburn Sands G.C.
(0908) 583596
West Hill, Aspley Guise
(18) 6248 yards

Beadlow Manor G. & C.C.
(0525) 60800
Shefford
(18) 6231 yards
(9) 3297 yards

Bedford & County G.C.
(0234) 52617
Green Lane, Clapham, Bedford
(18) 6347 yards

Bedfordshire G.C.
(0234) 61669
Bromham Road, Biddenham, Bedford
(18) 6172 yards

Dunstable Downs G.C.
(0582) 604472
Whipsnade Road, Dunstable
(18) 6184 yards

John O'Gaunt G.C.
(0767) 260252
Sutton Park, Sandy, Biggleswade
(18) 6513 yards (John O'Gaunt)
(18) 5869 yards (Carthagena)

Leighton Buzzard G.C.
(0525) 373525
Plantation Road, Leighton Buzzard
(18) 5366 yards

Millbrook G.C.
(0525) 712001
Millbrook, Ampthill
(18) 6473 yards

Mowsbury G.C.
(0234) 771042
Kimbolton Road, Bedford
(18) 6514 yards

South Beds G.C.
(0582) 591500
Warden Hill, Luton
(18) 6342 yards
(9) 4954 yards

Stockwood Park G.C.
(0582) 413704
London Road, Luton
(18) 5964 yards

Tilsworth G.C.
(0525) 210721
Dunstable Road, Tilsworth
(9) 5443 yards

Wyboston Lakes G.C.
(0480) 212501
Wyboston
(18) 5688 yards

BERKSHIRE

Bearwood G.C.
(0734) 760060
Mole Road, Sindlesham
(9) 5628 yards

Berkshire G.C.
(0990) 21496
Swinley Road, Ascot
(18) 6356 yards (Red)
(18) 6258 yards (Blue)

Calcot Park G.C.
(0734) 27124
Bath Road, Calcot
(18) 6283 yards

Downshire G.C.
(0344) 424066
Easthampstead Park, Wokingham
(18) 6382 yards

East Berkshire G.C.
(0344) 772041
Ravenswood Avenue, Crowthorne
(18) 6315 yards

Goring & Streatley G.C.
(0491) 873229
Rectory Road, Streatley-on-Thames
(18) 6255 yards

Hawthorn Hill G.C.
(0628) 75588
Drift Road, Maidenhead
(18) 6212 yards

Hurst G.C.
(0734) 345143
Hurst, Wokingham
(9) 3015 yards

Maidenhead G.C.
(0628) 24693
Shoppenhangers Road,
Maidenhead
(18) 6344 yards

Newbury & Crookham G.C.
(0635) 40035
Greenham, Newbury
(18) 5880 yards

Reading G.C.
(0734) 472909
Kidmore End Road, Reading
(18) 6283 yards

Royal Ascot G.C.
(0990) 25175
Winkfield Road, Ascot
(18) 5653 yards

Sonning G.C.
(0734) 693332
Duffield Road, Sonning-on-Thames
(18) 6355 yards

Sunningdale G.C.
(0990) 21681
Ridgemount Road, Sunningdale
(18) 6341 yards (Old)
(18) 6676 yards (New)

Sunningdale Ladies G.C.
(0990) 20507
Cross Road, Sunningdale
(18) 3622 yards

Swinley Forest G.C.
(0990) 20197
Coronation Road, South Ascot
(18) 6001 yards

Temple G.C.
(062882) 4795
Henley Road, Hurley
(18) 6206 yards

West Berks G.C.
(04882) 574
Chaddleworth, Newbury
(18) 7053 yards

Winter Hill G.C.
(06285) 27613
Grange Park, Cookham,
Maidenhead
(18) 6432 yards

BUCKINGHAMSHIRE

Abbey Hill G.C.
(0908) 563845
Two Ash, Milton Keynes
(18) 6505 yards

Beaconsfield G.C.
(0494) 676545
Seer Green, Beaconsfield
(18) 6469 yards

Buckingham GC.
(0280) 815566
Tingewick Road, Buckingham
(18) 6082 yards

Burnham Beeches G.C.
(06286) 61448
Green Lane, Burnham
(18) 6415 yards

Chesham & Ley Hill G.C.
(0494) 784541
Ley Hill, Chesham
(9) 5147 yards

Chiltern Forest G.C.
(0296) 631267
Halton, Aylesbury
(9) 5724 yards

Datchet G.C.
(0753) 43887
Buccleuch Road, Datchet
(9) 5978 yards

Denham G.C.
(0895) 832022
Tilehouse Lane, Denham
(18) 6439 yards

Ellesborough G.C.
(0296) 622114
Butler's Cross, Aylesbury
(18) 6207 yards

Farnham Park G.C.
(02814) 3332
Park Road, Stoke Poges
(18) 5847 yards

Flackwell Heath G.C.
(06285) 20929
High Wycombe
(18) 6150 yards

Gerrards Cross G.C.
(0753) 885300
Chalfont Park, Gerrards Cross
(18) 6305 yards

Harewood Downs G.C.
(02404) 2184
Cokes Lane, Chalfont St Giles
(18) 5958 yards

Iver G.C.
(0753) 655615
Hollow Hill Lane, Iver
(9) 6214 yards

Little Chalfont G.C.
(02404) 4877
Lodge Lane, Little Chalfont
(9) 5852 yards

Stoke Poges G.C.
(0753) 26385
Park Road, Stoke Poges
(18) 6654 yards

Weston Turville G.C.
(0296) 24084
New Road, Weston Turville,
Aylesbury
(13) 6782 yards

Wexham Park G.C.
(02816) 3217
Wexham Street, Wexham
(18) 5836 yards
(9) 2383 yards

Whiteleaf G.C.
(08444) 3097
Whiteleaf, Aylesbury
(9) 5391 yards

Windmill Hill G.C.
(0908) 78623
Tattenhoe Lane, Bletchley, Milton
Keynes
(18) 6773 yards

Woburn G. & C.C.
(0908) 370756
Bow Brickhill, Milton Keynes
(18) 6883 yards Duke's
(18) 6616 yards Duchess

CAMBRIDGESHIRE

Abbotsley G.C.
(0480) 215153
Eynesbury Hardwicke, St Neots
(18) 6214 yards

**Cambridgeshire
Moat House Hotel G.C.**
(0954) 80555
Bar Hill, Cambridge
(18) 6734 yards

Ely City G.C.
(0353) 2751
Cambridge Road, Ely
(18) 6686 yards

Girton G.C.
(0223) 276169
Dodford Lane, Cambridge
(18) 5927 yards

Gog Magog G.C.
(0223) 247626
Shelford Bottom, Cambridge
(18) 6354 yards (Old)
(9) 5833 yards (New)

March G.C.
(0354) 52364
Grange Rd, March
(9) 6278 yards

Orton Meadows G.C.
(0733) 237478
Ham Lane, Peterborough
(18) 5800 yards

Peterborough Milton G.C.
(0733) 380489
Milton Ferry, Peterborough
(18) 6431 yards

Ramsey G.C.
(0487) 812600
Abbey Terrace, Ramsey
(18) 6136 yards

St Ives G.C.
(0480) 68392
St Ives, Huntingdon
(9) 6052 yards

St Neots G.C.
(0480) 72363
Crosshall Rd, St Neots
(18) 6027 yards

Thorpe Wood G.C.
(0733) 267701
Nene Parkway, Peterborough
(18) 7086 yards

CHESHIRE

Alderley Edge G.C.
(0625) 585583
Brook Lane, Alderley Edge
(9) 5839 yards

Astbury G.C.
(0260) 272772
Peel Lane, Astbury, Congleton
(18) 6269 yards

Birchwood G.C.
(0925) 818819
Kelvin Close, Birchwood,
Warrington
(18) 6666 yards

Chapel-en-le-Frith G.C.
(0298) 813943
The Cockyard, Manchester Road,
Chapel-en-le-Frith
(18) 6065 yards

Chester G.C.
(0244) 677760
Curzon Park, Chester
(18) 6487 yards

Congleton G.C.
(0260) 273540
Biddulph Road, Congleton
(18) 6221 yards

Crewe G.C.
(0270) 584099
Fields Road, Haslington, Crewe
(18) 6277 yards

Davenport G.C.
(0625) 877319
Worton Hall, Middlewood Road,
Higher Poynton
(18) 6006 yards

Delamere Forest G.C.
(0606) 882807
Station Road, Delamere,
Northwich
(18) 6287 yards

Eaton G.C.
(0244) 680474
Eaton Park, Eccleston, Chester
(18) 6446 yards

Ellesmere Port G.C.
(051) 339 7689
Chester Road, Hooton
(18) 6432 yards

Helsby G.C.
(09282) 2021
Towers Lane, Helsby, Warrington
(18) 6262 yards

Knights Grange G.C.
(06065) 52780
Grange Lane, Winsford
(9) 6210 yards

Knutsford G.C.
(0565) 3355
Mereheath Lane, Knutsford
(9) 6288 yards

Leigh G.C.
(092576) 2943
Kenyon Hall,
Culcheth, Warrington
(18) 5853 yards

Lymm G.C.
(092575) 5020
Whitbarrow Road, Lymm
(18) 6304 yards

Macclesfield G.C.
(0625) 23227
The Hollins, Macclesfield
(9) 5974 yards

Malkins Bank G.C.
(0270) 765931
Betchton Road, Sandbach
(18) 6178 yards

Mere G. & C.C.
(0565) 830219
Mere, Knutsford
(18) 6849 yards

New Mills G.C.
(0663) 43816
Shaw Marsh, New Mills
(9) 5924 yards

Poulton Park G.C.
(0925) 812034
Cinnamon Brow, Warrington
(9) 5512 yards

Prestbury G.C.
(0625) 828241
Macclesfield Road, Prestbury
(18) 6359 yards

Runcorn G.C.
(09285) 74214
Clifton Road, Runcorn
(18) 6012 yards

Sandbach G.C.
(0270) 762117
Middlewich Road, Sandbach
(9) 5533 yards

Sandiway G.C.
(0606) 883247
Chester Road, Sandiway
(18) 6435 yards

Tytherington Club
(0625) 617622
Macclesfield
(18) 6717 yards

Upton-by-Chester G.C.
(0244) 381183
Upton Lane, Chester
(18) 5875 yards

Vicars Cross G.C.
(0244) 335174
Littleton, Chester
(18) 5804 yards

Walton Hall G.C.
(0925) 66775
Higher Walton, Warrington
(18) 6843 yards

Warrington G.C.
(0925) 61775
Appleton, Warrington
(18) 6217 yards

Widnes G.C.
(051) 424 2995
Highfield Road, Widnes
(18) 5719 yards

Widnes Municipal G.C.
(051) 424 6230
Dundalk Road, Widnes
(9) 5982 yards

Wilmslow G.C.
(056587) 2148
Great Warford, Mobberley,
Knutsford
(18) 6500 yards

CHANNEL ISLANDS

Alderney G.C.
(048182) 2835
Routes des Carriers, Alderney
(9) 2528 yards

La Moye G.C.
(0534) 43401
La Moye, St Brelade
(18) 6464 yards

Royal Guernsey G.C.
(0481) 47022
L'Ancresse, Guernsey
(18) 6206 yards

Royal Jersey G.C.
(0534) 54416
Grouville, Jersey
(18) 6106 yards

St Clements G.C.
(0534) 21938
St Clements, Jersey
(9) 3972 yards

CLEVELAND

Billingham G.C.
(0642) 554494
Sandy Lane, Billingham
(18) 6430 yards

Castle Eden & Peterlee G.C.
(0429) 836220
Castle Eden, Hartlepool
(18) 6297 yards

Cleveland G.C.
(0642) 483693
Queen Street, Redcar
(18) 6707 yards

Eaglescliffe G.C.
(0642) 780098
Yarm Road, Eaglescliffe
(18) 6275 yards

Hartlepool G.C.
(0429) 870282
Hart Warren, Hartlepool
(18) 6325 yards

Middlesborough G.C.
(0642) 311515
Marton, Middlesborough
(18) 6106 yards

Middlesborough Municipal G.C.
(0642) 315533
Ladgate Lane, Middlesborough
(18) 6314 yards

Saltburn-by-the Sea G.C.
(0287) 22812
Hob Hill, Saltburn-by-the-Sea
(18) 5803 yards

Seaton Carew G.C.
(0429) 266249
Tees Road, Seaton Carew
(18) 6604 yards

Teeside G.C.
(0642) 616516
Acklam Road, Thornaby
(18) 6472 yards

Wilton G.C.
(0642) 465265
Wilton Castle, Redcar
(18) 5774 yards

CORNWALL

Bude & North Cornwall G.C.
(0288) 2006
Burn View, Bude
(18) 6202 yards

Budock Vean Hotel G.C.
(0326) 250288
Mawnan Smith, Falmouth
(9) 5007 yards

Carlyon Bay Hotel G.C.
(072681) 4228
Carlyon Bay, St Austell
(18) 6463 yards

Falmouth G.C.
(0326) 40525
Swanpool Road, Falmouth
(18) 5581 yards

Isles of Scilly G.C.
(0720) 22692
St Mary's, Isles of Scilly
(9) 5974 yards

Launceston G.C.
(0566) 3442
St Stephen, Launceston
(18) 6409 yards

Looe Bin Down G.C.
(05034) 247
Widegates, Looe
(18) 5875 yards

Mullion G.C.
(0326) 240685
Curry, Helston
(18) 5616 yards

Newquay G.C.
(0637) 874354
Tower Road, Newquay
(18) 6140 yards

Perranporth G.C.
(0872) 573701
Budnick Hill, Perranporth
(18) 6208 yards

Praa Sands G.C.
(0736) 763445
Germoe Cross, Penzance
(9) 4036 yards

St Austell G.C.
(0726) 74756
Tregongeeves Lane, St Austell
(18) 5875 yards

St Enodoc G.C.
(020886) 3216
Rock, Wadebridge
(18) 6188 yards
(18) 4151 yards

St Mellion G. & C.C.
(0579) 50101
St Mellion, Saltash
(18) 6626 yards (Nicklaus)
(18) 5927 yards

Tehidy Park G.C.
(0209) 842208
Camborne
(18) 6222 yards

Trevose G. & C.C.
(0841) 520208
Constantine Bay, Padstow
(18) 6608 yards
(9) 1367 yards

Truro G.C.
(0872) 78684
Treliske, Truro
(18) 5347 yards

West Cornwall G.C.
(0736) 753401
Lelant, St Ives
(18) 6070 yards

Whitsand Bay Hotel G.C.
(0503) 30276
Portwrinkle, Torpoint
(18) 5512 yards

CUMBRIA

Alston Moor G.C.
(0498) 81675
The Hermitage, Alston
(9) 5380 yards

Appleby G.C.
(0930) 51432
Blackenber Moor,
Appleby-in-Westmoreland
(18) 5913 yards

Barrow G.C.
(0229) 24174
Hawcoat, Barrow-in-Furness
(18) 6209 yards

Brampton G.C.
(06977) 2255
Talkin Tarn, Brampton
(18) 6426 yards

Carlisle G.C.
(022872) 303
Aglionby, Carlisle
(18) 6278 yards

Cockermouth G.C.
(059681) 223
Embleton, Cockermouth
(18) 5496 yards

Dunnerholme G.C.
(0229) 62675
Duddon Road, Askam-in-Furness
(10) 6118 yards

Furness G.C.
(0229) 41232
Central Drive, Barrow-in-Furness
(18) 6374 yards

Grange Fell G.C.
(04484) 2536
Fell Road, Grange-over-Sands
(9) 5278 yards

Grange-over-Sands G.C.
(04484) 3180
Meathop Road, Grange-over-Sands
(18) 5660 yards

Kendal G.C.
(0539) 20840
The Heights, Kendal
(18) 5533 yards

Keswick G.C.
(07687) 72147
Threlkeld Hall, Keswick
(18) 6175 yards

Kirkby Lonsdale G.C.
(0468) 71483
Casterton Road, Kirkby Lonsdale
(9) 4058 yards

Maryport G.C.
(0900) 812605
Bank End, Maryport
(18) 6272 yards

Penrith G.C.
(0768) 62217
Salkeld Road, Penrith
(18) 6026 yards

St Bees School G.C.
(0946) 812105
Station Road, St Bees
(9) 5082 yards

Seascale G.C.
(09467) 28662
The Banks, Seascale
(18) 6372 yards

Sedbergh G.C.
(0587) 20993
Sedburgh
(9) 4134 yards

Silecroft G.C.
(0657) 4250
Silecroft, Millom
(9) 5627 yards

Silloth-on-Solway G.C.
(0965) 31304
Silloth-on-Solway, Carlisle
(18) 6343 yards

Stony Holme Municipal G.C.
(0228) 34856
St Aidans Road, Carlisle
(18) 5773 yards

Ulverston G.C.
(0229) 52806
Bardsea Park, Ulverston
(18) 6092 yards

Windermere G.C.
(09662) 3123
Cleabarrow, Windermere
(18) 5006 yards

Workington G.C.
(0900) 3460
Branthwaite Road, Workington
(18) 6202 yards

DERBYSHIRE

Alfreton G.C.
(0773) 832070
Wingfield Road, Oakerthorpe
(9) 5012 yards

Allestree Park G.C.
(0332) 550616
Allestree Hall, Derby
(18) 5749 yards

Ashbourne G.C.
(0335) 42077
Clifton, Ashbourne
(9) 5388 yards

Bakewell G.C.
(062981) 2307
Station Road, Bakewell
(9) 5240 yards

Breadsall Priory G. & C.C.
(0332) 832235
Moor Road, Morley, Derby
(18) 6402 yards

Burton-on-Trent G.C.
(0283) 44551
Ashby Road East, Burton-on-Trent
(18) 6555 yards

**Buxton &
High Peak G.C.**
(0298) 3453
Fairfield, Buxton
(18) 5954 yards

Cavendish G.C.
(0298) 5052
Gadley Lane, Buxton
(18) 5833 yards

Chesterfield G.C.
(0246) 566032
Walton, Chesterfield
(18) 6326 yards

**Chesterfield
Municipal G.C.**
(0246) 73887
Crow Lane, Chesterfield
(18) 6044 yards

Chevin G.C.
(0332) 841864
Golf Lane, Duffield
(18) 6057 yards

Derby G.C.
(0332) 766462
Shakespeare Street, Sinfin, Derby
(18) 6183 yards

Erewash Valley G.C.
(0602) 322984
Stanton-by-Dale, Ilkeston
(18) 6487 yards

**Glossop &
District G.C.**
(04574) 3117
Sheffield Road, Glossop
(11) 5726 yards

Ilkeston G.C.
(0602) 320304
West End Drive, Ilkeston
(9) 4116 yards

Kedleston Park G.C.
(0332) 840035
Kedleston, Quarndon
(18) 6636 yards

Matlock G.C.
(0629) 582191
Chesterfield Road, Matlock
(18) 5871 yards

Mickleover G.C.
(0332) 518662
Uttoxeter Road, Mickleover
(18) 5621 yards

Ormonde Fields G. & C.C.
(0773) 42987
Nottingham Road, Codnor, Ripley
(18) 6007 yards

Pastures G.C.
(0332) 513921
Pastures Hospital, Mickleover
(9) 5005 yards

Renishaw Park G.C.
(0246) 432044
Station Road, Renishaw
(18) 6253 yards

Shirlands G. & S.C.
(0773) 834935
Lower Delves, Shirland
(18) 6021 yards

Sickleholme G.C.
(0433) 51306
Bamford
(18) 6064 yards

Stanedge G.C.
(0246) 566156
Walton, Chesterfield
(9) 4867 yards

DEVON

Axe Cliff G.C.
(0297) 20499
Axemouth, Seaton
(18) 4998 yards

Bigbury G.C.
(0548) 810557
Bigbury-on-Sea, Kingsbridge
(18) 6038 yards

Chulmleigh G.C.
(0769) 80519
Leigh Road, Chulmleigh
(18) 1440 yards

Churston G.C.
(0803) 842751
Churston, Brixham
(18) 6201 yards

Downes Crediton G.C.
(03632) 3025
Hookway, Crediton
(18) 5858 yards

East Devon G.C.
(03954) 3370
North View Road,
Budleigh Salterton
(18) 6214 yards

Elfordleigh Hotel G. & C.C.
(0752) 336428
Plympton, Plymouth
(9) 5609 yards

Exeter G. & C.C.
(0392) 874139
Countess Wear, Exeter
(18) 5702 yards

Holsworthy G.C.
(0409) 253177
Kilatree, Holsworthy
(18) 5935 yards

Honiton G.C.
(0404) 44422
Honiton
(18) 5900 yards

Ilfracombe G.C.
(0271) 62176
Hele Bay, Ilfracombe
(18) 6227 yards

Manor House Hotel G. & C.C.
(0647) 40355
Princetown Road,
Moretonhampstead
(18) 6016 yards

Newton Abbot (Stover) G.C.
(0626) 62078
Bovey Road, Newton Abbot
(18) 5724 yards

Okehampton G.C.
(0837) 2113 .
Okehampton
(18) 5307 yards

Royal North Devon G.C.
(02372) 73817
Westward Ho!, Bideford
(18) 6449 yards

Saunton G.C.
(0271) 812436
Saunton, Braunton
(18) 6703 yards (East)
(18) 6322 yards (West)

Sidmouth G.C.
(0395) 513451
Cotmaton Road, Sidmouth
(18) 5188 yards

Staddon Heights G.C.
(0752) 402475
Plymstock, Plymouth
(18) 5861 yards

Tavistock G.C.
(0822) 612049
Down Road, Tavistock
(18) 6250 yards

Teignmouth G.C.
(06267) 4194
Exeter Road, Teignmouth
(18) 6142 yards

Thurlestone G.C.
(0548) 560405
Thurlestone, Kingsbridge
(18) 6337 yards

Tiverton G.C.
(0884) 252187
Post Hill, Tiverton
(18) 6227 yards

Torquay G.C.
(0803) 37471
St Marychurch,
Torquay
(18) 6251 yards

Torrington G.C.
(0805) 22229
Weare Trees, Torrington
(9) 4418 yards

Warren G.C.
(0626) 862255
Dawlish Warren
(18) 5968 yards

Wrangaton G.C.
(03647) 3229
Wrangaton, South Brent
(9) 5790 yards

Yelverton G.C.
(0822) 852824
Golf Links Road, Yelverton
(18) 6288 yards

DORSET

Ashley Wood G.C.
(0258) 52253
Wimborne Road, Blandford Forum
(9) 6227 yards

Boscombe G.C.
(0202) 36198
Queen's Park, Bournemouth
(18) 6505 yards

Bridport & West Dorset G.C.
(0308) 22597
East Cliff, West Bay, Bridport
(18) 5246 yards

Broadstone G.C.
(0202) 692595
Wentworth Drive, Broadstone
(18) 6204 yards

Came Down G.C.
(030 581) 2531
Came Down, Dorchester
(18) 6121 yards

Christchurch G.C.
(0202) 473817
Iford Bridge, Christchurch
(9) 4824 yards

Ferndown G.C.
(0202) 874602
119 Golf Links Road, Ferndown
(18) 6442 yards (Old Course)
(9) 5604 yards (New Course)

Highcliffe Castle G.C.
(04252) 72210
107 Lymington Road, Highcliffe-on-Sea
(18) 4732 yards

Isle of Purbeck G.C.
(0929) 44361
Studland, Swanage
(18) 6248 yards
(9) 2022 yards

Knighton Heath G.C.
(0202) 572633
Francis Avenue, West Howe, Bournemouth
(18) 6206 yards

Lakey Hill G.C.
(0929) 471776
Hyde, Wareham
(18) 6146 yards

Lyme Regis G.C.
(02974) 2963
Timber Hill, Lyme Regis
(18) 6262 yards

Meyrick Park G.C.
(0202) 290871
Central Drive, Bournemouth
(18) 5878 yards

Parkstone G.C.
(0202) 707138
Links Road, Parkstone
(18) 6250 yards

Sherborne G.C.
(0935) 814431
Higher Clatcombe, Sherborne
(18) 5768 yards

Weymouth G.C.
(0305) 773981
Links Road, Westham, Weymouth
(18) 5985 yards

DURHAM

Aycliffe G.C.
(0325) 318390
Newton Aycliffe
(9) 6054 yards

Barnard Castle G.C.
(0833) 38355
Marmire Road, Barnard Castle
(18) 5838 yards

Beamish Park G.C.
(091) 3701382
Beamish, Stanley
(18) 6205 yards

Birtley G.C.
(091) 4102207
Portobello Road, Birtley
(9) 5154 yards

Bishop Auckland G.C.
(0388) 663648
Durham Road, Bishop Auckland
(18) 6420 yards

Blackwell Grange G.C.
(0325) 464464
Briar Close, Blackwell, Darlington
(18) 5609 yards

Brancepeth Castle G.C.
(091) 3780075
Brancepeth Village, Durham
(18) 6300 yards

Chester-le-Street G.C.
(091) 3883218
Lumley Park, Chester-le-Street
(18) 6054 yards

Consett & District G.C.
(0207) 502186
Elmfield Road, Consett
(18) 6001 yards

Crook G.C.
(0388) 762429
Low Job's Hill, Crook
(18) 6089 yards

Darlington G.C.
(0325) 463936
Haughton Grange, Darlington
(18) 6272 yards

Dinsdale Spa G.C.
(0325) 332297
Middleton St. George, Darlington
(18) 6078 yards

Durham City G.C.

(091) 3780069
Langley Moor, Durham
(18) 6118 yards

Mount Oswald G.C.

(091) 3867527
South Road, Durham
(18) 6009 yards

Roseberry Grange G.C.

(091) 3700660
Grange Villa, Chester-le-Street
(18) 5628 yards

Seaham G.C.

(091) 5812354
Dawdon, Seaham
(18) 5972 yards

South Moor G.C.

(0207) 232848
The Middles, Craghead, Stanley
(18) 6445 yards

Stressholme G.C.

(0325) 461002
Snipe Lane, Darlington
(18) 6511 yards

EAST SUSSEX

Ashdown Forest Hotel G.C.

(034282) 4866
Chapel Lane, Forest Row
(18) 5433 yards

Brighton and Hove G.C.

(0273) 556482
Dyke Road, Brighton
(9) 5722 yards

Cooden Beach G.C.

(04243) 2040
Cooden, Bexhill
(18) 6411 yards

Crowborough Beacon G.C.

(08926) 61511
Beacon Road, Crowborough
(18) 6279 yards

Dale Hill G.C.

(0580) 200112
Ticehurst, Wadhurst
(18) 6035 yards

The Dyke G.C.

(079156) 296
Dyke Road, Brighton
(18) 6557 yards

Eastbourne Downs G.C.

(0323) 20827
East Dean Road, Eastbourne
(18) 6635 yards

East Brighton G.C.

(0273) 603989
Roedean Road, Brighton
(18) 6291 yards

Hastings G.C.

(0424) 52981
Battle Road, St. Leonards-on-Sea
(18) 6073 yards

Highwoods G.C.

(0424) 212625
Ellerslie Lane, Bexhill-on-Sea
(18) 6218 yards

Hollingbury Park G.C.

(0273) 552010
Ditching Road, Brighton
(18) 6415 yards

Horam Park G.C.

(04353) 3477
Chiddingly Road, Horam
(9) 2600 yards

Lewes G.C.

(0273) 473074
Chapel Hill, Lewes
(18) 5951 yards

Peacehaven G.C.

(0273) 514049
Brighton Road, Newhaven
(9) 5235 yards

Piltdown G.C.

(082572) 2033
Piltdown, Uckfield
(18) 6059 yards

Pyecombe G.C.

(07918) 5372
Clayton Hill, Pyecombe
(18) 6234 yards

Royal Ashdown Forest G.C.

(034282) 2018
Chapel Lane, Forest Row
(18) 6439 yards

Royal Eastbourne G.C.

(0323) 29738
Paradise Drive, Eastbourne
(18) 6084 yards
(9) 2147 yards

Rye G.C.

(0797) 225241
Camber, Near Rye
(18) 6301 yards
(18) 6141 yards (Jubilee)

Seaford G.C.

(0323) 892442
East Blatchington, Seaford
(18) 6241 yards

Seaford Head G.C.

(0323) 894843
Southdown Road, Seaford
(18) 5812 yards

Waterhall G.C.

(0273) 508658
Mill Road, Brighton
(18) 5615 yards

West Hove G.C.

(0273) 419738
Old Shoreham Road, Hove
(18) 6130 yards

Willingdon G.C.

(0323) 32383
Southdown Road, Eastbourne
(18) 6049 yards

ESSEX

Abridge G. & C.C.

(04028) 396
Stapleford Tawney, Abridge
(18) 6703 yards

Ballards Gore G.C.

(03706) 8924
Gore Road, Canewdon, Rochford
(18) 7062 yards

Basildon G.C.
(0268) 3849
Clay Hill Lane, Basildon
(18) 6122 yards

Belfairs Park G.C.
(0702) 525345
Eastwood Road, Leigh-on-Sea
(18) 5871 yards

Belhus Park G.C.
(0708) 854260
Belhus Park, South Ockendon
(18) 5501 yards

Bentley G.C.
(0277) 73179
Ongar Road, Brentwood
(18) 6709 yards

Birch Grove G.C.
(0206) 34276
Layer Road, Colchester
(9) 2828 yards

Boyce Hill G.C.
(0268) 793625
Vicarage Hill, South Benfleet
(18) 5882 yards

Braintree G.C.
(0376) 24117
Kings Lane, Stisted, Braintree
(18) 6026 yards

Bunsay Downs G.C.
(024541) 2648
Woodham Walter, Maldon
(18) 5826 yards

Burnham-on-Crouch G.C.
(0621) 782282
Creeksea, Burnham-on-Crouch
(9) 5866 yards

Canon's Brook G.C.
(0279) 21482
Elizabeth Way, Harlow
(18) 6745 yards

Channels G.C.
(0245) 440005
Belsteads Farm Lane, Little
Waltham, Chelmsford
(18) 6033 yards

Chelmsford G.C.
(0245) 256483
Widford, Chelmsford
(18) 5912 yards

Clacton G.C.
(0255) 421919
West Road, Clacton-on-Sea
(18) 6217 yards

Colchester G.C.
(0206) 853396
Braiswick, Colchester
(18) 6319 yards

Forrester Park G.C.
(0621) 891406
Great Totham, Maldon
(9) 5350 yards

Frinton G.C.
(02556) 4618
Esplanade, Frinton-on-Sea
(18) 6259 yards

Harwich & Dovercourt G.C.
(0255) 503616
Parkeston, Harwich
(9) 5692 yards

Havering G.C.
(0708) 22942
Lower Bedfords Road, Romford
(18) 5687 yards

Maldon G.C.
(0621) 53212
Beeleigh Landford, Maldon
(9) 6197 yards

Maylands G. & C.C.
(04023) 73080
Harold Park, Romford
(18) 6351 yards

Orsett G.C.
(0375) 891352
Brentwood Road, Orsett
(18) 6575 yards

Pipps Hill G.C.
(0268) 523456
Cranes Farm Road, Basildon
(9) 5658 yards

Rochford Hundred G.C.
(0702) 544302
Rochford Hall, Rochford
(18) 6255 yards

Romford G.C.
(0708) 40986
Gidea Park, Romford
(18) 6377 yards

Saffron Walden G.C.
(0799) 22786
Windmill Hill, Saffron Walden
(18) 6608 yards

Skips G.C.
(04023) 48234
Tysea Hill, Stapleford Abbotts
(18) 6146 yards

Stoke-by-Nayland G.C.
(0206) 262836
Leavenheath, Colchester
(18) 6471 yards (Gainsborough)
(18) 6498 yards (Constable)

Theydon Bois G.C.
(0378) 3054
Theydon Road, Epping
(18) 5472 yards

Thorndon Park G.C.
(0277) 811666
Ingrave, Brentwood
(18) 6455 yards

Thorpe Hall G.C.
(0702) 582205
Thorpe Hall Avenue, Thorpe Bay
(18) 6259 yards

Three Rivers G. & C.C.
(0621) 828631
Stow Road, Purleigh
(18) 6609 yards (Kings)
(9) 2142 yards

Towerlands G.C.
(0376) 26802
Panfield Road, Braintree
(9) 5396 yards

Upminster G.C.
(04022) 22788
Hall Lane, Upminster
(18) 5926 yards

Woodhall Spa

Warley Park G.C.
(0277) 224891
Little Warley, Brentwood
(18) 6261 yards
(9) 3166 yards

Warren G.C.
(024541) 3258
Woodham Walter, Maldon
(18) 6211 yards

GLOUCESTERSHIRE

Cirencester G.C.
(0285) 652465
Cheltenham Road, Bagendon,
Cirencester
(18) 6021 yards

Cleeve Hill G.C.
(0242) 672592
Cleeve Hill, Cheltenham
(18) 6217 yards

Cotswold Hills G.C.
(0242) 515264
Ullenwood, Cheltenham
(18) 6716 yards

Gloucester Hotel G. & C.C.
(0452) 411331
Robinswood Hill, Gloucester
(18) 6135 yards

Lilley Brook G.C.
(0242) 526785
Cirencester Road, Charlton Kings,
Cheltenham
(18) 6226 yards

Lydney G.C.
(0594) 42614
Lakeside Avenue, Lydney
(9) 5382 yards

Minchinhampton G.C.
(045383) 3866 (New)
(045383) 2642 (Old)
Minchinhampton, Stroud
(18) 6295 yards (Old Course)
(18) 6675 yards (New Course)

Painswick G.C.
(0452) 812180
Painswick, Stroud
(18) 4780 yards

Royal Forest of Dean G.C.
(0594) 32583
Lords Hill, Coleford
(18) 5519 yards

Stinchcombe Hill G.C.
(0453) 2015
Stinchcombe Hill, Dursley
(18) 5710 yards

Tewkesbury Park Hotel G.C.
(0684) 295405
Lincoln Green Lane, Tewkesbury
(18) 6533 yards

Westonbirt G.C.
(045383) 3860
Westonbirt, Tetbury
(9) 4504 yards

GREATER LONDON

Addington G.C.
(01) 777 6057
Shirley Church Road, Croydon
(18) 6242 yards

Addington Court G.C.
(01) 657 0281
Featherbed Lane,
Addington, Croydon
(18) 5577 yards (Old)
(18) 5513 yards (New)

Addington Palace G.C.
(01) 654 3061
Gravel Hill, Addington, Croydon
(18) 6262 yards

Arkley G.C.
(01) 449 0394
Rowley Green Road, Barnet
(9) 6045 yards

Ashford Manor G.C.
(0784) 252049
Fordbridge Road, Ashford
(18) 6343 yards

Banstead Downs G.C.
(01) 642 2284
Burdon Lane, Belmont, Sutton
(18) 6169 yards

Beckenham Place Park G.C.
(01) 650 2292
Beckenham Hill Road, Beckenham
(18) 5722 yards

Bexley Heath G.C.
(01) 303 6951
Mount Road, Bexley Heath
(9) 5239 yards

Brent Valley G.C.
(01) 567 1287
Church Road, Hanwell W7
(18) 5426 yards

Bushey G.C.
(01) 950 2215
High Street, Bushey
(9) 6000 yards

Bush Hill Park G.C.
(01) 360 5738
Winchmore Hill, N21
(18) 5809 yards

Chigwell G.C.
(01) 500 2059
High Road, Chigwell
(18) 6279 yards

Chingford G.C.
(01) 529 5708
Station Road, Chingford E4
(18) 6136 yards

Chislehurst G.C.
(01) 467 2782
Camden Place, Chislehurst
(18) 5128 yards

Coombe Hill G.C.
(01) 942 2284
Golf Club Drive, Kingston Hill
(18) 6286 yards

Coombe Wood G.C.
(01) 942 0388
George Road, Kingston Hill
(18) 5210 yards

Coulsdon Court G.C.
(01) 660 0468
Coulsdon Road, Coulsdon
(18) 6030 yards

Crews Hill G.C.
(01) 363 6674
Cattlegate Road, Crews Hill
(18) 6208 yards

Croham Hurst G.C.
(01) 657 2075
Croham Road, South Croydon
(18) 6274 yards

Cuddington G.C.
(01) 393 0952
Banstead Road, Banstead
(18) 6282 yards

Dulwich & Sydenham Hill G.C.
(01) 693 3961
College Road, SE21
(18) 6051 yards

Dyrham Park G.C.
(01) 440 3361
Galley Lane, Barnet
(18) 6369 yards

Ealing G.C.
(01) 997 0937
Perivale Lane, Greenford
(18) 6216 yards

Elstree G.C.
(01) 953 6115
Watling Street, Elstree
(18) 5245 yards

Eltham Warren G.C.
(01) 850 4477
Bexley Road, Eltham SE9
(9) 5840 yards

Enfield G.C.
(01) 363 3970
Old Park Road South,
Windmill Hill, Enfield
(18) 6137 yards

Fairlop Waters G.C.
(01) 500 9911
Barkingside, Ilford
(18) 6288 yards

Finchley G.C.
(01) 346 2436
Frith Lane, NW7
(18) 6411 yards

Fulwell G.C.
(01) 977 2733
Hampton Hill
(18) 6490 yards

Greenford G.C.
(01) 578 3949
Rockware Avenue, Greenford
(9) 4418 yards

Grim's Dyke G.C.
(01) 428 4539
Oxhey Lane, Hatch End, Pinner
(18) 5598 yards

Hadley Wood G.C.
(01) 449 4328
Beech Hill, Hadley Wood
(18) 6473 yards

Hainault Forest G.C.
(01) 500 2131
Chigwell Row, Hainault Forest
(18) 5754 yards (No. 1)
(18) 6445 yards (No. 2)

Hampstead G.C.
(01) 455 7089
Winnington Road, N2
(9) 5812 yards

Harefield Place G.C.
(0895) 31169
The Drive, Harefield Place,
Uxbridge
(18) 5711 yards

Hartsbourne G. & C.C.
(01) 950 1113
Bushey Heath
(18) 6305 yards
(9) 5432 yards

Haste Hill G.C.
(09274) 26485
The Drive, Northwood
(18) 5794 yards

Hendon G.C.
(01) 346 6023
Devonshire Road, NW7
(18) 6241 yards

Highgate G.C.
(01) 340 3745
Denewood Road, Highgate N6
(18) 5964 yards

Hillingdon G.C.
(0895) 33956
Dorset Way, Hillingdon
(9) 5469 yards

Home Park G.C.
(01) 977 2423
Hampton Wick, Kingston
(18) 6497 yards

Horsenden Hill G.C.
(01) 902 4555
Woodland Rise, Greenford
(9) 1618 yards

Hounslow Heath G.C.
(01) 570 5271
Staines Road, Hounslow
(18) 5820 yards

Ilford G.C.
(01) 554 2930
Wanstead Park Road, Ilford
(18) 5710 yards

Langley Park G.C.
(01) 650 2090
Barnfield Wood Road, Beckenham
(18) 6488 yards

Leaside G.C.
(01) 803 3611
Picketts Lock Centre, Edmonton
(9) 4978 yards

London Scottish G.C.
(01) 788 0135
Windmill Enclosure,
Wimbledon Common SW19
(18) 5486 yards

Magpie Hall Lane G.C.
(01) 462 7014
Magpie Hall Lane, Bromley
(9) 5538 yards

Malden G.C.
(01) 942 0654
Traps Lane, New Malden
(18) 6315 yards

Mill Hill G.C.
(01) 959 2339
Barnet Way, Mill Hill NW7
(18) 6309 yards

Mitcham G.C.
(01) 648 4197
Carshalton Road, Mitcham
Junction
(18) 5931 yards

Muswell Hill G.C.
(01) 888 1764
Rhodes Avenue, Wood Green N22
(18) 6470 yards

North Middlesex G.C.
(01) 445 1604
Friern Barnet Lane, N20
(18) 5611 yards

Northwood G.C.
(09274) 25329
Rickmansworth Road, Northwood
(18) 6464 yards

Oaks Park Sports Centre G.C.
(01) 643 8363
Woodmansterne Road, Carshalton
(18) 5873 yards

Old Ford Manor G.C.
(01) 440 9185
Hadley Green, Barnet
(18) 6449 yards

Perivale Park G.C.
(01) 578 1693
Ruislip Road East, Greenford
(9) 5334 yards

Pinner Hill G.C.
(01) 866 0963
South View Road, Pinner Hill
(18) 6293 yards

Purley Downs G.C.
(01) 657 8347
Purley Downs Road, Purley
(18) 6237 yards

Richmond G.C.
(01) 940 4351
Sudbrook Park, Richmond
(18) 5965 yards

Richmond Park G.C.
(01) 940 3205
Richmond Park, SW15
(18) 5940 yards
(18) 5969 yards

Roehampton G.C.
(01) 876 5505
Roehampton Lane
(18) 6057 yards

Royal Blackheath G.C.
(01) 850 1795
Court Road, Eltham
(18) 6216 yards

Royal Epping Forest G.C.
(01) 529 2195
Forest Approach, Chingford
(18) 6220 yards

Royal Mid-Surrey G.C.
(01) 940 1894
Old Deer Park, Richmond
(18) 6331 yards (Outer)
(18) 5446 yards (Inner)

Royal Wimbledon G.C.
(01) 946 2125
29 Camp Road, Wimbledon
(18) 6300 yards

Ruislip G.C.
(0895) 638835
Ickenham Road, Ruislip
(18) 5235 yards

Sandy Lodge G.C.
(09274) 25429
Sandy Lodge Lane, Northwood
(18) 6340 yards

Selsdon Park Hotel G.C.
(01) 657 8811
Addington Road, Sanderstead
(18) 6402 yards

Shirley Park G.C.
(01) 654 1143
Addiscombe Road, Croydon
(18) 6210 yards

Shooters Hill G.C.
(01) 854 6368
Eaglesfield Road, Shooters Hill
(18) 5736 yards

Shortlands G.C.
(01) 460 2471
Meadow Road, Shortlands,
Bromley
(9) 5261 yards

Sidcup G.C.
(01) 300 2150
Hurst Road, Sidcup
(9) 5692 yards

South Herts G.C.
(01) 445 2035
Links Drive, Totteridge
(18) 6470 yards

Stanmore G.C.
(01) 954 2599
Gordon Avenue, Stanmore
(18) 5982 yards

Strawberry Hill G.C.
(01) 894 0165
Wellesley Road, Twickenham
(9) 4762 yards

Sudbury G.C.
(01) 902 3713
Bridgewater Road, Wembley
(18) 6282 yards

Sundridge Park G.C.
(01) 460 0278
Garden Road, Bromley
(18) 6410 yards (East)
(18) 6027 yards (West)

Surbiton G.C.
(01) 398 3101
Woodstock Lane, Chessington
(18) 6211 yards

Thames Ditton & Esher G.C.
(01) 398 1551
Portsmouth Road, Esher
(9) 5415 yards

Trent Park G.C.
(01) 366 7432
Bramley Road, Southgate
(18) 6008 yards

Twickenham G.C.
(01) 979 0032
Staines Road, Twickenham
(9) 6014 yards

Wanstead G.C.
(01) 989 3938
Overton Drive, Wanstead
(18) 6211 yards

West Middlesex G.C.
(01) 574 3450
Greenford Road, Southall
(18) 6242 yards

Whitewebbs G.C.
(01) 363 2951
Clay Hill, Enfield
(18) 5755 yards

Wimbledon Common G.C.
(01) 946 7571
Camp Road, Wimbledon Common
(18) 5486 yards

Wimbledon Park G.C.
(01) 946 1250
Home Park Road, Wimbledon
(18) 5465 yards

Woodcote Park G.C.
(01) 668 2788
Meadow Hill, Coulsdon
(18) 6624 yards

Wyke Green G.C.
(01) 560 8777
Syon Lane, Isleworth
(18) 6242 yards

GREATER MANCHESTER

Altrincham Municipal G.C.
(061) 928 0761
Stockport Road, Timperley,
Altrincham
(18) 6204 yards

Ashton-in-Makerfield G.C.
(0942) 727745
Gardwood Park, Liverpool Road,
Ashton-in-Makerfield
(18) 6160 yards

Ashton-on-Mersey G.C.
(061) 973 3220
Church Lane, Sale
(9) 6242 yards

Ashton-under-Lyne G.C.
(061) 330 1537
Kings Road, Ashton-under-Lyne
(18) 6157 yards

Blackley G.C.
(061) 643 4116
Victoria Avenue East, Blackley
(18) 6235 yards

Bolton G.C.
(0204) 43067
Lostock Park, Bolton
(18) 6215 yards

Bolton Municipal G.C.
(0204) 42336
Links Road, Lostock, Bolton
(18) 6012 yards

Bolton Old Links G.C.
(0204) 42307
Chorley Old Road, Bolton
(18) 6406 yards

Brackley G.C.
(061) 790 6076
Bullows Road, Little Hulton
(9) 6006 yards

Bramhall G.C.
(061) 766 2213
Ladythorn Road, Bramhall
(18) 6300 yards

Bramhall Park G.C.
(061) 485 3119
Manor Road, Bramhall
(18) 6214 yards

Breightmet G.C.
(0204) 27381
Redbridge, Ainsworth
(9) 6407 yards

Brookdale G.C.
(061) 681 8996
Woodhouses, Failsworth
(18) 5878 yards

Bury G.C.
(061) 766 2213
Blackford Bridge, Bury
(18) 5961 yards

Castle Hawk G.C.
(0706) 40841
Castleton, Rochdale
(18) 6316 yards

Cheadle G.C.
(061) 485 4540
Shiers Drive, Cheadle
(9) 5006 yards

Chorlton-Cum-Hardy G.C.
(061) 881 5830
Barlow Hall Road, Chorlton
(18) 6004 yards

Crompton & Royton G.C.
(061) 624 2154
High Barn, Royton, Oldham
(18) 6121 yards

Davyhulme Park G.C.
(061) 748 2260
Gleneagles Road, Davyhulme
(18) 6237 yards

Deane G.C.
(0204) 651808
Junction Road, Deane, Bolton
(18) 5511 yards

Denton G.C.
(061) 336 3218
Manchester Road, Denton
(18) 6290 yards

Didsbury G.C.
(061) 998 2811
Ford Lane, Northenden
(18) 6273 yards

Disley G.C.
(06632) 2071
Jackson's Edge, Disley
(18) 5977 yards

Dukinfield G.C.
(061) 338 2669
Yew Tree Lane, Dukinfield
(18) 5544 yards

Dunham Forest G. & C.C.
(061) 928 2605
Oldfield Lane, Altrincham
(18) 6636 yards

Dunscar G.C.
(0204) 53321
Bromley Cross, Bolton
(18) 5995 yards

Ellesmere G.C.
(061) 790 7108
Old Clough Lane, Worsley
(18) 5957 yards

Fairfield G. & S.C.
(061) 370 2292
Booth Road, Andenshaw
(18) 5664 yards

Flixton G.C.
(061) 748 2116
Church Road, Flixton, Urmston
(9) 6441 yards

Gathurst G.C.
(02575) 2432
Shevington
(9) 6308 yards

Gatley G.C.
(061) 437 2091
Styal Road, Heald Green
(9) 5934 yards

Great Lever &
Farnworth G.C.
(0204) 72550
Lever Edge Lane, Bolton
(18) 5859 yards

Greenmount G.C.
(020488) 3712
Greenmount, Bury
(9) 4920 yards

Hale G.C.
(061) 980 4225
Rappax Road, Hale
(9) 5734 yards

Harwood G.C.
(0204) 28028
Harwood, Bolton
(9) 6028 yards

Hazel Grove G.C.
(061) 483 7272
Buxton Road, Hazel Grove
(18) 6300 yards

Heaton Moor G.C.
(061) 432 6458
Heaton Mersey, Stockport
(18) 5876 yards

Heaton Park G.C.
(061) 798 0295
Heaton Park, Prestwich
(18) 5849 yards

Horwich G.C.
(0204) 696298
Horwich, Bolton
(9) 5404 yards

Houldsworth G.C.
(061) 224 4571
Wingate House, Levenshulme
(18) 6078 yards

Lowes Park G.C.
(061) 764 1231
Walmersley, Bury
(9) 6003 yards

Manchester G.C.
(061) 643 3202
Rochdale Road, Middleton
(18) 6450 yards

Marple G.C.
(061) 427 6364
Hawk Green, Marple, Stockport
(18) 5506 yards

Mellor & Townscliffe G.C.
(061) 427 2208
Mellor, Stockport
(18) 5925 yards

Mirrlees G.C.
(061) 483 1000
Bramhall Moor Lane, Hazel Grove
(9) 6102 yards

North Manchester G.C.
(061) 643 9033
Manchester Old Road, Middleton
(18) 6542 yards

Northenden G.C.
(061) 998 4738
Palatine Road, Northenden
(18) 6435 yards

Oldham G.C.
(061) 624 4986
Lees New Road, Oldham
(18) 5045 yards

Pike Fold G.C.
(061) 740 1136
Cooper Lane, Victoria Avenue,
Blackley
(9) 5789 yards

Prestwich G.C.
(061) 773 2544
Hilton Lane, Prestwich M25
(18) 4712 yards

Reddish Vale G.C.
(061) 480 2359
Southcliffe Road, Reddish,
Stockport
(18) 6048 yards

Ringway G.C.
(061) 980 2630
Hale Barns, Altrincham
(18) 6494 yards

Rochdale G.C.
(0706) 43818
Bagslate, Rochdale
(18) 5981 yards

Romiley G.C.
(061) 430 7257
Goosehouse Green, Romiley
(18) 6357 yards

Saddleworth G.C.
(04577) 3653
Uppermill, Oldham
(18) 5961 yards

Sale G.C.
(061) 973 1638
Golf Road, Sale
(18) 6351 yards

Springfield Park G.C.
(0706) 49801
Marland, Rochdale
(18) 5209 yards

Stamford G.C.
(04575) 4829
Huddersfield Road, Stalybridge
(18) 5619 yards

Stand G.C.
(061) 766 2214
Ashbourne Grove, Whitefield
(18) 6411 yards

Stockport G.C.
(061) 427 4425
Offerton Road, Offerton, Stockport
(18) 6319 yards

Swinton Park G.C.
(061) 794 0861
East Lanes Road, Swinton
(18) 6675 yards

Tunshill G.C.
(0706) 342095
Milnrow, Rochdale
(9) 5812 yards

Turton G.C.
(0204) 852235
Bromley Cross, Bolton
(9) 5805 yards

Walmersley G.C.
(061) 764 0018
Garretts Close, Walmersley
(9) 6114 yards

Werneth G.C.
(061) 624 1190
Garden Suburb, Oldham
(18) 5296 yards

Werneth Low G.C.
(061) 368 7388
Werneth Low, Hyde
(9) 5734 yards

Westhoughton G.C.
(0942) 811085
Westhoughton, Bolton
(9) 5834 yards

Whitefield G.C.
(061) 766 2904
Higher Lane, Whitefield
(18) 6106 yards

Wigan G.C.
(0257) 421360
Arley Hall, Haigh, Wigan
(9) 6058 yards

Wigan Metropolitan G.C.
(0942) 401107
Haigh Hall Park, Wigan
(18) 6423 yards

William Wroe G.C.
(061) 748 8680
Pennybridge Lane, Flixton
(18) 4395 yards

Withington G.C.
(061) 445 9544
Palatine Road, West Didsbury
(18) 6411 yards

Worsley G.C.
(061) 789 4202
Monton Green, Eccles
(18) 6217 yards

HAMPSHIRE

Alresford G.C.
(0962) 733746
Cheriton Road, Alresford
(18) 5986 yards

Alton G.C.
(0420) 82042
Old Odiham Road, Alton
(9) 5699 yards

Ampfield Par Three G.C.
(0794) 68480
Winchester Road, Ampfield
(18) 2478 yards

Andover G.C.
(0264) 58040
Winchester Road, Andover
(9) 5933 yards

Army G.C.
(0252) 540638
Laffans Road, Aldershot
(18) 6579 yards

Barton-on-Sea G.C.
(0425) 615308
Marine Drive, Barton-on-Sea
(18) 5565 yards

Basingstoke G.C.
(0256) 465990
Kempshott Park, Basingstoke
(18) 6309 yards

Basingstoke Hospitals G.C.
(0256) 20347
Aldermaston Road, Basingstoke
(9) 5480 yards

Bishopswood G.C.
(07356) 5213
Bishopswood Lane, Tadley,
Basingstoke
(9) 6474 yards

Blackmoor G.C.
(04203) 2775
Golf Lane, White Hill, Bordon
(18) 6213 yards

Bramshaw G.C.
(0703) 813433
Brook, Lyndhurst
(18) 6233 yards (Manor)
(18) 5774 yards (Forest)

Brockenhurst Manor G.C.
(0590) 23332
Sway Road, Brockenhurst
(18) 6216 yards

Burley G.C.
(04253) 2431
Burley, Ringwood
(9) 6224 yards

Corhampton G.C.
(0489) 877279
Sheeps Pond Lane, Droxford,
Southampton
(18) 6088 yards

Dibden G.C.
(0703) 845596
Dibden, Southampton
(18) 6206 yards

Dunwood Manor G.C.
(0794) 40549
Shootash Hill, Romsey
(18) 5959 yards

Fleming Park G.C.
(0703) 612797
Magpie Lane, Eastleigh
(18) 4436 yards

Gosport and Stokes Bay G.C.
(0705) 527941
Haslar, Gosport
(9) 5806 yards

Great Salterns G.C.
(0705) 664549
Eastern Road, Portsmouth
(18) 5970 yards

Hartley Wintney G.C.
(025126) 4211
London Road, Hartley Wintney
(9) 6096 yards

Hayling G.C.
(0705) 464446
Ferry Road, Hayling Island
(18) 6489 yards

Hockley G.C.
(0962) 713165
Twyford, Winchester
(18) 6260 yards

Lee-on-the-Solent G.C.
(0705) 551170
Brune Lane, Lee-on-the-Solent
(18) 6022 yards

Liphook G.C.
(0428) 723785
Wheatsheaf Enclosure, Liphook
(18) 6207 yards

Meon Valley Hotel G. & C.C.
(0329) 833455
Sandy Lane, Shedfield
(18) 6519 yards

New Forest G.C.
(042128) 2450
Lyndhurst
(18) 5748 yards

North Hants G.C.
(0252) 616443
Minley Road, Fleet
(18) 6257 yards

Old Thorns Hotel & G.C.
(0428) 724555
Longmoor Road, Liphook
(18) 6447 yards

Petersfield G.C.
(0730) 62386
Heath Road, Petersfield
(18) 5751 yards

Portsmouth G.C.
(0705) 372210
Crookhorn Lane, Woodley,
Portsmouth
(18) 6259 yards

Romsey G.C.
(0703) 732218
Nursling, Southampton
(18) 5752 yards

Rowlands Castle G.C.
(070541) 2784
Links Lane, Rowlands Castle
(18) 6627 yards

Royal Winchester G.C.
(0962) 52462
Sarum Road, Winchester
(18) 6218 yards

Southampton G.C.
(0703) 790732
Golf Course Road, Bassett,
Southampton
(18) 6218 yards
(9) 2391 yards

Southwick Park G.C.
(0705) 380131
Pinsley Drive, Southwick
(18) 5970 yards

Southwood G.C.
(0252) 548700
Ively Road, Farnborough
(18) 5553 yards

Stoneham G.C.
(0703) 769272
Bassett, Southampton
(18) 6310 yards

Tylney Park G.C.
(0256) 722079
Rotherwick, Basingstoke
(18) 6150 yards

Waterlooville G.C.
(0705) 263388
Idsworth Road, Cowplain,
Portsmouth
(18) 6647 yards

HEREFORD & WORCESTER

Belmont House G.C.
(0432) 277445
Belmont, Hereford
(18) 6448 yards

Blackwell G.C.
(021) 445 1994
Blackwell, Bromsgrove
(18) 6105 yards

Broadway G.C.
(0386) 853683
Willersey Hill, Broadway
(18) 6211 yards

Churchill & Blakedown G.C.
(0562) 700200
Blakedown, Kidderminster
(9) 5399 yards

Droitwich G. & C.C.
(0905) 774344
Ford Lane, Droitwich
(18) 6036 yards

Evesham G.C.
(0386) 860395
Fladbury Cross, Pershore
(9) 6418 yards

Habberley G.C.
(0562) 745756
Habberley, Kidderminster
(9) 5440 yards

Herefordshire G.C.
(0432) 71219
Wormsley, Hereford
(18) 6036 yards

Kidderminster G.C.
(0562) 822303
Russell Road, Kidderminster
(18) 6156 yards

Kington G.C.
(0544) 230340
Bradnor Hill, Kington
(18) 5830 yards

Leominster G.C.
(0568) 2863
Ford Bridge, Leominster
(9) 5314 yards

Little Lakes G.C.
(0299) 266385
Lye Head, Bewdley
(9) 6204 yards

Redditch G.C.
(0527) 43309
Callow Hill, Redditch
(18) 6671 yards

Ross-on-Wye G.C.
(098982) 267
Gorsley, Ross-on-Wye
(18) 6500 yards

Tolladine G.C.
(0905) 21074
Tolladine Road, Worcester
(9) 5630 yards

Worcester G. & C.C.
(0905) 422555
Boughton Park, Worcester
(18) 5890 yards

Worcestershire G.C.
(06845) 5992
Wood Farm, Malvern Wells
(18) 6449 yards

HERTFORDSHIRE

Aldenham G. & C.C.
(092385) 7889
Radlett Road, Aldenham
(18) 6455 yards

Ashridge G.C.
(044284) 2244
Little Gaddesden, Berkhamsted
(18) 6508 yards

Batchwood Hall G.C.
(0727) 33349
Batchwood Drive, St. Albans
(18) 6463 yards

Berkhamsted G.C.
(04427) 5832
The Common, Berkhamsted
(18) 6568 yards

Bishop's Stortford G.C.
(0279) 54715
Dunhow Road, Bishop's Stortford
(18) 6440 yards

Boxmoor G.C.
(0442) 42434
Box Lane, Hemel Hempstead
(9) 4854 yards

Brickendon Grange G.C.
(099286) 258
Brickendon, Hertford
(18) 6315 yards

Royal St Georges

Brookman's Park G.C.
(0707) 52487
Golf Club Road, Hatfield
(18) 6438 yards

Bushey Hall G.C.
(0923) 25802
Bushey Hall Drive, Bushey
(18) 6071 yards

Chadwell Springs G.C.
(0920) 3647
Hertford Road, Ware
(9) 6418 yards

Cheshunt Park G.C.
(0992) 24009
Park Lane, Cheshunt
(18) 6608 yards

Chorleywood G.C.
(09278) 2009
Common Road, Chorleywood
(9) 5676 yards

East Herts G.C.
(0920) 821978
Hammels Park, Buntingford
(18) 6449 yards

Harpenden G.C.
(05827) 2580
Hammonds End, Harpenden
(18) 6363 yards

Harpenden Common G.C.
(05827) 5959
East Common, Harpenden
(18) 5613 yards

Knebworth G.C.
(0438) 812752
Deards End Lane, Knebworth
(18) 6428 yards

Letchworth G.C.
(0462) 683203
Letchworth Lane, Letchworth
(18) 6082 yards

Little Hay G.C.
(0442) 833798
Bovingdon, Hemel Hempstead
(18) 6610 yards

Mid Herts G.C.
(058283) 2242
Gustard Wood, Wheathampstead
(18) 6094 yards

Moor Park G.C.
(0923) 773146
Moor Park, Rickmansworth
(18) 6713 yards (High)
(18) 5815 yards (West)

Panshanger G.C.
(0707) 333350
Herns Lane, Welwyn Garden City
(18) 6538 yards

Hatfield London Country Club
(0707) 42624
Bedwell Park, Essendon
(18) 6878 yards

Porters Park G.C.
(09276) 4127
Shenley Hill, Radlett
(18) 6313 yards

Potters Bar G.C.
(0707) 52020
Darkes Lane, Potters Bar
(18) 6273 yards

Redbourn G.C.
(058285) 3493
Kingsbourne Green Lane,
Redbourn
(18) 6407 yards

Rickmansworth G.C.
(0923) 773163
Moor Lane, Rickmansworth
(18) 4412 yards

Royston G.C.
(0763) 42696
Baldock Road, Royston
(18) 6032 yards

Stevenage G.C.
(043888) 424
Aston, Stevenage
(18) 6451 yards

Verulam G.C.
(0727) 53327
London Road, St Albans
(18) 6432 yards

Welwyn Garden City G.C.
(0707) 325243
High Oaks Road, Welwyn Garden
City
(18) 6200 yards

West Herts G.C.
(0923) 36484
Cassiobury Park, Watford
(18) 6488 yards

Whipsnade Park G.C.
(044284) 2330
Studham Lane, Dagnall
(18) 6812 yards

HUMBERSIDE
Beverley & East Riding G.C.
(0482) 869519
The Westwood, Beverley
(18) 5937 yards

Boothferry G.C.
(0430) 430364
Spaldington, Goole
(18) 6651 yards

Bridlington G.C.
(0262) 674721
Belvedere Road, Bridlington
(18) 6320 yards

Brough G.C.
(0482) 667374
Cave Road, Brough
(18) 6012 yards

Cleethorpes G.C.
(0472) 812059
Kings Road, Cleethorpes
(18) 6015 yards

Driffield G.C.
(0377) 44069
Sunderlandwick, Driffield
(9) 6225 yards

Elsham G.C.
(0652) 680291
Barton Road, Elsham
(18) 6420 yards

Flamborough Head G.C.
(0262) 850333
Flamborough, Bridlington
(18) 5438 yards

Ganstead G.C.
(0482) 811121
Coniston, Hull
(9) 5769 yards

Grimsby G.C.
(0472) 42630
Littlecoates Road, Grimsby
(18) 6058 yards

Hainsworth Park G.C.
(0964) 542362
Driffield
(9) 5350 yards

Hessle G.C.
(0482) 650171
Cottingham, Hull
(18) 6638 yards

Holme Hall G.C.
(0724) 862078
Bottesford, Scunthorpe
(18) 6475 yards

Hornsea G.C.
(0964) 534989
Rolston Road, Hornsea
(18) 6470 yards

Hull G.C.
(0482) 658919
Packman Lane, Kirk Ella, Hull
(18) 6242 yards

Normanby Hall G.C.
(0724) 720226
Normanby Park, Scunthorpe
(18) 6398 yards

Scunthorpe G.C.
(0724) 866561
Burringham Road, Scunthorpe
(18) 6281 yards

Sutton Park G.C.
(0482) 74242
Holderness Road, Hull
(18) 6251 yards

Withernsea G.C.
(0964) 612214
Chesnut Avenue, Withernsea
(9) 5112 yards

ISLE OF MAN
Castletown G.C.
(0624) 822125
Fort Island, Castletown
(18) 6804 yards

Douglas G.C.
(0624) 75952
Pulrose Road, Douglas
(18) 6080 yards

Howstrake G.C.
(0624) 20430
Grondle Road, Onchan
(18) 5367 yards

Peel G.C.
(0624) 843456
Rheast Lane, Peel
(18) 5914 yards

Ramsey G.C.
(0624) 812244
Brookfield Avenue, Ramsey
(18) 6019 yards

Rowany G.C.
(0624) 834108
Rowany Drive, Port Erin
(18) 5813 yards

ISLE OF WIGHT

Cowes G.C.
(0983) 292303
Crossfield Avenue, Cowes
(9) 5880 yards

Freshwater Bay G.C.
(0983) 752955
Afton Downs, Freshwater Bay
(18) 5628 yards

Newport G.C.
(0983) 525076
St. George's Down, Newport
(9) 5704 yards

Osborne G.C.
(0983) 295421
Osborne, East Cowes
(9) 6286 yards

Ryde G.C.
(0983) 614809
Binstead Road, Ryde
(9) 5220 yards

Shanklin & Sandown G.C.
(0983) 403217
The Fairway, Sandown
(18) 6000 yards

Ventnor G.C.
(0983) 853326
Steephill Down Road, Ventnor
(9) 5910 yards

KENT

Ashford G.C.
(0233) 620180
Sandyhurst Lane, Ashford
(18) 6246 yards

Barnehurst G.C.
(0322) 523746
Mayplace Road, East Barnehurst
(9) 5320 yards

Bearsted G.C.
(0622) 38198
Ware Street, Bearsted, Maidstone
(18) 6253 yards

Broome Park G. & C.C.
(0227) 831701
Barham, Canterbury
(18) 6610 yards

Canterbury G.C.
(0227) 453532
Scotland Hills, Canterbury
(18) 6209 yards

Cherry Lodge G.C.
(0959) 72250
Jail Lane, Biggin Hill
(18) 6908 yards

Chestfield G.C.
(022779) 2365
Chestfield, Whitstable
(18) 6126 yards

Cobtree Manor Park G.C.
(0622) 53276
Chatham Road, Boxley, Maidstone
(18) 5701 yards

Cranbrook G.C.
(0580) 712833
Benenden Road, Cranbrook
(18) 6128 yards

Cray Valley G.C.
(0689) 37909
Sandy Lane, St Paul's Cray,
Orpington
(18) 6338 yards

Darenth Valley G.C.
(09592) 2944
Station Road, Shoreham
(18) 6356 yards

Dartford G.C.
(0322) 26455
Dartford Heath, Dartford
(18) 5914 yards

Deangate Ridge G.C.
(0634) 251180
Hoo, Rochester
(18) 6300 yards

Edenbridge G. & C.C.
(0732) 865097
Crouch House Road, Edenbridge
(18) 6635 yards

Faversham G.C.
(079589) 561
Belmont Park, Faversham
(18) 5979 yards

Gillingham G.C.
(0634) 53017
Woodlands Road, Gillingham
(18) 5911 yards

Hawkhurst G.C.
(0580) 752396
High Street, Hawkhurst
(9) 5769 yards

Herne Bay G.C.
(0227) 373964
Eddington, Herne Bay
(18) 5466 yards

High Elms G.C.
(0689) 58175
High Elms Road, Downe
(18) 6210 yards

Holtye G.C.
(034286) 635
Holtye Common, Cowden,
Edenbridge
(9) 5289 yards

Hythe Imperial G.C.
(0303) 67554
Princes Parade, Hythe
(9) 5583 yards

Knole Park G.C.
(0732) 452150
Seal Hollow Road, Sevenoaks
(18) 6249 yards

Lamberhurst G.C.
(0892) 890241
Church Road, Lamberhurst
(18) 6277 yards

Leeds Castle G.C.
(062780) 467
Leeds Castle, Maidstone
(9) 6017 yards

Littlestone G.C.
(0679) 63355
St Andrews Road, Littlestone,
New Romney
(18) 6417 yards

Lullingstone Park G.C.
(0959) 34542
Park Gate, Chelsfield, Orpington
(18) 6674 yards
(9) 2432 yards

Mid Kent G.C.
(0474) 68035
Singlewell Road, Gravesend
(18) 6206 yards

Nevill G.C.
(0892) 25818
Benhall Mill Road,
Tunbridge Wells
(18) 6336 yards

North Foreland G.C.
(0843) 62140
Convent Road, Broadstairs
(18) 6382 yards

Poult Wood G.C.
(0732) 364039
Higham Lane, Tonbridge
(18) 5569 yards

Prince's G.C.
(0304) 613797
Sandwich Bay, Sandwich
(18) 6923 yards
(9) 3134 yards

**Rochester & Cobham
Park G.C.**
(047482) 3411
Park Dale, Rochester
(18) 6467 yards

Royal Cinque Ports G.C.
(0304) 374007
Golf Road, Deal
(18) 6744 yards

Royal St George's G.C.
(0304) 613090
Sandwich
(18) 6857 yards

Ruxley G.C.
(0689) 71490
St Paul's Cray, Orpington
(18) 5017 yards

St Augustine's G.C.
(0843) 590333
Cliffsend, Ramsgate
(18) 5138 yards

Sene Valley G.C.
(0303) 68513
Sene, Folkestone
(18) 6320 yards

Sheerness G.C.
(0795) 662585
Powe Station Road, Sheerness
(18) 6500 yards

**Sittingbourne & Milton Regis
G.C.**
(0795) 842261
Newington, Sittingbourne
(18) 6121 yards

Tenterden G.C.
(05806) 3987
Woodchurch Road, Tenterden
(9) 5119 yards

Tunbridge Wells G.C.
(0892) 23034
Langton Road, Tunbridge Wells
(9) 4684 yards

Walmer & Kingsdown G.C.
(0304) 373256
Kingsdown, Deal
(18) 6451 yards

Westgate & Birchington G.C.
(0843) 31115
Domneva Road, Westgate-on-Sea
(18) 4926 yards

West Kent G.C.
(0689) 51323
Downe, Orpington
(18) 6392 yards

West Malling G.C.
(0732) 844785
Addington, Maidstone
(18) 6142 yards

Whitstable & Seasalter G.C.
(0227) 272020
Collingwood Road, Whitstable
(18) 5276 yards

Wildernesse G.C.
(0732) 61199
Seal, Sevenoaks
(18) 6478 yards

Woodlands Manor G.C.
(09592) 3806
Woodlands, Sevenoaks
(18) 5858 yards

Wrotham Heath G.C.
(0732) 884800
Comp, Sevenoaks
(9) 5823 yards

LANCASHIRE

Accrington & District G.C.
(0254) 35070
West End, Oswaldtwistle,
Accrington
(18) 5954 yards

Ashton & Lea G.C.
(0772) 720374
Blackpool Road, Lea, Preston
(18) 6286 yards

Bacup G.C.
(0706) 873170
Maden Road, Bacup
(9) 5652 yards

Baxenden & District G.C.
(0254) 34555
Top o' th' Meadow, Baxenden,
Accrington
(9) 5740 yards

Beacon Park G.C.
(0695) 622700
Dalton, Up Holland, Wigan
(18) 5996 yards

Blackburn G.C.
(0254) 55942
Beardwood Brow, Blackburn
(18) 6099 yards

Blackpool North Shore G.C.
(0253) 52054
Devonshire Road, Blackpool
(18) 6440 yards

Blackpool Park G.C.
(0253) 31004
North Park Drive, Blackpool
(18) 6060 yards

Burnley G.C.
(0282) 24328
Glen View, Burnley
(18) 5891 yards

Chorley G.C.
(025 72) 63024
Charnock, Chorley
(18) 6277 yards

Clitheroe G.C.
(0200) 22292
Whalley Road, Clitheroe
(18) 6311 yards

Colne G.C.
(0282) 67158
Skipton Old Road, Colne
(9) 5961 yards

Darwen G.C.
(0254) 71287
Winter Hill, Darwen
(18) 5752 yards

Dean Wood G.C.
(0695) 622219
Lafford Lane, Up Holland,
Skelmersdale
(18) 6097 yards

Duxbury Park G.C.
(02572) 65380
Duxbury Park, Chorley
(18) 6390 yards

Fairhaven G.C.
(0253) 736741
Lytham Hall Park, Ansdell,
Lytham St Annes
(18) 6883 yards

Fishwick Hall G.C.
(0772) 798300
Farringdon Park, Preston
(18) 6203 yards

Fleetwood G.C.
(03917) 3661
Princes Way, Fleetwood
(18) 6437 yards

Green Haworth G.C.
(0254) 37580
Green Haworth, Accrington
(9) 5513 yards

Heysham G.C.
(0254) 51011
Trumacar Park, Heysham
(18) 6224 yards

Hindley Hall G.C.
(0942) 55991
Hall Lane, Hindley
(18) 5875 yards

Ingol G. & S.C.
(0772) 734556
Ingol, Preston
(18) 6345 yards

Knott End G.C.
(0253) 810576
Wyreside, Knott End on Sea,
Blackpool
(18) 5852 yards

Lancaster G. & C.C.
(0524) 751247
Ashton-with-Stodday, Lancaster
(18) 6442 yards

Lansil G.C.
(0524) 67143
Caton Road, Lancaster
(9) 5608 yards

Leyland G.C.
(0772) 436457
Wigan Road, Leyland
(18) 6105 yards

Longridge G.C.
(077478) 3291
Jeffrey Hill, Longridge
(18) 5678 yards

Lytham Green Drive G.C.
(0253) 737390
Ballam Road, Lytham
(18) 6043 yards

Marsden Park G.C.
(0282) 67525
Townhouse Road, Nelson
(18) 5806 yards

Morecambe G.C.
(0254) 412841
Bare, Morecambe
(18) 5766 yards

Nelson G.C.
(0282) 64583
Brierfield, Nelson
(18) 5961 yards

Ormskirk G.C.
(0695) 72227
Lathom, Ormskirk
(18) 6333 yards

Penwortham G.C.
(0772) 744630
Penwortham, Preston
(18) 5915 yards

Pleasington G.C.
(0254) 22177
Pleasington, Blackburn
(18) 6445 yards

Poulton-le-Fylde G.C.
(0253) 892444
Breck Road, Poulton-le-Fylde
(9) 5752 yards

Preston G.C.
(0772) 700011
Fulwood, Preston
(18) 6249 yards

Rishton G.C.
(0254) 884442
Eachill Links, Rishton
(9) 6094 yards

Rossendale G.C.
(0706) 213056
Haslinden, Rossendale
(18) 6267 yards

Royal Lytham & St Annes G.C.
(0253) 724206
Links Gate, Lytham St Annes
(18) 6673 yards

St Annes Old Links G.C.
(0253) 723597
Highbury Road, St Annes, Lytham
(18) 6616 yards

Shaw Hill G. & C.C.
(02572) 69221
Whittle-le-Woods,
Chorley
(18) 6467 yards

Silverdale G.C.
(0524) 701300
Redbridge Lane, Silverdale,
Carnworth
(9) 5262 yards

Todmorden G.C.
(070681) 2986
Stone Road, Todmorden
(9) 5818 yards

Towneley G.C.
(0282) 38473
Towneley Park, Burnley
(9) 5840 yards

Whalley G.C.
(025482) 2236
Whalley, Blackburn
(9) 5953 yards

Whittaker G.C.
(0706) 78310
Whittaker Lane, Littleborough
(9) 5636 yards

Wilpshire G.C.
(0254) 49558
Wilpshire, Blackburn
(18) 5911 yards

LEICESTERSHIRE

Birstall G.C.
(0533) 674322
Station Road, Birstall, Leicester
(18) 6203 yards

Charnwood Forest G.C.
(0509) 890259
Breakback Lane, Woodhouse Eaves
(9) 6202 yards

Cosby G.C.
(0533) 864759
Chapel Lane, Cosby
(18) 6277 yards

Enderby G.C.
(0533) 849388
Mill Lane, Enderby
(9) 4356 yards

Glen Gorse G.C.
(0533) 714159
Glen Road, Oadby, Leicester
(18) 6641 yards

Hinckley G.C.
(0455) 615014
Leicester Road, Hinckley
(18) 6578 yards

Humberstone Heights G.C.
(0533) 764674
Gipsy Lane, Leicester
(18) 6444 yards

Kibworth G.C.
(053753) 2301
Weir Road, Kibworth Beauchamp
(18) 6282 yards

Kirby Muxloe G.C.
(0533) 393457
Kirby Muxloe, Leicester
(18) 6303 yards

Leicestershire G.C.
(0533) 738825
Evington Lane, Leicester
(18) 6312 yards

Lingdale G.C.
(0509) 890035
Joe Moores Lane,
Woodhouse Eaves
(9) 6114 yards

Longcliffe G.C.
(0509) 239129
Snell's Nook Lane, Loughborough
(18) 6551 yards

Luffenham Heath G.C.
(0780) 720205
Ketton, Stamford
(18) 6254 yards

Lutterworth G.C.
(04555) 2532
Rugby Road, Lutterworth
(18) 5570 yards

Market Harborough G.C.
(0858) 63684
Oxenden Road,
Market Harborough
(9) 6080 yards

Melton Mowbray G.C.
(0664) 62118
Waltham Road, Melton Mowbray
(9) 6168 yards

Oadby G.C.
(0533) 709052
Leicester Road, Oadby
(18) 6228 yards

Rothley Park G.C.
(0533) 302809
Westfield Lane, Rothley
(18) 6487 yards

R.A.F. North Luffenham
(0780) 720041
North Luffenham, Oakham
(18) 5629 yards

Rushcliffe G.C.
(050982) 2959
Stocking Lane, East Leake,
Loughborough
(18) 6057 yards

Scraptoft G.C.
(0533) 419000
Beeby Road, Scraptoft
(18) 6166 yards

Ullesthorpe G.C.
(0455) 209023
Ullesthorpe, Luttersworth
(18) 6048 yards

Western Park G.C.
(0533) 872339
Scudmore Road, Leicester
(18) 6532 yards

Willesley Park G.C.
(0530) 414596
Tamworth Road,
Ashby-de-la-Zouch
(18) 6310 yards

LINCOLNSHIRE

Belton Park G.C.
(0476) 67399
Londonthorpe Road, Grantham
(9) 6412 yards
(9) 6101 yards
(9) 5857 yards

Blankney G.C.
(0526) 20202
Blankney, Lincoln
(18) 6232 yards

Boston G.C.
(0205) 50589
Horncastle Road, Boston
(18) 5795 yards

Burghley Park G.C.
(0780) 53789
Stamford
(18) 6133 yards

Canwick Park G.C.
(0522) 22166
Canwick Park, Lincoln
(18) 6257 yards

Carholme G.C.
(0522) 33263
Carholme Road, Lincoln
(18) 6086 yards

Lincoln G.C.
(042771) 721
Torksey, Lincoln
(18) 6400 yards

Louth G.C.
(0507) 603681
Crowtree Lane, Louth
(18) 6502 yards

Market Rasen and District G.C.
(0673) 842416
Legsby Road, Market Rasen
(18) 6031 yards

North Shore G.C.
(0754) 3298
North Shore Road, Skegness
(18) 6134 yards

Sandilands G.C.
(0521) 41617
Sandilands, Mablethorpe
(18) 5995 yards

Seacroft G.C.
(0754) 3020
Seacroft, Skegness
(18) 6478 yards

Sleaford G.C.
(05298) 273
South Rauceby, Sleaford
(18) 6443 yards

Spalding G.C.
(077585) 386
Surfleet, Spalding
(18) 5807 yards

Stoke Rochford G.C.
(047683) 275
Stoke Rochford, Grantham
(18) 6204 yards

Sutton Bridge G.C.
(0406) 350323
Sutton Bridge, Spalding
(9) 5850 yards

Thonock G.C.
(0427) 3088
Thonock, Gainsborough
(18) 5824 yards

Woodhall Spa G.C.
(0526) 52511
The Broadway, Woodhall Spa
(18) 6866 yards

MERSEYSIDE

Allerton Municipal G.C.
(051) 428 1046
Allerton, Liverpool
(18) 5459 yards

Alt G.C.
(0704) 35268
Park Road West, Southport
(18) 5939 yards

Arrowe Park G.C.
(051) 677 1527
Arrow Park, Woodchurch,
Birkenhead
(18) 6377 yards

Bidston G.C.
(051) 630 6650
Leasowe, Wirral
(18) 6207 yards

Bootle G.C.
(051) 928 1371
Dunningsbridge Road, Bootle
(18) 6362 yards

Bowring G.C.
(051) 489 5985
Roby Road, Huyton
(9) 5592 yards

Brackenwood G.C.
(051) 608 3093
Bebington, Wirral
(18) 6285 yards

Bromborough G.C.
(051) 334 2978
Raby Hall Road, Bromborough
(18) 6650 yards

Caldy G.C.
(051) 625 1818
Links Hey Road, Caldy, Wirral
(18) 6665 yards

Childwall G.C.
(051) 487 9871
Naylor's Road, Liverpool
(18) 6425 yards

Eastham Lodge G.C.
(051) 327 3003
Ferry Road, Eastham, Wirral
(15) 5826 yards

Formby G.C.
(07048) 72164
Golf Road, Formby
(18) 6871 yards

Formby Ladies G.C.
(07048) 73493
Golf Road, Formby
(18) 5374 yards

Grange Park G.C.
(0744) 26318
Prescot Road, St Helens
(18) 6480 yards

Haydock Park G.C.
(09252) 6944
Golborne Park, Newton-le-Willows
(18) 6014 yards

Hesketh G.C.
(0704) 36897
Cambridge Road, Southport
(18) 6478 yards

Heswall G.C.
(051) 342 1237
Cottage Lane, Heswall, Wirral
(18) 6472 yards

Hillside G.C.
(0704) 67169
Hastings Road, Southport
(18) 6850 yards

Hoylake Municipal G.C.
(051) 632 2956
Carr Lane, Hoylake
(18) 6312 yards

Huyton & Prescot G.C.
(051) 489 3948
Hurst Park, Huyton
(18) 5738 yards

Leasowe G.C.
(051) 677 5852
Leasowe Road, Moreton, Wirral
(18) 6204 yards

Lee Park G.C.
(051) 487 3882
Childwall Valley Road,
Liverpool
(18) 6024 yards

Liverpool Municipal G.C.
(051) 546 5435
Ingoe Lane, Kirkby
(18) 6571 yards

Prenton G.C.
(051) 608 1053
Golf Links Road, Prenton,
Birkenhead
(18) 6379 yards

Royal Birkdale G.C.
(0704) 67920
Waterloo Road, Southport
(18) 6968 yards

Royal Liverpool G.C.
(051) 632 3101
Meols Drive, Hoylake, Wirral
(18) 6780 yards

Sherdley Park G.C.
(0744) 813149
Elton Road, St. Helens
(18) 5941 yards

**Southport &
Ainsdale G.C.**
(0704) 78000
Bradshaws Lane, Ainsdale,
Southport
(18) 6603 yards

Southport Municipal G.C.
(0704) 35286
Park Road West, Southport
(18) 6253 yards

Southport Old Links G.C.
(0704) 24294
Moors Lane, Southport
(9) 6486 yards

Wallasey G.C.
(051) 691 1024
Bayswater Road, Wallasey
(18) 6607 yards

Warren G.C.
(051) 639 5730
Grove Road, Wallasey
(9) 5914 yards

West Derby G.C.
(051) 228 1034
Yew Tree Lane, West Derby,
Liverpool
(18) 6333 yards

West Lancashire G.C.
(051) 924 1076
Hall Road West, Blundellsands,
Liverpool
(18) 6756 yards

Wirral Ladies G.C.
(051) 652 1255
Budston Road, Oxon, Birkenhead
(18) 4966 yards

Woolton G.C.
(051) 486 2298
Doe Park, Woolton, Liverpool
(18) 5706 yards

NORFOLK

Barnham Broom Hotel G.C.
(060545) 393
Honingham Road,
Barnham Broom
(18) 6603 yards

Bawburgh G.C.
(0603) 746390
Long Lane, Bawburgh
(9) 5278 yards

Dereham G.C.
(0362) 693122
Quebec Road, Dereham
(9) 6255 yards

Diss G.C.
(0379) 2847
Stuston, Diss
(9) 5900 yards

Eaton G.C.
(0603) 51686
Newmarket Road, Norwich
(18) 6125 yards

Fakenham G.C.
(0328) 2867
The Racecourse, Fakenham
(9) 5879 yards

Gorleston G.C.
(0493) 661911
Warren Road, Gorleston
Great Yarmouth
(18) 6279 yards

Great Yarmouth & Caister G.C.
(0493) 728699
Beach House, Caister-on-Sea
(18) 6235 yards

Hunstanton G.C.
(04853) 2811
Golf Course Road, Old Hunstanton
(18) 6670 yards

Kings Lynn G.C.
(055387) 654
Castle Rising, Kings Lynn
(18) 6552 yards

**Links Country Park
Hotel & G.C.**
(026375) 691
West Runton
(9) 4814 yards

Mundesley G.C.
(0263) 720095
Mundesley, Norwich
(9) 5376 yards

Royal Cromer G.C.
(0263) 512884
Overstrand Road, Cromer
(18) 6508 yards

Royal Norwich G.C.
(0603) 429928
Hellesdon, Norwich
(18) 6603 yards

Royal West Norfolk G.C.
(0485) 210233
Brancaster
(18) 6302 yards

Ryston Park G.C.
(0366) 382133
Denver, Downham Market
(9) 6292 yards

Sheringham G.C.
(0263) 823488
Weybourne Road, Sheringham
(18) 6430 yards

Sprowston Park G.C.
(0603) 410657
Wroxham Road, Sprowston,
Norwich
(18) 5985 yards

Swaffham G.C.
(0760) 21611
Clay Road, Swaffham
(9) 6252 yards

Thetford G.C.
(0842) 2169
Brandon Road, Thetford
(18) 6504 yards

NORTH YORKSHIRE

Aldwark Manor G.C.
(03473) 8146
Alne, York
(18) 5172 yards

Bedale G.C.
(0677) 22451
Leyburn Road, Bedale
(18) 5599 yards

Bentham G.C.
(0468) 61018
Robin Lane, Bentham
(9) 5752 yards

Catterick Garrison G.C.
(0748) 833268
Leyburn Road, Catterick Garrison
(18) 6336 yards

Easingwold G.C.
(0347) 21486
Stillington Road, Easingwold
(18) 6222 yards

Filey G.C.
(0723) 513293
West Avenue, Filey
(18) 6030 yards

Fulford G.C.
(0904) 412882
Heslington Lane, Fulford, York
(18) 6779 yards

Ganton G.C.
(0944) 70329
Ganton, Scarborough
(18) 6693 yards

Ghyll G.C.
(0282) 842466
Ghyll Brow, Barnoldswick
(9) 5708 yards

Harrogate G.C.
(0423) 862999
Starback, Harrogate
(18) 6183 yards

Heworth G.C.
(0904) 424618
Mancastergate, York
(11) 6078 yards

Kirkbymoorside G.C.
(0751) 31525
Manor Vale, Kirkbymoorside
(18) 5958 yards

Knaresborough G.C.
(0423) 862690
Boroughbridge Road,
Knaresborough
(18) 6281 yards

Malton & Norton G.C.
(0653) 697912
Norton, Malton
(18) 6411 yards

Masham G.C.
(0765) 89379
Masham, Ripon
(9) 5338 yards

Oakdale G.C.
(0423) 67162
Oakdale, Harrogate,
(18) 6456 yards

Pannal G.C.
(0423) 872628
Follifoot Road, Pannal, Harrogate
(18) 6659 yards

Pike Hills G.C.
(0904) 708756
Copmanthorpe, York
(18) 6048 yards

Richmond G.C.
(0748) 4775
Bend Hagg, Richmond
(18) 5704 yards

Ripon City G.C.
(0765) 700411
Palace Road, Ripon
(9) 5752 yards

The Belfry

Scarborough North Cliff G.C.
(0723) 360786
Burniston Road, Scarborough
(18) 6425 yards

Scarborough South Cliff G.C.
(0723) 374737
Deepdale Avenue, Scarborough
(18) 6085 yards

Selby G.C.
(075782) 785
Mill Lane, Selby
(18) 6246 yards

Settle G.C.
(07292) 3921
Giggleswick, Settle
(9) 4900 yards

Skipton G.C.
(0756) 2128
Grassington Road, Skipton
(18) 6087 yards

Thirsk & Northallerton G.C.
(0845) 22170
Thornton-le-Street, Thirsk
(9) 6087 yards

Whitby G.C.
(0947) 600660
Low Straggleton, Whitby
(18) 5710 yards

York G.C.
(0904) 490304
Lords Manor Lane, Strensall,
York
(18) 6275 yards

NORTHAMPTON-SHIRE

Cherwell Edge G.C.
(0295) 711591
Chacombe, Nr. Banbury
(18) 5925 yards

Cold Ashby G.C.
(0604) 740548
Cold Ashby
(18) 5957 yards

Daventry & District G.C.
(0327) 702829
Norton Road, Daventry
(9) 5555 yards

Delapre G.C.
(0604) 64036
Nene Valley Way, Northampton
(18) 6293 yards

Kettering G.C.
(0536) 511104
Headlands, Kettering
(18) 6035 yards

Kingsthorpe G.C.
(0604) 710610
Kingsley Road, Northampton
(18) 6006 yards

Northampton G.C.
(0604) 719453
Kettering Road, Northampton
(18) 6002 yards

Northamptonshire County G.C.
(0604) 843025
Church Brampton, Northampton
(18) 6503 yards

Oundle G.C.
(0832) 73267
Oundle
(18) 5507 yards

Priors Hall G.C.
(0536) 67546
Stamford Road, Weldon
(18) 6677 yards

Rushden & District G.C.
(0933) 312197
Kimbolton Road, Chelveston
(9) 6381 yards

Staverton Park G.C.
(0327) 705911
Staverton, Daventry
(18) 6634 yards

Wellingborough G.C.
(0933) 677234
Harrowden Hall, Wellingborough
(18) 6604 yards

Woodlands G.C.
(032736) 291
Farthingstone, Towcester
(18) 6330 yards

NORTHUMBERLAND

Allendale G.C.
(091) 2675875
Allendale, Hexham
(9) 4488 yards

Alnmouth G.C.
(0665) 830368
Foxton Hall, Alnmouth
(18) 6414 yards

Alnmouth Village G.C.
(0665) 830370
Marine Road, Alnmouth
(9) 6078 yards

Alnwick G.C.
(0665) 602499
Swansfield Park, Alnwick
(9) 5379 yards

Arcot Hall G.C.
(091) 236 2794
Dudley, Cramlington
(18) 6389 yards

Bamburgh Castle G.C.
(06684) 321
Bamburgh
(18) 5465 yards

Bedlingtonshire G.C.
(0670) 822457
Acorn Bank, Bedlington
(18) 6825 yards

Bellingham G.C.
(0660) 20530
Boggle Hole, Bellingham
(9) 5226 yards

Berwick-upon-Tweed G.C.
(0289) 87348
Goswick, Berwick-upon-Tweed
(18) 6399 yards

Blyth G.C.
(0670) 356514
New Delaval, Blyth
(18) 6533 yards

Dunstanburgh Castle G.C.
(066576) 562
Embleton
(18) 6357 yards

Hexham G.C.
(0434) 603072
Spital Park, Hexham
(18) 6272 yards

Magdalene Fields G.C.
(0289) 306384
Berwick-upon-Tweed
(18) 6551 yards

Morpeth G.C.
(0670) 512065
The Common, Morpeth
(18) 6215 yards

Newbiggin-by-the Sea G.C.
(0670) 817833
Newbiggin-by-the-Sea
(18) 6444 yards

Prudhoe G.C.
(0661) 32466
Eastwood Park, Prudhoe
(18) 5812 yards

Rothbury G.C.
(0669) 20718
Old Race Course, Rothbury
(9) 5650 yards

Seahouses G.C.
(0665) 720794
Bednell Road, Seahouses
(18) 5399 yards

Stocksfield G.C.
(0661) 843041
New Ridley, Stocksfield
(18) 5594 yards

Tynedale G.C.
(0434) 605701
Tyne Green, Hexham
(9) 5706 yards

Warkworth G.C.
(0665) 711596
Warkworth, Morpeth
(9) 5817 yards

NOTTINGHAMSHIRE

Beeston Fields G.C.
(0602) 257062
Beeston Fields, Nottingham
(18) 6404 yards

Bulwell Forest G.C.
(0602) 278008
Hucknall Road, Bulwell,
Nottingham
(18) 5606 yards

Bulwell Hall Park G.C.
(0602) 278021
Lawton Drive, Bulwell
(18) 6218 yards

Chilwell Manor G.C.
(0602) 258958
Meadow Lane, Chilwell,
Nottingham
(18) 6379 yards

Coxmoor G.C.
(0623) 557359
Coxmoor Road, Sutton-in-Ashfield
(18) 6501 yards

Edwalton Municipal G.C.
(0602) 234775
Edwalton, Nottingham
(9) 3336 yards

Kilton Forest G.C.
(0909) 486563
Blyth Road, Worksop
(18) 6569 yards

Lindrick G.C.
(0909) 475820
Lindrick Common, Worksop
(18) 6615 yards

Mansfield Woodhouse G.C.
(0623) 23521
Leeming Lane, Mansfield
(9) 2150 yards

Mapperley C.C.
(0602) 265611
Mapperley Plains,
Nottingham
(18) 6224 yards

Newark G.C.
(063684) 282
Coddington, Newark
(18) 6486 yards

Notts G.C.
(0623) 753225
Hollinwell, Derby Road,
Kirby-in-Ashfield
(18) 7020 yards

Oxton G.C.
(0602) 653545
Oxton, Southwell
(18) 6630 yards

Radcliffe-on-Trent G.C.
(06073) 3000
Cropwell Road, Radcliffe-on-Trent
(18) 6423 yards

Retford G.C.
(0777) 703733
Ordsall, Retford
(9) 6230 yards

Sherwood Forest G.C.
(0623) 26689
Eakring Road, Mansfield
(18) 6709 yards

Stanton-on-the-Wolds G.C.
(06077) 2044
Stanton-on-the-Wolds, Keyworth
(18) 6379 yards

Wollaton Park G.C.
(0602) 787574
Wollaton Park, Nottingham
(18) 6494 yards

Worksop G.C.
(0909) 477731
Windmill Lane, Worksop
(18) 6651 yards

OXFORDSHIRE

Badgemore Park G.C.
(0491) 572206
Henley-on-Thames
(18) 6112 yards

Burford G.C.
(099 382) 2583
Burford
(18) 6405 yards

Chesterton County G.C.
(0869) 241204
Chesterton, Bicester
(18) 6496 yards

Chipping Norton G.C.
(0608) 2383
Southcombe, Chipping Norton
(9) 5280 yards

Frilford Heath G.C.
(0865) 390428
Frilford Heath, Abingdon
(18) 6768 yards (Red)
(18) 6006 yards (Green)

Henley G.C.
(0491) 575742
Harpsden, Henley-on-Thames
(18) 6329 yards

Huntercombe G.C.
(0491) 641207
Nuffield, Henley-on-Thames
(18) 6257 yards

North Oxford G.C.
(0865) 54924
Banbury Road, Oxford
(18) 5805 yards

Southfield G.C.
(0865) 242158
Hill Top Road, Oxford
(18) 6230 yards

Tadmarton Heath G.C.
(0608) 737278
Wiggington, Banbury
(18) 5917 yards

SHROPSHIRE

Bridgnorth G.C.
(0742) 2400
Stanley Lane, Bridgnorth
(18) 6673 yards

Church Stretton G.C.
(0694) 722281
Trevor Hill, Church Stretton
(18) 5008 yards

Hawkstone Park Hotel & G.C.
(093924) 611
Weston-under-Redcastle,
Shrewsbury
(18) 6465 yards (Hawkstone)
(18) 5368 yards (Weston)

Hill Valley G. & C.C.
(0948) 3584
Terrick Road, Whitchurch
(18) 6884 yards
(9) 5106 yards

Lilleshall Hall G.C.
(0952) 604776
Lilleshall, Newport
(18) 5891 yards

Llanymynech G.C.
(0691) 830542
Pant, Oswestry
(18) 6114 yards

Ludlow G.C.
(058477) 285
Bromfield, Ludlow
(18) 6239 yards

Market Drayton G.C.
(0630) 2266
Sutton, Market Drayton
(18) 6170 yards

Meole Brace G.C.
(0743) 64050
Meole Brace
(9) 5830 yards

Oswestry G.C.
(069188) 535
Aston Park, Oswestry
(18) 6046 yards

Shifnal G.C.
(0952) 460330
Decker Hill, Shifnal
(18) 6422 yards

Shrewsbury G.C.
(074372) 2976
Condover, Shrewsbury
(18) 6212 yards

Telford Hotel G. & C.C.
(0952) 585642
Greay Hay, Telford
(18) 6228 yards

Wrekin G.C.
(0952) 44032
Wellington, Telford
(18) 5699 yards

SOMERSET

Brean G.C.
(027875) 467
Brean, Burnham-on-Sea
(18) 5566 yards

Burnham and Berrow G.C.
(0278) 785760
St Christopher's Way,
Burnham-on-Sea
(18) 6547 yards
(9) 6550 yards

Enmore Park G.C.
(027867) 481
Enmore, Bridgewater
(18) 6443 yards

**Minehead and West
Somerset G.C.**
(0643) 2057
The Warren, Minehead
(18) 6131 yards

Taunton and Pickeridge G.C.
(082342) 240
Corfe, Taunton
(18) 5927 yards

Vivary Park G.C.
(0823) 333875
Taunton
(18) 4620 yards

Wells G.C.
(0749) 72868
East Horrington Road, Wells
(18) 5288 yards

Windwhistle G. & S.C.
(046030) 231
Cricket St Thomas, Chard
(12) 6055 yards

Yeovil G.C.
(0935) 22965
Sherborne Road, Yeovil
(18) 6139 yards

SOUTH YORKSHIRE

Abbeydale G.C.
(0742) 360763
Twentywell Lane, Dore, Sheffield
(18) 6419 yards

Austerfield Park G.C.
(0302) 710850
Cross Lane, Austerfield
(18) 6824 yards

Barnsley G.C.
(0226) 382954
Staincross, Barnsley
(18) 6048 yards

Beauchief Municipal G.C.
(0742) 367274
Abbey Lane, Sheffield
(18) 5428 yards

Birley Wood G.C.
(0742) 389198
Birley Lane, Sheffield
(18) 6275 yards

Concord Park G.C.
(0742) 613605
Shiregreen Lane, Sheffield
(18) 4280 yards

Crookhill Park G.C.
(0709) 863466
Conisbrough, Doncaster
(18) 5846 yards

Doncaster G.C.
(0302) 868404
Bescarr, Doncaster
(18) 6230 yards

Doncaster Town Moor G.C.
(0302) 535458
Belle Vue, Doncaster
(18) 6081 yards

Dore & Totley G.C.
(0742) 369872
Broadway Road, Sheffield
(18) 6301 yards

Grange Park G.C.
(0709) 559497
Upper Wortley Road, Rotherham
(18) 6461 yards

Hallamshire G.C.
(0742) 302153
Sandygate, Sheffield
(18) 6396 yards

Hallowes G.C.
(0246) 413734
Hallowes Lane, Dronfield, Sheffield
(18) 6366 yards

Hickleton G.C.
(0709) 893506
Hickleton, Doncaster
(18) 6401 yards

Hillsborough G.C.
(0742) 349151
Worrall Road, Sheffield
(18) 6100 yards

Lees Hall G.C.
(0742) 552900
Hemsworth Road, Norton,
Sheffield
(18) 6137 yards

Phoenix G.C.
(0709) 370759
Brinsworth, Rotherham
(18) 6170 yards

Rotherham G.C.
(0709) 850812
Thrybergh Park, Rotherham
(18) 6324 yards

Serlby Park G.C.
(0777) 818268
Serlby, Doncaster
(18) 5325 yards

Silkstone G.C.
(0226) 244796
Field Head, Silkstone, Barnsley
(18) 6045 yards

Sitwell Park G.C.
(0709) 541046
Shrogswood Road Rotherham
(18) 6203 yards

Stocksbridge & District G.C.
(0742) 882408
Royd Lane, Townend, Deepcar
(15) 5055 yards

Tankersley Park G.C.
(0742) 468247
High Green, Sheffield
(18) 6241 yards

Tinsley Park G.C.
(0742) 560237
Darnall, Sheffield
(18) 6045 yards

Wath G.C.
(0709) 878677
Abdy Rawmarsh, Rotherham
(9) 5606 yards

Wheatley G.C.
(0302) 831655
Armthorpe Road, Doncaster
(18) 6345 yards

Wortley G.C.
(0742) 885294
Hermit Hill Lane, Wortley,
Sheffield
(18) 5960 yards

SUFFOLK

Aldeburgh G.C.
(072 885) 2890
Saxmundham Road, Aldeburgh
(18) 6330 yards
(9) 2114 yards

Beccles G.C.
(0502) 712479
The Common, Beccles
(9) 5392 yards

**Bungay &
Waveny Valley G.C.**
(0986) 2337
Outney Common, Bungay
(18) 5944 yards

Bury St Edmunds G.C.
(0284) 5978
Tuthill, Bury St Edmunds
(18) 6615 yards

Felixstowe Ferry G.C.
(0394) 286834
Ferry Road, Felixstowe
(18) 6042 yards

Flempton G.C.
(028484) 291
Flempton, Bury St Edmunds
(9) 6050 yards

Fornham Park G.C.
(0284) 63426
Fornham St. Martin,
Bury St. Edmunds
(18) 6212 yards

Haverhill G.C.
(0440) 61951
Coupals Road, Haverhill
(9) 5708 yards

Ipswich G.C.
(0473) 78941
Purdis Heath, Ipswich
(18) 6405 yards
(9) 3860 yards

Links G.C.
(0638) 663000
Cambridge Road, Newmarket
(18) 6402 yards

Newton Green G.C.
(0787) 77501
Newton Green, Sudbury
(9) 5442 yards

Rookery Park G.C.
(0502) 60380
Carlton Colville, Lowestoft
(18) 6649 yards

**Royal Worlington
& Newmarket G.C.**
(0638) 712216
Worlington, Bury St Edmunds
(9) 6218 yards

Rushmere G.C.
(0473) 75648
Rushmere Heath, Ipswich
(18) 6287 yards

Southwold G.C.
(0502) 723248
The Common, Southwold
(9) 6001 yards

Stowmarket G.C.
(04493) 473
Onehouse, Stowmarket
(18) 6119 yards

Thorpeness G.C.
(072885) 2176
Thorpeness
(18) 6241 yards

Waldringfield Heath G.C.
(0473) 726821
Waldringfield, Woodbridge
(18) 5837 yards

Woodbridge G.C.
(03943) 2038
Bromeswell Heath,
Woodbridge
(18) 6314 yards
(9) 4486 yards

STAFFORDSHIRE

Alsager G. & C.C.
(0270) 875700
Alsager Road, Alsager
(18) 6192 yards

Beau Desert G.C.
(05438) 2626
Hazel Slade, Cannock
(18) 6285 yards

Branston G.C.
(0283) 43207
Branston, Burton-on-Trent
(18) 6480 yards

Brocton Hall G.C.
(0785) 661901
Brocton, Stafford
(18) 6095 yards

Burslem G.C.
(0782) 87006
High Lane, Tunstall,
Stoke-on-Trent
(9) 5354 yards

Craythorne G.C.
(0283) 64329
Stretton, Burton-on-Trent
(18) 5230 yards

Drayton Park G.C.
(0827) 251139
Drayton Park, Tamworth
(18) 6414 yards

Greenway Hall G.C.
(0782) 503158
Stockton Brook, Stoke-on-Trent
(18) 5676 yards

Ingestre Park G.C.
(0889) 270845
Ingestre, Weston, Stafford
(18) 6376 yards

Leek G.C.
(0538) 385889
Cheadle Road, Leek
(18) 6240 yards

Leek Westwood G.C.
(0538) 383060
Newcastle Road, Leek
(9) 5501 yards

Newcastle-under-Lyme G.C.
(0782) 617006
Whitmore Road, Newcastle
(18) 6450 yards

Newcastle Municipal G.C.
(0782) 627596
Keele Road, Newcastle
(18) 6301 yards

Stafford Castle G.C.
(0785) 3821
Newport Road, Stafford
(9) 6347 yards

Stone G.C.
(0785) 813103
Filleybrooks, Stone
(9) 6272 yards

Tamworth G.C.
(0827) 53850
Eagle Drive, Tamworth
(18) 6695 yards

Trentham G.C.
(0782) 658109
Barlaston Old Road, Trentham,
Stoke-on-Trent
(18) 6644 yards

Trentham Park G.C.
(0782) 658800
Trentham Park, Trentham,
Stoke-on-Trent
(18) 6403 yards

Uttoxeter G.C.
(08893) 4844
Wood Lane, Uttoxeter
(9) 5695 yards

Whittington Barracks G.C.
(0543) 432317
Tamworth Road, Lichfield
(18) 6457 yards

Wolstanton G.C.
(0782) 622413
Dimsdale Old Hall, Newcastle
(18) 5807 yards

SURREY

Barrow Hills G.C.
(0276) 72037
Longcross, Chertsey
(18) 3090 yards

Betchworth Park G.C.
(0306) 882052
Reigate Road, Dorking
(18) 6266 yards

Bramley G.C.
(0483) 892696
Godden Hill, Bramley
(18) 5910 yards

Burhill G.C.
(0932) 227345
Walton-on-Thames
(18) 6224 yards

Camberley Heath G.C.
(0276) 23258
Golf Drive, Camberley
(18) 6402 yards

Chipstead G.C.
(07375) 55781
How Lane, Coulsdon
(18) 5454 yards

Crondall G.C.
(0252) 850880
Oak Park, Heath Lane, Crondall
(18) 6233 yards

Dorking G.C.
(0306) 886917
Chart Park, Dorking
(9) 5106 yards

Drift G.C.
(04865) 4641
The Drift, East Horsley
(18) 6404 yards

Effingham G.C.
(0372) 52203
Guildford Road, Effingham
(18) 6488 yards

Epsom G.C.
(03727) 21666
Longdown Lane, Epsom
(18) 5725 yards

Farnham G.C.
(02518) 2109
The Sands, Farnham
(18) 6313 yards

Fernfell G. & C.C.
(0483) 276626
Barhatch Lane, Cranleigh
(18) 5236 yards

Foxhills G.C.
(093287) 2050
Stonehill Road, Ottershaw
(18) 6658 yards
(18) 6406 yards

Gatton Manor Hotel & G.C.
(030679) 555
Ockley, Dorking
(18) 6902 yards

Guildford G.C.
(0483) 63941
High Path Road, Merrow,
Guildford
(18) 6080 yards

Hankley Common G.C.
(025125) 2493
Tilford, Farnham
(18) 6403 yards

Hindhead G.C.
(042873) 4614
Churt Road, Hindhead
(18) 6357 yards

Hoebridge G.C.
(04862) 22611
Old Woking Road, Old Woking
(18) 6587 yards

Kingswood G.C.
(0737) 832188
Sandy Lane, Kingswood
(18) 6821 yards

Laleham G.C.
(09328) 564211
Laleham Reach, Chertsey
(18) 6203 yards

Leatherhead G.C.
(037284) 3966
Kingston Road, Leatherhead
(18) 6069 yards

Limpsfield Chart G.C.
(088388) 2106
Limpsfield, Oxted
(9) 5718 yards

Moore Place G.C.
(0372) 63533
Portsmouth Road, Esher
(9) 3512 yards

New Zealand G.C.
(09323) 42891
Woodham Lane, Woodham,
Weybridge
(18) 6012 yards

North Downs G.C.
(088385) 2057
Northdown Road, Woldingham
(18) 5787 yards

Puttenham G.C.
(0483) 810498
Puttenham
(18) 5367 yards

R.A.C. Country Club
(03722) 76311
Woodcote Park, Epsom
(18) 6672 yards
(18) 5520 yards

Walton Heath

Redhill & Reigate G.C.
(0737) 240777
Pendleton Road, Redhill
(18) 5193 yards

Reigate Heath G.C.
(0737) 242610
Reigate Heath, Reigate
(9) 5554 yards

St George's Hill G.C.
(0932) 847758
St George's Hill, Weybridge
(18) 6492 yards
(9) 4562 yards

Sandown Park G.C.
(0372) 63340
Moor Lane, Esher
(9) 5658 yards

Shillinglee Park G.C.
(0428) 53237
Chiddingfold, Godalming
(9) 2500 yards

Silvermere G.C.
(0932) 66007
Redhill Road, Cobham
(18) 6333 yards

Tandridge G.C.
(0883) 712733
Oxted
(18) 6260 yards

Tyrell's Wood G.C.
(0372) 376025
Tyrell's Wood, Leatherhead
(18) 6219 yards

Walton Heath G.C.
(073781) 2380
Tadworth
(18) 6813 yards (Old)
(18) 6659 yards (New)

Wentworth G.C.
(09904) 2201
Virginia Water
(18) 6945 yards (West)
(18) 6176 yards (East)

West Byfleet G.C.
(09323) 43433
Sheerwater Road, West Byfleet
(18) 6211 yards

West Hill G.C.
(04867) 4365
Bagshot Road, Brookwood
(18) 6307 yards

West Surrey G.C.
(04868) 21275
Enton Green, Godalming
(18) 6247 yards

Windlemere G.C.
(09905) 8727
Windlesham Road, West End,
Woking
(9) 5346 yards

Woking G.C.
(04862) 60053
Pond Road, Hook Heath, Woking
(18) 6322 yards

Worplesdon G.C.
(04867) 2277
Heath House Road, Woking
(18) 6422 yards

TYNE AND WEAR

Backworth G.C.
(091) 2681048
Backworth, Shiremoor
(9) 5930 yards

Boldon G.C.
(091) 536 5360
Dip Lane, East Boldon
(18) 6319 yards

City of Newcastle G.C.
(091) 2851775
Three Mile Bridge, Gosforth
(18) 6508 yards

Garesfield G.C.
(0207) 561278
Chopwell
(18) 6610 yards

Gosforth G.C.
(091) 285 3495
Broadway East, Gosforth
(18) 6030 yards

Gosforth Park G.C.
(091) 236 4480
High Gosforth Park, Gosforth
(18) 6200 yards

Heworth G.C.
(0632) 692137
Heworth, Gateshead
(18) 6442 yards

Hobson Municipal G.C.
(0207) 70941
Hobson, Burnopfield
(18) 6502 yards

Houghton-le-Spring G.C.
(091) 584 1198
Copt Hill, Houghton-le-Spring
(18) 6248 yards

Newcastle United G.C.
(091) 286 9998
Ponteland Road, Cowgate,
Newcastle
(18) 6498 yards

Northumberland G.C.
(091) 236 2498
High Gosforth Park, Newcastle
(18) 6629 yards

Ponteland G.C.
(0661) 22689
Bell Villas, Ponteland, Newcastle
(18) 6512 yards

Ravensworth G.C.
(091) 487 2843
Wrekenton, Gateshead
(18) 5872 yards

Ryton G.C.
(091) 413 3737
Clara Vale, Ryton
(18) 6034 yards

South Shields G.C.
(091) 456 8942
Cleadon Hills, South Shields
(18) 6264 yards

Tynemouth G.C.
(091) 257 4578
Spital Dean, Tynemouth,
North Shields
(18) 6351 yards

Tyneside G.C.
(091) 413 2742
Westfield Lane, Ryton
(18) 6055 yards

Wallsend G.C.
(091) 262 8989
Bigges Main, Wallsend
(18) 6601 yards

Washington G.C.
(091) 417 8346
Cellar Road, Washington
(18) 6604 yards

Wearside G.C.
(091) 534 2518
Coxgreen, Sunderland
(18) 6204 yards

Westerhope G.C.
(091) 286 9125
Westerhope, Newcastle
(18) 6468 yards

Whickham G.C.
(091) 488 7309
Hollinside Park, Newcastle
(18) 6129 yards

Whitburn G.C.
(091) 529 4210
Lizard Lane, South Shields
(18) 6035 yards

Whitley Bay G.C.
(091) 252 0180
Claremount Road, Whitley Bay
(18) 6712 yards

WARWICKSHIRE

Atherstone G.C.
(08277) 714579
The Outwoods, Atherstone
(18) 6239 yards

Kenilworth G.C.
(0926) 58517
Crew Lane, Kenilworth
(18) 6408 yards

Leamington & Country G.C.
(0926) 28014
Whitnash, Leamington Spa
(18) 6430 yards

Newbold Comyn G.C.
(0926) 21157
Newbold Terrace East,
Leamington Spa
(18) 6430 yards

Nuneaton G.C.
(0203) 347810
Whitestone, Nuneaton
(18) 6368 yards

Purley Chase G.C.
(0203) 395 348
Ridge Lane, Nuneaton
(18) 6604 yards

Rugby G.C.
(0788) 75134
Clifton Road, Rugby
(18) 5457 yards

Stratford-upon-Avon G.C.
(0789) 205749
Tiddington Road, Stratford
(18) 6309 yards

Warwick G.C.
(0926) 494316
The Racecourse, Warwick
(9) 5364 yards

Welcombe Hotel & G.C.
(0789) 295252
Warwick Road,
Stratford-upon-Avon
(18) 6202 yards

WEST MIDLANDS

The Belfry
(0675) 470301
Lichfield Road, Wishaw,
Sutton Coldfield
(18) 6975 yards (Brabazon)
(18) 6127 yards (Derby)

Bloxwich G.C.
(0922) 405724
Stafford Road, Bloxwich
(18) 6286 yards

Boldmere G.C.
(021) 354 3379
Monmouth Drive, Sutton Coldfield
(18) 4463 yards

Brand Hall G.C.
(021) 552 2195
Heron Road, Oldbury, Warley
(18) 5813 yards

Calderfields G.C.
(0922) 32243
Aldridge Road, Walsall
(18) 6636 yards

City of Coventry G.C.
(0203) 85032
Brandon Lane, Coventry
(18) 6530 yards

Cocks Moor Woods G.C.
(021) 444 3584
Alcester Road South, Kings Heath,
Birmingham
(18) 5888 yards

Copt Heath G.C.
(05645) 2650
Warwick Road, Knowle, Solihull
(18) 6504 yards

Coventry G.C.
(0203) 414152
Finham Park, Coventry
(18) 6613 yards

Dartmouth G.C.
(021) 588 2131
Vale Street, West Bromwich
(9) 6060 yards

Druids Heath G.C.
(0922) 55595
Stonnall Road, Aldridge
(18) 6914 yards

Dudley G.C.
(0384) 53719
Turners Hill, Dudley
(18) 5715 yards

Edgbaston G.C.
(021) 454 1736
Church Road, Edgbaston
(18) 6118 yards

Enville G.C.
(0384) 872074
Highgate Common, Stourbridge
(18) 6541 yards

Forest of Arden G. & C.C.
(0676) 22118
Maxstone Lane, Meriden, Coventry
(18) 6867 yards

Fulford Heath G.C.
(0564) 822806
Tanners Green Lane, Wythall
(18) 6256 yards

Gay Hill G.C.
(021) 430 8544
Alcester Road, Hollywood,
Birmingham
(18) 6532 yards

Grange G.C.
(0203) 451465
Copeswood, Coventry
(9) 6002 yards

Great Barr G.C.
(021) 357 1232
Chapel Lane, Birmingham
(18) 6545 yards

Hagley C.C.
(0562) 883701
Wassell Grove, Stourbridge
(18) 6353 yards

Halesowen G.C.
(021) 501 3606
The Leasowes, Halesowen
(18) 5673 yards

Handsworth G.C.
(021) 554 0599
Sunningdale Close, Handsworth,
Birmingham
(18) 6297 yards

Harborne G.C.
(021) 427 1728
Tennal Road, Harborne,
Birmingham
(18) 6240 yards

Hatchford Brook G.C.
(021) 743 9821
Coventry Road, Sheldon,
Birmingham
(18) 6164 yards

Hearsall G.C.
(0203) 713470
Beechwood Avenue, Coventry
(18) 5951 yards

Hill Top G.C.
(021) 554 4463
Park Lane, Handsworth,
Birmingham
(18) 6200 yards

Himley Hall G.C.
(0902) 895207
Himley Hall Park, Dudley
(9) 3090 yards

Kings Norton G.C.
(0564) 826706
Brockhill Lane, Weatheroak,
Alvechurch
(18) 6754 yards
(9) 3290 yards

Ladbrook Park G.C.
(05644) 2264
Poolhead Lane,
Tanworth-in-Arden, Solihull
(18) 6407 yards

Lickey Hills G.C.
(021) 453 3159
Rednal, Birmingham
(18) 6010 yards

Little Aston G.C.
(021) 353 2066
Streetly, Sutton Coldfield
(18) 6724 yards

Maxstone Park G.C.
(0203) 64915
Castle Lane, Coleshill, Birmingham
(18) 6437 yards

Moor Hall G.C.
(021) 308 6130
Moor Hall Park, Sutton Coldfield
(18) 6249 yards

Moseley G.C.
(021) 444 4957
Springfield Road, Kings Heath,
Birmingham
(18) 6227 yards

North Warwickshire G.C.
(0676) 22259
Hampton Lane, Meriden, Coventry
(9) 6362 yards

North Worcestershire G.C.
(021) 475 1047
Northfield, Birmingham
(18) 5919 yards

Olton G.C.
(021) 705 7296
Mirfield Road, Solihull
(18) 6229 yards

Oxley Park G.C.
(0902) 25445
Bushbury, Wolverhampton
(18) 6153 yards

Penn G.C.
(0902) 341142
Penn Common, Wolverhampton
(18) 6449 yards

Pype Hayes G.C.
(021) 351 1014
Walmley, Sutton Coldfield
(18) 5811 yards

Robin Hood G.C.
(021) 706 0061
St Bernards Road, Solihull
(18) 6609 yards

Sandwell Park G.C.
(021) 553 4637
Birmingham Road, West Bromwich
(18) 6470 yards

Shirley G.C.
(021) 744 6001
Stratford Road, Solihull
(18) 6445 yards

South Staffordshire G.C.
(0902) 751065
Danescourt Road, Tettenhall,
Wolverhampton
(18) 6538 yards

Stourbridge G.C.
(0384) 395566
Pedmore, Stourbridge
(18) 6178 yards

Sutton Coldfield G.C.
(021) 353 9633
Thornhill Road, Sutton Coldfield
(18) 6541 yards

Walmley G.C.
(021) 373 0029
Wylde Green, Sutton Coldfield
(18) 6340 yards

Walsall G.C.
(0922) 613512
The Broadway, Walsall
(18) 6232 yards

Warley G.C.
(021) 429 2440
Lightwood Hill, Warley
(9) 5212 yards

WEST SUSSEX

Bognor Regis G.C.
(0243) 821929
Downview Road, Felpham, Bognor
Regis
(18) 6238 yards

Copthorne G.C.
(0342) 712508
Borers Arms Road, Copthorne
(18) 6505 yards

Cottesmore G.C.
(0293) 28256
Buchan Hill, Crawley
(18) 6097 yards (North)
(18) 5321 yards (South)

Cowdray Park G.C.
(073081) 3599
Midhurst
(18) 6212 yards

Effingham Park G.C.
(0342) 716528
Copthorne
(9) 1749 yards

Goodwood G.C.
(0243) 774968
Goodwood, Chichester
(18) 6370 yards

Ham Manor G.C.
(0903) 783288
Angmering
(18) 6216 yards

Haywards Heath G.C.
(0444) 414457
High Beech Lane, Haywards Heath
(18) 6202 yards

Hill Barn G.C.
(0903) 37301
Hill Barn Lane, Worthing
(18) 6224 yards

Ifield G. & C.C.
(0293) 20222
Rusper Road, Ifield, Crawley
(18) 6289 yards

Littlehampton G.C.
(0903) 717170
Rope Walk, Littlehampton
(18) 6202 yards

Mannings Heath G.C.
(0403) 210228
Goldings Lane, Mannings Heath
(18) 6402 yards

Selsey G.C.
(0243) 602203
Golf Links Lane, Selsey
(9) 5932 yards

Tilgate G.C.
(0293) 30103
Titmus Drive, Tilgate, Crawley
(18) 6359 yards

West Chiltington G.C.
(07983) 3574
Broadford Road, West Chiltington
(18) 5969 yards

West Sussex G.C.
(07982) 2563
Pulborough
(18) 6156 yards

Worthing G.C.
(0903) 60801
Links Road, Worthing
(18) 6519 yards (Lower)
(18) 5243 yards (Upper)

WEST YORKSHIRE

Alwoodley G.C.
(0532) 681680
Wigton Lane, Alwoodley, Leeds
(18) 6686 yards

Baildon G.C.
(0274) 595162
Baildon, Shipley
(18) 6085 yards

Ben Rhydding G.C.
(0943) 608759
Ben Rhydding, Ilkley
(9) 4711 yards

Bingley St Ives G.C.
(0274) 562506
Harden, Bingley
(18) 6480 yards

Bradford G.C.
(0943) 75570
Hawksworth Lane, Guisley
(18) 6259 yards

Bradford Moor G.C.
(0274) 638313
Pollard Lane, Bradford
(9) 5854 yards

Bradley Park G.C.
(0484) 39988
Bradley Road, Huddersfield
(18) 6100 yards

Branshaw G.C.
(0535) 43235
Oakworth, Keighley
(18) 5790 yards

City of Wakefield G.C.
(0924) 376214
Luspet Park, Wakefield
(18) 6405 yards

Clayton G.C.
(0724) 880047
Thornton View Road, Clayton,
Bradford
(9) 5527 yards

Cleckheaton & District G.C.
(0274) 877851
Bradford Road, Cleckheaton
(18) 5994 yards

Crosland Heath G.C.
(0484) 653262
Crosland Heath, Huddersfield
(18) 5962 yards

Dewsbury District G.C.
(0924) 492399
Sands Lane, Mirfield
(18) 6226 yards

East Bierley G.C.
(0274) 681023
South View Road, Bierley, Bradford
(9) 4692 yards

Elland G.C.
(0484) 26085
Leach Lane, Elland
(9) 5526 yards

Fulneck G.C.
(0532) 565191
Pudsey
(9) 5432 yards

Garforth G.C.
(0532) 863308
Long Lane, Garforth, Leeds
(18) 6327 yards

Gott's Park G.C.
(0532) 638232
Armley Ridge Road, Leeds
(18) 4449 yards

Halifax G.C.
(0422) 244171
Union Lane, Ogden, Halifax
(18) 6038 yards

Halifax Bradley Hall G.C.
(0422) 70231
Holywell Green, Halifax
(18) 6213 yards

Hanging Heaton G.C.
(0924) 461729
Bennett Lane, Dewsbury
(9) 5874 yards

Headingley G.C.
(0532) 679573
Back Church Lane, Adel, Leeds
(18) 6238 yards

Headley G.C.
(0274) 833481
Thornton, Bradford
(9) 4918 yards

Horsforth G.C.
(0532) 585200
Horsforth, Leeds
(18) 6293 yards

Howley Hall G.C.
(0924) 478417
Scotchman Lane, Morley, Leeds
(18) 6209 yards

Huddersfield G.C.
(0484) 26203
Fixby Hall, Huddersfield
(18) 6424 yards

Ilkley G.C.
(0943) 600214
Myddleton, Ilkley
(18) 6249 yards

Keighley G.C.
(0535) 604778
Howden Park, Keighley
(18) 6139 yards

Leeds G.C.
(0532) 658775
Elmete Lane, Roundhay, Leeds
(18) 6097 yards

Lightcliffe G.C.
(0422) 202459
Knowle Top Road, Lightcliffe
(9) 5888 yards

Longley Park G.C.
(0484) 22304
Maple Street, Huddersfield
(9) 5269 yards

Low Laithes G.C.
(0924) 274667
Flushdyke, Ossett
(18) 6440 yards

Marsden G.C.
(0484) 844253
Hemplow, Marsden
(9) 5702 yards

Meltham G.C.
(0484) 850227
Meltham, Huddersfield
(18) 6145 yards

Middleton Park G.C.
(0532) 700449
Middleton Park, Leeds
(18) 5233 yards

Moor Allerton G.C.
(0532) 661154
Coal Road, Wike, Leeds
(9) 3242 yards
(9) 3138 yards
(9) 3441 yards

Moortown G.C.
(0532) 686521
Harrogate Road, Leeds
(18) 6503 yards

Mount Skip G.C.
(0422) 842896
Wadsworth, Hebden Bridge
(9) 5114 yards

Normanton G.C.
(0924) 220134
Syndale Road, Normanton
(9) 5284 yards

Northcliffe G.C.
(0274) 596731
High Bank Lane
(18) 6093 yards

Otley G.C.
(0943) 463403
West Busk Lane, Otley
(18) 6225 yards

Outlane G.C.
(0422) 74762
Outlane, Huddersfield
(18) 5590 yards

Painthorpe G.C.
(0924) 255083
Crigglestone, Wakefield
(9) 4108 yards

Phoenix Park G.C.
(0274) 667178
Phoenix Park, Thornbury
(9) 4982 yards

Pontefract & District G.C.
(0977) 792115
Park Lane, Pontefract
(18) 6227 yards

Queensbury G.C.
(0274) 882155
Brighouse Road, Queensbury
(9) 5102 yards

Rawdon G.C.
(0532) 506040
Rawdon, Leeds
(9) 5964 yards

Riddlesden G.C.
(0535) 602148
Riddleston, Keighley
(18) 4247 yards

Roundhay G.C.
(0532) 661686
Park Lane, Leeds
(9) 5166 yards

Sand Moor G.C.
(0532) 683925
Alwoodley Lane, Leeds
(18) 6429 yards

Scarcroft G.C.
(0532) 892311
Skye Lane, Leeds
(18) 6426 yards

Shipley G.C.
(0274) 568652
Cottingley Bridge, Bingley
(18) 6203 yards

Silsden G.C.
(0535) 52998
Silsden, Keighley
(14) 4780 yards

South Bradford G.C.
(0274) 676911
Odsal, Bradford
(9) 6004 yards

South Leeds G.C.
(0532) 771676
Gipsy Lane, Leeds
(18) 5835 yards

Temple Newsam G.C.
(0532) 645624
Temple Newsam Road, Leeds
(18) 6448 yards
(18) 6029 yards

Wakefield G.C.
(0924) 255380
Sandal, Wakefield
(18) 6626 yards

West Bowling G.C.
(0274) 393207
Rooley Lane, Bradford
(18) 5756 yards

West Bradford G.C.
(0274) 42767
Haworth Road, Bradford
(18) 5752 yards

West End G.C.
(0422) 53068
Highroad Well, Halifax
(18) 6003 yards

Wetherby G.C.
(0937) 62527
Linton Lane, Wetherby
(18) 6244 yards

Whitwood G.C.
(0997) 558596
Whitwood, Castleford
(9) 6176 yards

Woodhall Hills G.C.
(0532) 554594
Calverley, Rudsey
(18) 6102 yards

Woodsome Hall G.C.
(0484) 602971
Fenay Bridge, Huddersfield
(18) 6068 yards

WILTSHIRE

Bremhill Park G.C.
(0793) 782946
Shrivenham, Swindon
(18) 6040 yards

Brinkworth G.C.
(066641) 277
Brinkworth,
Chippenham
(18) 6086 yards

Broome Manor G.C.
(0793) 32403
Pipers Way, Swindon
(18) 6359 yards
(9) 5610 yards

Chippenham G.C.
(0249) 652040
Malmesbury Road, Chippenham
(18) 5540 yards

High Post G.C.
(0722) 73356
Great Durnford, Salisbury
(18) 6267 yards

Kingsdown G.C.
(0225) 73219
Kingsdown, Corsham
(18) 6445 yards

Marlborough G.C.
(0672) 52147
The Common, Marlborough
(18) 6440 yards

North Wilts G.C.
(038068) 627
Bishops Cannings, Devizes
(18) 6450 yards

R.A.F. Upavon G.C.
(0980) 630787
R.A.F. Upavon, Pewsey
(9) 5597 yards

Salisbury & South Wilts G.C.
(0722) 742645
Netherhampton, Salisbury
(18) 6189 yards
(9) 4848 yards

Swindon G.C.
(067284) 287
Ogbourne St George, Marlborough
(18) 6226 yards

Tidworth Garrison G.C.
(0980) 42321
Bulford Road, Tidworth
(18) 5990 yards

West Wilts G.C.
(0985) 212110
Elm Hill, Warminster
(18) 5701 yards

SCOTLAND

BORDERS

Duns G.C.
(0361) 83327
Hardens Road, Duns
(9) 5826 yards

Eyemouth G.C.
(08907) 50551
Gunsgreen Road, Eyemouth
(9) 5446 yards

Galashiels G.C.
(0896) 3724
Ladhope Recreation Ground,
Galashiels
(18) 5309 yards

Hawick G.C.
(0450) 72293
Vertish Hill, Hawick
(18) 5929 yards

Innerliethen G.C.
(0896) 830951
Innerliethen Water
(9) 5820 yards

Jedburgh G.C.
(0835) 63587
Dunion Road, Jedburgh
(9) 5520 yards

Kelso G.C.
(0573) 23009
Racecourse Road, Kelso
(18) 6066 yards

Lauder G.C.
(05782) 409
Galashiels Road, Lauder
(9) 6002 yards

Melrose G.C.
(089682) 2855
Dingleton, Melrose
(9) 5464 yards

Minto G.C.
(0450) 72267
Minto Village, Denholm, Hawick
(18) 5460 yards

Peebles G.C.
(0721) 20153
Kirkland Street, Peebles
(18) 6137 yards

St Boswells G.C.
(0835) 22359
St Boswells
(9) 5054 yards

Selkirk G.C.
(0750) 20621
The Hill, Selkirk
(9) 5560 yards

West Linton G.C.
(0968) 60256
West Linton
(18) 5835 yards

CENTRAL

Aberfoyle G.C.
(087 72) 441
Braval, Aberfoyle, Stirling
(18) 5205 yards

Alloa G.C.
(0259) 722745
Schawpark, Sauchie, Alloa
(18) 6230 yards

Alva G.C.
(0259) 60431
Beauclerc Street, Alva
(9) 4574 yards

Bonnybridge G.C.
(0324) 812645
Larbert Road, Bonnybridge
(9) 6058 yards

Braehead G.C.
(0259) 722078
Cambus, Alloa
(18) 6013 yards

Bridge of Allan G.C.
(0786) 2332
Sunnylaw, Bridge of Allan
(9) 4932 yards

Buchanan Castle G.C.
(0360) 60307
Drymen
(18) 6032 yards

Callander G.C.
(0877) 30090
Aveland Road, Callander
(18) 5125 yards

Dollar G.C.
(02594) 400
Brewlands House, Dollar
(18) 5144 yards

Dunblane New G.C.
(0786) 823711
Perth Road, Dunblane
(18) 5878 yards

Falkirk G.C.
(0324) 611061
Stirling Road, Falkirk
(18) 6090 yards

Falkirk Tryst G.C.
(0324) 562091
Burnhead Road, Larbert
(18) 6053 yards

Glenbervie G.C.
(0324) 562605
Stirling Road, Larbert
(18) 6452 yards

Grangemouth G.C.
(0324) 711500
Polmont, Falkirk
(18) 6339 yards

Muckhart G.C.
(025981) 423
Dramburn Road, Muckhart, Dollar
(18) 6115 yards

Polmont G.C.
(0324) 711277
Maddison, Falkirk
(9) 6088 yards

Stirling G.C.
(0786) 64098
Queens Road, Stirling
(18) 6409 yards

Tillicoultry G.C.
(0259) 50741
Alva Road, Tillicoultry
(9) 5256 yards

Tulliallan G.C.
(0259) 30897
Alloa Road, Kincardine, Alloa
(18) 5982 yards

DUMFRIES & GALLOWAY

Castle Douglas G.C.
(0556) 2801
Abercromby Road, Castle Douglas
(9) 5408 yards

Colvend G.C.
(055663) 398
Sandyhills, Dalbeattie
(9) 4208 yards

Dumfries & County G.C.
(0387) 62045
Edinburgh Road, Dumfries
(18) 5914 yards

Dumfries & Galloway G.C.
(0387) 63848
Laurieston Avenue, Dumfries
(18) 5782 yards

Kirkcudbright G.C.
(0557) 30542
Stirling Crescent, Kirkcudbright
(18) 5598 yards

Langholm G.C.
(0541) 80429
Langholm
(9) 2872 yards

Lochmaben G.C.
(038781) 0552
Castlehill Gate, Lochmaben
(9) 5338 yards

Lockerbie G.C.
(05762) 2165
Currie Road, Lockerbie
(18) 5228 yards

Moffatt G.C.
(06833) 20020
Coateshill, Moffatt
(18) 5218 yards

Newton Stewart G.C.
(0671) 2172
Newton Stewart
(9) 5512 yards

Portpatrick (Dunskey) G.C.
(0776) 83215
Portpatrick, Stranraer
(18) 5644 yards

Powfoot G.C.
(04612) 2866
Cummertrees, Annan
(18) 6283 yards

Sanquhar G.C.
(06592) 577
Old Barr Road, Sanquhar
(9) 5144 yards

Southerness G.C.
(038788) 677
Southerness
(18) 6554 yards

Stranraer G.C.
(0776) 87245
Creachmore, Stranraer
(18) 6300 yards

Thornhill G.C.
(0848) 30546
Blacknest, Thornhill
(18) 6011 yards

Wigtown & Bladnoch G.C.
(09884) 3354
Wigtown
(9) 5462 yards

Wigtownshire County G.C.
(05813) 420
Mains of Park, Glenluce
(9) 5826 yards

FIFE

Aberdour G.C.
(0383) 860353
Seaside Place, Aberdour
(18) 5469 yards

Anstruther G.C.
(0333) 311966
Anstruther
(9) 4504 yards

Auchterderran G.C.
(0592) 721579
Woodend Road, Cardenden
(9) 5250 yards

Balbirnie Park G.C.
(0592) 752006
Balbirnie Park, Markinch,
Glenrothes
(18) 6444 yards

Ballingry G.C.
(0592) 860086
Crosshill, Lochgelly
(9) 6244 yards

Burntisland Golf House Club
(0592) 874093
Dodhead, Burntisland
(18) 5871 yards

Canmore G.C.
(0383) 726098
Venturefair Avenue, Dunfermline
(18) 5474 yards

Crail Golfing Society
(0333) 50278
Balcomie Clubhouse, Fifeness,
Crail
(18) 5720 yards

Cupar G.C.
(0334) 53549
Cupar
(9) 5074 yards

Dunfermline G.C.
(0383) 723534
Pitfirrane, Crossford, Dunfermline
(18) 6271 yards

Dunnikier Park G.C.
(0592) 267462
Dunnikier Way, Kirkcaldy
(18) 6601 yards

Glenrothes G.C.
(0592) 758686
Golf Course Road, Glenrothes
(18) 6444 yards

Golf House Club (Elie)
(0333) 330301
Elie, Leven
(18) 6241 yards

Kinghorn G.C.
(0592) 890345
Macduff Crescent, Kinghorn
(18) 5269 yards

Kirkcaldy G.C.
(0592) 203258
Balwearie Road, Kirkcaldy
(18) 6007 yards

Ladybank G.C.
(0337) 30814
Annsmuir, Ladybank
(18) 6617 yards

Leslie G.C.
Leslie 741449
Balsillie Laws, Leslie
(9) 4686 yards

Leven Links
(0333) 23509
Links Road, Leven
(18) 6434 yards

Leven Municipal
(0333) 27057
Leven Links
(18) 5403 yards

Lochgelly G.C.
(0592) 780174
Cartmore Road, Lochgelly
(18) 5491 yards

Lundin Links
(0333) 320202
Golf Road, Lundin Links
(18) 6377 yards

Lundin Ladies G.C.
(0333) 320022
Woodiela Road, Lundin Links
(9) 4730 yards

Pitreavie G.C.
(0383) 722591
Queensferry Road, Dunfermline
(18) 6086 yards

St Andrews
(0334) 75757
St Andrews
(18) 6933 yards (Old)
(18) 6604 yards (New)
(18) 6284 yards (Jubilee)
(18) 5971 yards (Eden)
(9) (Balgove)

St Michaels G.C.
(033483) 365
Leuchars
(9) 5510 yards

Saline G.C.
(0383) 852591
Kineddar Hill, Saline
(9) 5302 yards

Scotscraig G.C.
(0382) 730880
Golf Road, Tayport
(18) 6486 yards

Thornton G.C.
(0592) 771111
Station Road, Thornton
(18) 6177 yards

GRAMPIAN

Aboyne G.C.
(0339) 2328
Formaston Park, Aboyne
(18) 5330 yards

Auchinbale G.C.
(05612) 407
Auchinblae
(9) 4748 yards

Auchmill G.C.
(0224) 642121
Auchmill, Aberdeen
(9) 5500 yards

Ballater G.C.
(0338) 55567
Ballater
(18) 6106 yards

Balnagesk G.C.
(0224) 876407
St. Fittick's Road, Aberdeen
(18) 5975 yards

Banchory G.C.
(03302) 2365
Kinneskie, Banchory
(18) 5271 yards

Braemar G.C.
(033083) 618
Cluniebank, Braemar
(18) 5011 yards

Buckpool G.C.
(0542) 32236
Barhill Road, Buckie
(18) 6257 yards

Cruden Bay G.C.
(0779) 812285
Aulton Road, Cruden Bay
(18) 6401 yards (Championship)
(9) 4710 yards (St. Olaf)

Cullen G.C.
(0542) 40685
The Links, Cullen
(18) 4610 yards

Deeside G.C.
(0224) 86797
Bieldside, Aberdeen
(18) 5972 yards

Duff House Royal G.C.
(02612) 2062
Barnyards, Banff
(18) 6161 yards

Dufftown G.C.
(0340) 20325
Dufftown
(9) 4556 yards

Elgin G.C.
(0343) 2338
Birnie Road, Elgin
(18) 6401 yards

Fraserburgh G.C.
(0346) 28287
Philarth, Fraserburgh
(18) 6217 yards

Hazelhead G.C.
(0224) 317336
Hazelhead Park, Aberdeen
(18) 6595 yards
(9) 5205 yards

Huntly G.C.
(0466) 2643
Cooper Park, Huntly
(18) 5399 yards

Inverallochy G.C.
(03465) 2324
Inverlallochy, Fraserburgh
(18) 5137 yards

Inverurie G.C.
(0467) 24080
Blackhall Road, Inverurie
(18) 5703 yards

Keith G.C.
(05422) 2469
Fife Park, Keith
(18) 5745 yards

Kings Links
(0224) 632269
Kings Links, Aberdeen
(18) 6520 yards

Kintore G.C.
(0467) 32631
Kintore, Inverurie
(9) 5240 yards

McDonald G.C.
(0358) 20576
Hospital Road, Ellon
(18) 5986 yards

Moray G.C.
(034381) 2018
Stotfield Road, Lossiemouth
(18) 6258 yards (New)
(18) 6643 yards (Old)

Murcar G.C.
(0224) 704370
Bridge of Don, Aberdeen
(18) 6240 yards

Newburgh-on-Ythan G.C.
(03586) 389
Millend, Newburgh
(9) 6404 yards

Old Meldrum G.C.
(06512) 2212
Old Meldrum
(9) 5252 yards

Peterhead G.C.
(0779) 72149
Craigewan Links, Peterhead
(18) 6070 yards

Royal Aberdeen G.C.
(0224) 702221
Balgownie, Bridge of Don,
Aberdeen
(18) 6372 yards
(18) 4003 yards

Royal Tarlair G.C.
(0261) 32897
Buchan Street, Macduff
(18) 5866 yards

Spey Bay G.C.
(0343) 820424
Spey Bay, Fochabers
(18) 6059 yards

Stonehaven G.C.
(0569) 62124
Cowie, Stonehaven
(18) 5103 yards

Strathiene G.C.
(0542) 31798
Buckie
(18) 5957 yards

Tarland G.C.
(033981) 413
Tarland, Aboyne
(9) 5812 yards

Torphine G.C.
(033982) 493
Golf Road, Torphine
(9) 2330 yards

Turriff G.C.
(0888) 62745
Rosehall, Turriff
(18) 6105 yards

Westhill G.C.
(0224) 740159
Westhill, Skene
(18) 5866 yards

HIGHLAND

Abernethy G.C.
(047982) 637
Nethybridge
(9) 2484 yards

Alness G.C.
(0349) 883877
Ardross Road, Alness
(9) 4718 yards

Boat-of-Garten G.C.
(047983) 282
Boat-of-Garten
(18) 5720 yards

Bonar Bridge G.C.
(054982) 248
Bonar Bridge
(9) 4616 yards

Brora G.C.
(0408) 21475
Golf Road, Brora
(18) 6110 yards

Carrbridge G.C.
(047986) 674
Carrbridge
(9) 5250 yards

Forres G.C.
(0309) 72949
Muiryshade, Forres
(18) 6141 yards

Fort Augustus G.C.
(0320) 6460
Markethill, Fort Augustus
(9) 5454 yards

Fortrose & Rosemarkie G.C.
(0381) 20529
Ness Road East, Fortrose
(18) 5964 yards

Fort William G.C.
(0397) 4464
North Road, Fort William
(18) 5640 yards

Gairloch G.C.
(0445) 2407
Gairloch
(9) 4186 yards

Garmouth & Kingston G.C.
(034387) 388
Garmouth Road, Fochabers
(18) 5649 yards

Golspie G.C.
(04083) 3266
Ferry Road, Golspie
(18) 5763 yards

Grantown-on-Spey G.C.
(0479) 2667
Golf Course Road, Grantown-on-
Spey
(18) 5672 yards

Hopeman G.C.
(0348) 830578
Hopeman
(18) 5439 yards

Invergordon G.C.
(0349) 852116
Cromlet Drive, Invergordon
(9) 6028 yards

Inverness G.C.
(0463) 239882
Culcabock Road, Inverness
(18) 6226 yards

Kingussie G.C.
(05402) 374
Bynack Road, Kingussie
(18) 5466 yards

Lybster G.C.
(05932) 359
Main Street, Lybster
(9) 3770 yards

Muir of Ord G.C.
(0463) 870825
Great Northern Road, Muir of Ord
(18) 5022 yards

Nairn G.C.
(0667) 53208
Seabank Road, Nairn
(18) 6436 yards

Nairn Dunbar G.C.
(0667) 52741
Lochloy Road, Nairn
(18) 6431 yards

Newtonmore G.C.
(05403) 328
Golf Course Road, Newtonmore
(18) 5890 yards

Orkney G.C.
(0856) 2457
Grainbank, Kirkwall, Orkney
(18) 5406 yards

Reay G.C.
(084781) 288
Reay, Thurso
(18) 5876 yards

Royal Dornoch G.C.
(0862) 810219
Golf Road, Dornoch
(18) 6577 yards
(9) 2485 yards

Sconser G.C.
(0478) 2364
Sconser, Isle of Skye
(9) 4796 yards

Shetland G.C.
(059584) 369
Dale, Shetland
(18) 5791 yards

Stornoway G.C.
(0851) 2240
Lady Lever Park, Stornoway,
Isle of Lewis
(18) 5119 yards

Strathpeffer Spa G.C.
(0997) 21219
Strathpeffer
(18) 4813 yards

Stromness G.C.
(0856) 850772
Ness, Stromness, Orkney
(18) 4665 yards

Tain G.C.
(0862) 2314
Tain
(18) 6222 yards

Tarbat G.C.
(086287) 519
Portmahomack
(9) 4656 yards

Thurso G.C.
(0847) 63807
Newlands of Geise, Thurso
(18) 5818 yards

Torvean G.C.
(0463) 237543
Glenurquart Road, Inverness
(18) 4308 yards

Western Isles G.C.
(0688) 2020
Stronsaule, Tobermory, Isle of Mull
(9) 4920 yards

Wick G.C.
(0955) 2726
Reiss, Wick
(18) 5976 yards

LOTHIAN

Baberton G.C.
(031) 453 4911
Juniper Green, Edinburgh
(18) 6098 yards

Bathgate G.C.
(0506) 630505
Edinburgh Road, Bathgate
(18) 6326 yards

Braids United G.C.
(031) 447 6666
Braids Hill Approach, Edinburgh
(18) 5731 yards (No. 1)
(18) 4832 yards (no. 2)

Broomieknowe G.C.
(031) 663 9317
Golf Course Road, Bonnyrigg
(18) 6046 yards

Bruntsfield Links Golfing Society
(031) 336 1479
Barnton Avenue, Edinburgh
(18) 6407 yards

Craigmillar Park G.C.
(031) 667 2837
Observatory Road, Edinburgh
(18) 5846 yards

Dalmahoy C.C.
(031) 333 2055
Dalmahoy, Kirknewton
(18) 6664 yards (East)
(18) 5212 yards (West)

Deer Park G. & C.C.
(0506) 38843
Livingston
(18) 6636 yards

Duddingston G.C.
(031) 661 7688
Duddingston Road, Edinburgh
(18) 6647 yards

Dunbar G.C.
(0368) 62317
East Links, Dunbar
(18) 6426 yards

Dundas Park G.C.
(031) 331 3090
South Queensferry
(9) 6026 yards

East Links G.C.
(0620) 2340
East Links, North Berwick
(18) 6079 yards

Gifford G.C.
(062081) 267
Station Road, Gifford
(9) 6138 yards

Glencorse G.C.
(0968) 77189
Milton Bridge, Penicuik
(18) 5205 yards

Greenburn G.C.
(0501) 70292
Bridge Street, Fauldhouse
(18) 6210 yards

Gullane G.C.
(0620) 842255
Gullane
(18) 6479 yards (No. 1)
(18) 6127 yards (No. 2)
(18) 5035 yards (No. 3)

Honourable Company of Edinburgh Golfers (Muirfield)
(0620) 842123
Muirfield, Gullane
(18) 6941 yards

Kilspindie G.C.
(0875) 358
Aberlady
(18) 5410 yards

Kingsknowe G.C.
(031) 441 1145
Lanark Road, Edinburgh
(18) 5979 yards

Linlithgow G.C.
(0506) 842585
Braehead, Linlithgow
(18) 5858 yards

Longniddry G.C.
(0875) 52141
Links Road, Longniddry
(18) 6210 yards

Lothianburn G.C
(031) 445 2288
Biggar Road, Edinburgh
(18) 5671 yards

Luffness New G.C.
(0620) 843336
Aberlady
(18) 6085 yards

Merchants of Edinburgh G.C.
(031) 447 1219
Craighill Gardens, Edinburgh
(18) 4889 yards

Mortonhall G.C.
(031) 447 6974
Braid Road, Edinburgh
(18) 6557 yards

Murrayfield G.C.
(031) 337 3478
Murrayfield Road, Edinburgh
(18) 5727 yards

Muirfield (see Hon. Co. of Edinburgh Golfers)

Musselburgh G.C.
(031) 665 2005
Monktonhall, Musselburgh
(18) 6623 yards

Newbattle G.C.
(031) 663 2123
Abbey Road, Dalkeith
(18) 6012 yards

North Berwick G.C.
(0620) 2135
West Links, Beach Road,
North Berwick
(18) 6298 yards

Prestonfield G.C.
(031) 667 9665
Piestfield Road North, Edinburgh
(18) 6216 yards

Ratho Park G.C.
(031) 333 1752
Ratho, Newbridge
(18) 6028 yards

Royal Burgess Golfing Society
(031) 339 2075
Whitehouse Road, Barton,
Edinburgh
(18) 6604 yards

Royal Musselburgh G.C.
(0875) 810276
Prestongrange House, Prestonpans
(18) 6204 yards

Silverknowes G.C.
(031) 336 5359
Silverknowes, Parkway, Edinburgh
(18) 6210 yards

Swanston G.C.
(031) 445 2239
Swanston Road, Edinburgh
(18) 5024 yards

Torphin Hill G.C.
(031) 441 1100
Torphin Road, Colinton,
Edinburgh
(18) 5030 yards

Turnberry

Turnhouse G.C.
(031) 339 7701
Turnhouse Road, Edinburgh
(18) 6171 yards

Uphall G.C.
(0506) 856404
Uphall
(18) 5567 yards

West Lothian G.C.
(0506) 826030
Airngath Hill, Linlithgow
(18) 6629 yards

Winterfield G.C.
(0368) 62564
North Road, Dunbar
(18) 5053 yards

STRATHCLYDE

Airdrie G.C.
(02364) 62195
Rochsoles, Airdrie
(18) 6004 yards

Alexandra Park Municipal G.C.
(041) 556 3711
Alexandra Parade, Glasgow
(9) 4562 yards

Annanhill G.C.
(0563) 21644
Irvine Road, Kilmarnock
(18) 6269 yards

Ardeer G.C.
(0294) 64035
Greenhead, Stevenston
(18) 6630 yards

Ayr Belleisle G.C.
(0292) 41258
Belleisle Park, Ayr
(18) 6540 yards (Belleisle)
(18) 5244 yards (Seafield)

Ayr Dalmilling G.C.
(0292) 263893
Westwood Avenue, Ayr
(18) 5401 yards

Ballochmyle G.C.
(0290) 50469
Ballochmyle, Mauchline
(18) 5952 yards

Balmore G.C.
(041) 332 0392
Balmore, Torrance
(18) 5735 yards

Barshaw G.C.
(041) 884 2533
Barshaw Park, Paisley
(18) 5703 yards

Bearsden G.C.
(041) 942 2351
Thorn Road, Bearsden, Glasgow
(9) 5977 yards

Beith G.C.
(05055) 2011
Bigholm, Beith
(9) 5488 yards

Bellshill G.C.
(0698) 745124
Orbiston, Bellshill
(18) 6607 yards

Biggar G.C.
(0899) 20618
Broughton Road, Biggar
(18) 5256 yards

Bishopbriggs G.C.
(041) 772 1810
Brackenbrae Road, Bishopbriggs,
Glasgow
(18) 6041 yards

Blairbeth G.C.
(041) 634 3355
Rutherglen, Glasgow
(18) 5448 yards

Blairmore & Strone G.C.
(036984) 676
Blairmore, Argyll
(9) 4224 yards

Bonnyton G.C.
(03553) 2256
Eaglesham, Glasgow
(18) 6252 yards

Bothwell Castle G.C.
(0698) 853177
Blantyre Road, Bothwell, Glasgow
(18) 6432 yards

Brodick G.C.
(0770) 2513
Brodick, Isle of Arran
(18) 4404 yards

Bute G.C.
(0700) 83242
Kilchaltan Bay, Bute
(9) 5594 yards

Calderbraes G.C.
(0698) 813425
Roundknowe Road, Uddingston
(9) 5186 yards

Caldwell G.C.
(050585) 616
Uplawnmoor
(18) 6102 yards

Cambuslang G.C.
(041) 641 3130
Westburn Drive, Cambuslang,
Glasgow
(9) 6072 yards

Campsie G.C.
(0360) 0244
Crow Road, Lennoxtown, Glasgow
(18) 5517 yards

Caprington G.C.
(0563) 23702
Ayr Road, Kilmarnock
(18) 5718 yards

Cardross G.C.
(0389) 841350
Main Road, Cardross, Dumbarton
(18) 6466 yards

Carluke G.C.
(0555) 71070
Hallcraig, Carluke
(18) 5805 yards

Carnwath G.C.
(0555) 840251
Main Street, Carnwath
(18) 5860 yards

Carradale G.C.
(05833) 624
Carradale, Argyll
(9) 4774 yards

Cathcart Castle G.C.
(041) 638 9449
Mearns Road, Clarkston, Glasgow
(18) 5832 yards

Cathkin Braes G.C.
(041) 634 4007
Cathkin Road, Rutherglen,
Glasgow
(18) 6266 yards

Cawder G.C.
(041) 772 7101
Cadder Road, Bishopbriggs,
Glasgow
(18) 6229 yards (Cawder)
(18) 5877 yards (Keir)

Clober G.C.
(041) 956 1685
Craigton Road, Milngavie
(18) 5068 yards

Clydebank & District G.C.
(0389) 73289
Hardgate, Clydebank
(18) 5815 yards

Clydebank Municipal G.C.
(041) 952 6372
Overtoun Road, Clydebank
(18) 5349 yards

Cochrane Castle G.C.
(0505) 20146
Craigston, Johnstone
(18) 6226 yards

Colonsay G.C.
(09512) 316
Isle of Colonsay
(18) 4775 yards

Colville Park G.C.
(0698) 63017
Jerviston Estate, Motherwell
(18) 6208 yards

Corrie G.C.
(077081) 223
Corrie, Isle of Arran
(9) 3896 yards

Cowal G.C.
(0396) 5673
Kirn, Dunoon
(18) 5820 yards

Cowglen G.C.
(041) 632 0556
Barhead Road, Glasgow
(18) 5976 yards

Crow Wood G.C.
(041) 779 1943
Muirhead, Chryston
(18) 6209 yards

Cumbernauld Municipal G.C.
(02367) 28138
Cumbernauld
(18) 6412 yards

Dougalston G.C.
(041) 956 5750
Milngavie, Glasgow
(18) 6683 yards

Douglas Park G.C.
(041) 942 2220
Hillfoot, Bearsden, Glasgow
(18) 5957 yards

Douglas Water G.C.
(0555) 2295
Douglas Water, Lanark
(9) 5832 yards

Drumpellier G.C.
(0236) 24139
Drumpellier, Coatbridge
(18) 6227 yards

Dullatur G.C.
(02367) 27847
Dullatur, Glasgow
(18) 6253 yards

Dumbarton G.C.
(0389) 32830
Broadmeadow, Dumbarton
(18) 5981 yards

Dunaverty G.C.
(No tel.)
Southend, Campbeltown, Argyll
(18) 4597 yards

Easter Moffat G.C.
(0236) 21864
Mansion House, Plains, Airdrie
(18) 6221 yards

East Kilbride G.C.
(03552) 47728
Chapelside Road, Nerston,
East Kilbride
(18) 6419 yards

East Renfrewshire G.C.
(03555) 258
Pilmuir, Newton Mearns, Glasgow
(18) 6097 yards

Eastwood G.C.
(03555) 280
Muirshield, Newton Mearns,
Glasgow
(18) 5864 yards

Elderslie G.C.
(0505) 23956
Main Road, Elderslie
(18) 6004 yards

Erskine G.C.
(0505) 2302
Bishopston
(18) 6287 yards

Fereneze G.C.
(041) 881 1519
Fereneze Avenue, Barrhead,
Glasgow
(18) 5821 yards

Girvan G.C.
(0465) 4272
Golf Course Road, Girvan
(18) 5075 yards

Glasgow Gailes G.C.
(0294) 311247
Gailes, Irvine
(18) 6447 yards

Glasgow Killermont G.C.
(041) 942 2011
Killermont, Glasgow
(18) 5968 yards

Gleddoch G. & C.C.
(047554) 304
Langbank
(18) 6200 yards

Glencruitten G.C.
(0631) 62868
Glencruitten, Oban
(18) 4452 yards

Gourock G.C.
(0475) 33696
Cowal View, Gourock
(18) 6492 yards

Greenock G.C.
(0475) 20793
Forsyth Street, Greenock
(18) 5838 yards

Greenock Whinhill G.C.
(0475) 210641
Beith Road, Greenock
(18) 5454 yards

Haggs Castle G.C.
(041) 427 1157
Drumbreck Road, Glasgow
(18) 6464 yards

Hamilton G.C.
(0698) 282872
Riccarton, Ferniegair, Hamilton
(18) 6264 yards

Hayston G.C.
(041) 775 0882
Campsie Road, Kirkintilloch,
Glasgow
(18) 6042 yards

Helensburgh G.C.
(0436) 4173
East Abercromby Street,
Helensburgh
(18) 6058 yards

Hollandbush G.C.
(0555) 893484
Lesmahagow, Coalburn
(18) 6110 yards

Innellan G.C.
(0369) 3546
Innellan, Argyll
(9) 4878 yards

Irvine (Bogside) G.C.
(0294) 75979
Bogside, Irvine
(18) 6450 yards

Irvine Ravenspark G.C.
(0294) 79550
Kidsneuk Road, Irvine
(18) 6496 yards

Kilbirnie Place G.C.
(050582) 683398
Largs Road, Kilbirnie
(18) 5479 yards

Kilmacolm G.C.
(050587) 2695
Porterfield, Kilmacolm
(18) 5964 yards

Kilmarnock (Barassie) G.C.
(0292) 311077
Hillhouse Road, Barassie, Troon
(18) 6473 yards

Kilsyth Lennox G.C.
(0236) 822190
Tak-Ma-Doon Road, Kilsyth,
Glasgow
(9) 5944 yards

Kirkhill G.C.
(041) 641 8499
Greenlees Road, Cambuslang,
Glasgow
(18) 5889 yards

Kirkintilloch G.C.
(041) 776 1256
Todhill, Campsie Road,
Kirkintilloch
(18) 5269 yards

Knightswood G.C.
(041) 959 2131
Lincoln Avenue, Knightswood,
Glasgow
(9) 2717 yards

Kyles of Bute G.C.
(0700) 811355
Tighnabruaich, Argyll
(9) 4758 yards

Lamlash G.C.
(07706) 296
Lamlash, Isle of Arran
(18) 4681 yards

Lanark G.C.
(0555) 3219
The Moor, Lanark
(18) 6416 yards

Landoun G.C.
(0563) 821993
Edinburgh Road, Galston
(18) 5824 yards

Largs G.C.
(0475) 672497
Irvine Road, Largs
(18) 6257 yards

Larkhall G.C.
(0698) 881113
Burnhead Road, Larkhall
(9) 6236 yards

Leadhills G.C.
(06594) 222
Leadhills, Biggar
(9) 4062 yards

Lenzie G.C.
(041) 776 1535
Crosshill Road, Lenzie, Glasgow
(18) 5982 yards

Lethamhill G.C.
(041) 770 6220
Cumbernauld Road, Glasgow
(18) 6073 yards

Linn Park G.C.
(041) 637 5871
Simshill Road, Glasgow
(18) 4832 yards

Littlehill G.C.
(041) 772 1916
Auchinairn Road, Bishopbriggs,
Glasgow
(18) 6199 yards

Lochranza G.C.
(077083) 273
Brodick, Isle of Arran
(9) 3580 yards

Lochwinnoch G.C.
(0505) 842153
Burnfoot Road, Lochwinnoch
(18) 6223 yards

Machrie Hotel and G.C.
(0496) 2310
Machrie Hotel, Port Ellen, Isle of
Islay
(18) 6226 yards

Machrie Bay G.C.
(077084) 258
Machrie Bay, Isle of Arran
(9) 4246 yards

Machrihanish G.C.
(0586) 81213
Machrihanish, Campbeltown,
Argyll
(18) 6228 yards

Maybole G.C.
Maybole 82454
Memorial Park, Maybole
(9) 5270 yards

Millport G.C.
(0475) 530485
Golf Road, Millport,
Isle of Cumbrae
(18) 5831 yards

Milngavie G.C.
(041) 956 1619
Laigh Park, Milngavie, Glasgow
(18) 5818 yards

Mount Ellen G.C.
(0236) 782277
Johnston House, Gartcosh,
Glasgow
(18) 5525 yards

Paisley G.C.
(041) 884 2292
Braehead, Paisley
(18) 6424 yards

Pollok G.C.
(041) 632 4351
Barrhead Road, Glasgow
(18) 6257 yards

Port Bannatyne G.C.
(0700) 2009
Port Bannatyne, Isle of Bute
(13) 4654 yards

Port Glasgow G.C.
(0475) 704181
Port Glasgow
(18) 5712 yards

Prestwick G.C.
(0292) 77404
Links Road, Prestwick
(18) 6631 yards

Prestwick St Cuthbert G.C.
(0292) 79120
East Road, Prestwick
(18) 6470 yards

Prestwick St Nicholas G.C.
(0292) 77608
Grangemuir Road, Prestwick
(18) 5926 yards

Raiston G.C.
(041) 882 1349
Raiston, Paisley
(18) 6100 yards

Ranfurly Castle G.C.
(0505) 612609
Golf Road, Bridge of Weir
(18) 6284 yards

Renfrew G.C.
(041) 886 6692
Blythswood Estate,
Inchinnan Road, Renfrew
(18) 6818 yards

Gleneagles

Rothesay G.C.
(0700) 2244
Rothesay, Isle of Bute
(18) 5358 yards

Routenburn G.C.
(0475) 674289
Largs
(18) 5650 yards

Royal Troon G.C.
(0292) 311555
Craigend Road, Troon
(18) 6641 yards (Old)
(18) 6274 yards (Portland)

Sandyhills G.C.
(041) 778 1179
Sandyhills Road, Glasgow
(18) 6253 yards

Shiskine G.C.
(077086) 293
Blackwaterfoot, Isle of Arran
(12) 3000 yards

Shotts G.C.
(0501) 20431
Blairhead, Shotts
(18) 6125 yards

Skelmorlie G.C.
(0475) 520152
Skelmorlie
(13) 5056 yards

Strathaven G.C.
(0357) 20421
Overton Avenue, Glasgow Road,
Strathaven
(18) 6226 yards

Strathclyde Park G.C.
(0698) 66155
Motel Hill, Hamilton
(9) 6294 yards

Tarbert G.C.
(08802) 565
Kilberry Road, Tarbert, Argyll
(9) 4460 yards

Torrance House G.C.
(03552) 33451
Strathaven Road, East Kilbride,
Glasgow
(18) 6640 yards

Troon Municipal G.C.
(0292) 312464
Harling Drive, Troon
(18) 6687 yards (Lochgreen)
(18) 6327 yards (Darley)
(18) 4784 yards (Fullarton)

Turnberry Hotel
(0655) 31000
Turnberry Hotel, Turnberry
(18) 6956 yards (Ailsa)
(18) 6276 yards (Arran)

Vaul G.C.
(08792) 566
Scarinish, Isle of Tiree, Argyll
(9) 6246 yards

Western Gailes G.C.
(0294) 311649
Gailes, Irvine
(18) 6614 yards

Western Isles G.C.
(0688) 2020
Tobermory, Isle of Mull
(9) 4920 yards

West Kilbride G.C.
(0294) 823911
Fullerton Drive, West Kilbride
(18) 6348 yards

Whitecraigs G.C.
(041) 639 4530
Ayr Road, Giffnock, Glasgow
(18) 6230 yards

Whiting Bay G.C.
(07707) 487
Whiting Bay, Isle of Arran
(18) 4405 yards

Williamwood G.C.
(041) 637 2715
Clarkeston Road, Netherlee,
Glasgow
(18) 5878 yards

Windyhill G.C.
(041) 942 7157
Baljaffray Road, Bearsden,
Glasgow
(18) 6254 yards

Wishaw G.C.
(0698) 3782869
Cleland Road, Wishaw
(18) 6134 yards

TAYSIDE

Aberfeldy G.C.
(0887) 20203
Taybridge Road, Aberfeldy
(9) 5466 yards

Alyth G.C.
(08283) 2411
Pitcrocknie, Alyth
(18) 6226 yards

Arbroath G.C.
(0241) 72666
Elliot, Arbroath
(18) 6078 yards

Auchterarder G.C.
(07646) 2804
Auchterarder
(18) 5737 yards

Bishopshire G.C.
(0592) 860379
Kinnesswood
(9) 4360 yards

Blair Atholl G.C.
(079681) 274
Blair Atholl
(9) 5710 yards

Blairgowrie G.C.
(0250) 3116
Rosemount, Blairgowrie
(18) 6592 yards (Rosemount)
(18) 6865 yards (Lansdowne)
(9) 4614 yards (Wee)

Brechin G.C.
(03562) 2383
Trinity, Brechin
(18) 5267 yards

Caird Park G.C.
(0382) 44003
Mains Loan, Dundee
(18) 6303 yards

Camperdown (Municipal) G.C.
(0382) 68340
Camperdown Park, Dundee
(18) 6561 yards

Carnoustie
(0241) 53789
Links Parade, Carnoustie
(18) 6931 yards (Championship)
(18) 5935 yards (Burnside)
(18) 6445 yards (Buddon Links)

Comrie G.C.
(0764) 70544
Polinard, Comrie
(9) 5966 yards

Craigie Hill G.C.
(0738) 22644
Cherrybank, Perth
(18) 5379 yards

Crieff G.C.
(0764) 2909
(18) 6363 yards (Ferntower)
(9) 4772 yards (Dornock)

Dalmunzie G.C.
(025085) 226
Spittal of Glenshee, Blairgowrie
(9) 4458 yards

Downfield G.C.
(0382) 825595
Turnberry Avenue, Dundee
(18) 6899 yards

Dunkeld & Birnam G.C.
(03502) 524
Fungarth, Dunkeld
(9) 5264 yards

Dunning G.C.
(076484) 398
Rollo Park, Dunning
(9) 4836 yards

Edzell G.C.
(03564) 7283
High Street, Edzell, Brechin
(18) 6299 yards

Forfar G.C.
(0307) 63773
Cunninghill, Arbroath Road, Forfar
(18) 6255 yards

Glenalmond G.C.
(073888) 270
Trinity College, Glenalmond
(9) 5812 yards

Gleneagles Hotel
(07646) 3543
Gleneagles Hotel, Auchterarder
(18) 6452 yards (King's)
(18) 5964 yards (Queen's)
(18) 5719 yards (Glendevon)
(18) 4664 yards (Prince's)

Green Hotel G.C.
(0577) 63467
Green Hotel, Kinross
(18) 6339 yards

Killin G.C.
(05672) 312
Killin
(9) 5016 yards

King James VI G.C.

(0738) 32460
Moncrieffe Island, Perth
(18) 6037 yards

Kirriemuir G.C.

(0575) 73317
23 Bank Street, Kirriemuir, Angus
(18) 5591 yards

Letham Grange G. & G.C.

(0241) 89373
Letham Grange, Colliston,
Arbroath
(18) 6290 yards

Milnathort G.C.

(0577) 64069
South Street, Milnathort
(9) 5918 yards

Monifieth Golf Links

(0382) 533300
Ferry Road, Monifieth
(18) 6657 yards (Medal)
(18) 5123 yards (Ashludie)

Montrose Links

(0674) 72634
Trail Drive, Montrose
(18) 6451 yards (Medal)
(18) 4815 yards (Broomfield)

Murrayshall G.C.

(0738) 52784
Murrayshall, New Scone
(18) 6416 yards

Muthill G.C.

(0764) 3319
Peat Road, Muthill, Crieff
(9) 4742 yards

Panmure G.C.

(0241) 53120
Burnside Road, Barry
(18) 6302 yards

Pitlochry G.C.

(0796) 2792
Golf Course Road, Pitlochry
(18) 5811 yards

Royal Perth Golfing Society

(0738) 22265
Atholl Crescent, Perth
(18) 5141 yards

St Fillans G.C.

(076485) 312
St Fillans
(9) 5268 yards

Taymouth Castle G.C.

(08873) 228
Kenmore, Aberfeldy
(18) 6066 yards

WALES

CLWYD

Abergele & Pensarn G.C.
(0745) 824034
Tan-y-Goppa Road, Abergele
(18) 6086 yards

Denbigh G.C.
(074571) 4159
Henllan Road, Denbigh
(9) 5650 yards

Flint G.C.
(03526) 2186
Cornist Park, Flint
(9) 5829 yards

Hawarden G.C.
(0244) 531447
Groomsdale Lane, Hawarden
(9) 5735 yards

Holywell G.C.
(0352) 710040
Brynford, Holywell
(9) 6484 yards

Mold G.C.
(0352) 740318
Pantmywyn, Nr. Mold
(18) 5521 yards

Old Colwyn G.C.
(0492) 515581
Old Colwyn, Colwyn Bay
(9) 5268 yards

Old Padeswood G.C.
(0244) 547401
Station Road, Padeswood, Mold
(18) 6728 yards

Padeswood & Buckley G.C.
(0244) 542537
Station Lane, Padeswood
(18) 5746 yards

Prestatyn G.C.
(07456) 88353
Marine Road East, Prestatyn
(18) 6714 yards

Rhuddlan G.C.
(0745) 590675
Rhuddlan, Rhyl
(18) 6038 yards

Rhyl G.C.
(0745) 53171
Coast Road, Rhyl
(9) 6153 yards

Ruthin-Pwllglas G.C.
(08242) 4658
Ruthin-Pwllglas, Ruthin
(9) 5306 yards

St Melyd G.C.
(07456) 88858
Melyden Road, Prestatyn
(9) 5805 yards

Vale of Llangollen G.C.
(0978) 860050
Holyhead Road, Llangollen
(18) 6617 yards

Wrexham G.C.
(0978) 364268
Holt Road, Wrexham
(18) 6038 yards

DYFED

Aberystwyth G.C.
(0970) 615104
Bryn-y-Mor, Aberystwyth
(18) 5868 yards

Ashburnham G.C.
(05546) 2269
Cliff Terrace, Burry Port
(18) 7016 yards

Borth and Ynyslas G.C.
(097081) 202
Borth
(18) 6094 yards

Cardigan G.C.
(0239) 612035
Gwbert-on-Sea
(18) 6207 yards

Carmarthen G.C.
(0267) 87588
Blaenycoed Road, Carmarthen
(18) 6212 yards

Cilgywn G.C.
(0570) 45286
Llangybi
(9) 5318 yards

Glynhir G.C.
(0269) 850571
Glynhir Road, Llandybie,
Nr. Ammanford
(18) 6090 yards

Haverfordwest G.C.
(0437) 68409
Arnolds Down, Haverfordwest
(18) 5945 yards

Milford Haven G.C.
(06462) 2521
Milford Haven
(18) 6235 yards

Newport (Pembs) G.C.
(0239) 820244
Newport
(9) 6178 yards

St David's City G.C.
(0437) 720403
Whitesands Bay, St Davids
(9) 5695 yards

South Pembrokeshire G.C.
(0646) 682035
Defensible Barracks,
Pembroke Dock
(9) 5804 yards

Tenby G.C.
(0834) 2978
The Burrows, Tenby
(18) 6232 yards

GWENT

Blackwood G.C.
(0495) 223152
Cwmgelli, Blackwood
(9) 5304 yards

Caerleon G.C.
(0633) 420342
Caerleon, Newport
(9) 6184 yards

Greenmeadow G.C.
(06333) 626262
Treherbert Road, Cwmbran
(9) 6128 yards

Llanwern G.C.
(0633) 415233
Tennyson Avenue, Llanwern
(18) 6202 yards
(9) 5674 yards

Monmouth G.C.
(0600) 2212
Leasebrook Lane, Monmouth
(9) 5434 yards

Monmouthshire G.C.
(0873) 2606
Llanfoist, Abergavenny
(18) 6045 yards

Newport G.C.
(0633) 892683
Great Oak, Rogerstone, Newport
(18) 6370 yards

Pontnewydd G.C.
(0633) 32170
West Pontnewydd, Cwmbran
(10) 5321 yards

Pontypool G.C.
(04955) 3655
Trevethyn, Pontypool
(18) 6070 yards

Rolls of Monmouth G.C.
(0600) 5353
The Hendre, Monmouth
(18) 6723 yards

St Mellons G.C.
(0633) 680401
St Mellons, Nr Cardiff
(18) 6225 yards

St Pierre G. & C.C.
(02912) 5261
St Pierre Park, Chepstow
(18) 6700 yards (Old)
(18) 5762 yards (New)

Tredegar Park G.C.
(0633) 894433
Bassaleg Road, Newport
(18) 6044 yards

Tredegar and Rhymney G.C.
(0685) 840743
Rhymney
(9) 5564 yards

West Monmouthshire G.C.
(0495) 310233
Pond Road, Nantyglo
(18) 6097 yards

GWYNEDD

Aberdovey G.C.
(065472) 493
Aberdovey
(18) 6445 yards

Abersoch G.C.
(075881) 2622
Pwllheli, Abersoch
(9) 5722 yards

Bala G.C.
(0678) 520359
Penlan, Bala
(10) 4934 yards

Betws-y-Coed G.C.
(06902) 556
Betws-y-Coed
(9) 5030 yards

Caernarfon G.C.
(0286) 2643
Llanfaglan, Caernarfon
(18) 5859 yards

Caernarfonshire G.C.
(0492) 592423
Conway
(18) 6723 yards

Criccieth G.C.
(076671) 2154
Ednyfed Hill, Criccieth
(18) 5755 yards

Dolgellau G.C.
(0341) 422603
Pencefn Road, Dolgellau
(9) 4662 yards

Ffestiniog G.C.
(076) 676 2612
Blaenau Ffestiniog
(9) 4536 yards

Llandudno (Maesdu) G.C.
(0492) 76450
Hospital Road, Llandudno
(18) 6513 yards

Llanfairfechan G.C.
(0248) 680144
Llanfairfechan
(9) 6238 yards

Nefyn and District G.C.
(0758) 720966
Morfa Nefyn
(18) 6335 yards

North Wales G.C.
(0492) 75325
Bryniau Road, West Shore,
Llandudno
(18) 6132 yards

Penmaenmawr G.C.
(0492) 622085
Conway Old Road, Penmaenmawr
(9) 5031 yards

Portmadoc G.C.
(0766) 513828
Morfa Bychan, Portmadoc
(18) 5728 yards

Pwllheli G.C.
(0758) 612520
Golf Road, Pwllheli
(18) 6110 yards

Royal St David's G.C.
(0766) 780857
Harlech
(18) 6495 yards

St Deiniol G.C.
(0248) 353098
Bangor
(18) 5545 yards

ISLE OF ANGLESEY

Anglesey G.C.
(0407) 810219
Rhosneigr
(18) 6204 yards

Baron Hill G.C.
(0248) 810231
Beaumaris
(9) 5564 yards

Bull Bay G.C.
(0407) 830960
Almwch
(18) 6160 yards

Holyhead G.C.
(0407) 2022
Trearddur Bay, Holyhead
(18) 6090 yards

MID GLAMORGAN

Aberdare G.C.
(0685) 873387
Abernant, Aberdare
(18) 5875 yards

Bargoed G.C.
(0443) 830143
Hoelddu, Bargoed
(18) 6012 yards

Bryn Meadows G. & C.C.
(0495) 221905
The Bryn, Nr. Hengoed
(18) 5963 yards

Caerphilly G.C.
(0222) 863441
Mountain Road, Caerphilly
(14) 6063 yards

Castell Heights G.C.
(0222) 886666
Caerphilly
(9) 5376 yards

Creigiau G.C.
(0222) 890263
Creigiau
(18) 5736 yards

Llantrisant and Pontyclun G.C.
(0443) 222148
Talbot Green, Llantrisant
(12) 5712 yards

Maesteg G.C.
(0656) 732037
Mount Pleasant, Maesteg
(18) 5845 yards

Merthyr Tydfil G.C.
(0685) 3063
Cilsanws Mountain, Cefn Coed,
Merthyr Tydfil
(9) 5794 yards

Morlais Castle G.C.
(0685) 2822
Pant Dowlais, Merthyr Tydfil
(9) 6356 yards

Mountain Ash G.C.
(0443) 472265
Cefnpennar
(18) 5535 yards

Mountain Lakes G.C.
(0222) 861128
Caerphilly
(18) 6815 yards

Pontypridd G.C.
(0443) 402359
Tygwyn Road, Pontypridd
(18) 5650 yards

Pyle and Kenfig G.C.
(065671) 3093
Kenfig
(18) 6655 yards

Rhondda G.C.
(0443) 433204
Pontygwaith, Rhondda
(18) 6428 yards

Royal Porthcawl G.C.
(065671) 2251
Porthcawl
(18) 6605 yards

Southerndown G.C.
(0656) 880476
Ewenny, Bridgend
(18) 6615 yards

Whitehall G.C.
(0443) 740245
Nelson, Treharris
(9) 5750 yards

POWYS

Brecon G.C.
(0874) 2004
Llanfaes, Brecon
(9) 5218 yards

Builth Wells G.C.
(0982) 553296
Builth Wells
(9) 5458 yards

Cradoc G.C.
(0874) 3658
Penoyre Park, Cradoc
(18) 6318 yards

Llandrindod Wells G.C.
(0597) 2059
Llandrindod Wells
(18) 5759 yards

Machynlleth G.C.
(0654) 2000
Machynlleth
(9) 5734 yards

St Giles G.C.
(0686) 25844
Pool Road, Newtown
(9) 5864 yards

St Idloes G.C.
(05512) 2205
Penrhalt, Llanidloes
(9) 5210 yards

Welshpool G.C.
(0938) 3377
Golfa Hill, Welshpool
(18) 5708 yards

SOUTH GLAMORGAN

Brynhill G.C.
(0446) 733660
Port Road, Barry
(18) 6000 yards

Cardiff G.C.
(0222) 754772
Sherborne Avenue, Cyncoed,
Cardiff
(18) 6015 yards

Dinas Powis G.C.
(0222) 512727
Old High Walls, Dinas Powis
(18) 5377 yards

Glamorganshire G.C.
(0222) 701185
Lavernock Road, Penarth
(18) 6150 yards

Llanishen G.C.
(0222) 752205
Cwm-Lisvane, Cardiff
(18) 5296 yards

Radyr G.C.
(0222) 842408
Drysgol Road, Radyr
(18) 6031 yards

Wenvoe Castle G.C.
(0222) 594371
Wenvoe Castle, Cardiff
(18) 6411 yards

Whitchurch G.C.
(0222) 614660
Pantmawr Road, Whitchurch,
Cardiff
(18) 6245 yards

WEST GLAMORGAN

Clyne G.C.
(0792) 401989
Owls Lodge Lane, Mayals, Swansea
(18) 6312 yards

Fairwood Park G. & C.C.
(0792) 203648
Upper Killay, Swansea
(18) 6606 yards

Glynneath G.C.
(0639) 720679
Pontneathvaughan
(9) 5742 yards

Inco G.C.
(0792) 844216
Clydach, Swansea
(18) 5976 yards

Langland Bay G.C.
(0792) 66023
Langland Bay, Swansea
(18) 5812 yards

Morriston G.C.
(0792) 796528
Claremont Road, Morriston,
Swansea
(18) 5722 yards

Neath G.C.
(0639) 3615
Cadoxton, Neath
(18) 6460 yards

Palleg G.C.
(0639) 842524
Lower Cwmtwrch, Swansea
(9) 3209 yards

Pennard G.C.
(044128) 3131
Southgate Road, Southgate
(18) 6266 yards

Pontardawe G.C.
(0792) 863118
Cefn Llan, Pontardawe
(18) 6061 yards

Swansea Bay G.C.
(0792) 812198
Jersey Marine, Neath
(18) 6302 yards

St Pierre, Chepstow

NORTHERN IRELAND

CO. ANTRIM

Ballycastle G.C.
(026) 5762536
Ballycastle
(18) 5902 yards

Ballyclare G.C.
(09603) 22051
Springvale Road, Ballyclare
.(9) 6708 yards

Ballymena G.C.
(026) 6861487
Raceview Road, Ballymena
(18) 5168 yards

Bushfoot G.C.
(026) 5731317
Portballintrae, Bushmills
(9) 5572 yards

Cairndhu G.C.
(0574) 83324
Coast Road, Ballygally, Larne
(18) 6112 yards

Carrickfergus G.C.
(09603) 63713
North Road, Carrickfergus
(18) 5789 yards

Cushendall G.C.
(026) 6771318
Shore Road, Cushendall
(9) 4678 yards

Dunmurry G.C.
(0232) 621402
Dunmurry Lane, Dunmurry, Belfast
(18) 5832 yards

Greenisland G.C.
(023) 862236
Upper Road, Greenisland
(9) 5951 yards

Larne G.C.
(09603) 72043
Ferris Bay, Islandmagee, Larne
(9) 6114 yards

Lisburn G.C.
(08462) 77216
Eglantine Road, Lisburn
(18) 6255 yards

Massereene G.C.
(08494) 62096
Lough Road, Antrim
(18) 6554 yards

Royal Portrush G.C.
(0265) 822311
Bushmills Road, Portrush
(18) 6810 yards (Dunluce)
(18) 6259 yards (Valley)
(9) 1187 yards

Whitehead G.C.
(09603) 72792
McCrae's Brae, Whithead
(18) 6412 yards

CO. ARMAGH

County Armagh G.C.
(0861) 522501
Newry Road, Armagh
(18) 6184 yards

Craigavon Golf & Ski Centre
(0762) 42413
Silverwood, Lurgan
(18) 6496 yards

Lurgan G.C.
(0762) 322087
Lurgan
(18) 6380 yards

Portadown G.C.
(0762) 335356
Carrickblacker, Portadown
(18) 6119 yards

Trandragee G.C.
(0762) 840727
Trandragee, Craigavon
(18) 6084 yards

BELFAST

Balmoral G.C.
(0232) 381514
Lisburn Road, Belfast
(18) 6250 yards

Belvoir Park G.C.
(0232) 491693
Newtown, Breda, Belfast
(18) 6476 yards

Cliftonville G.C.
(0232) 744158
Westland Road, Belfast
(9) 6240 yards

Fortwilliam G.C.
(0232) 771770
Downview Avenue, Belfast
(18) 5642 yards

The Knock G.C.
(02318) 3251
Summerfield, Dundonald, Belfast
(18) 6292 yards

Malone G.C.
(0232) 612695
Upper Malone Road, Dunmurry
(18) 6433 yards

Ormeau G.C.
(0232) 641069
Ravenhill Road, Belfast
(9) 5306 yards

Shandon Park G.C.
(0232) 797859
Shandon Park, Belfast
(18) 6252 yards

CO. DOWN

Ardglass G.C.
(0396) 841219
Castle Place, Ardglass
(18) 6500 yards

Banbridge G.C.
(08206) 22342
Huntly Road, Banbridge
(12) 5879 yards

Bangor G.C.
(0247) 270922
Broadway, Bangor
(18) 6450 yards

Carnalea G.C.
(0247) 270368
Carnalea
(18) 5513 yards

Clandeboye G.C.
(0247) 271767
Conlig, Newtownards
(18) 6650 yards (Dufferin)
(18) 5634 yards (Ava)

Donaghadee G.C.
(0237) 883624
Warren Road, Donaghadee
(18) 6099 yards

Downpatrick G.C.
(0396) 2152
Saul Road, Downpatrick
(18) 6196 yards

Helen's Bay G.C.
(0247) 852601
Helen's Bay, Bangor
(9) 5638 yards

Holywood G.C.
(02317) 2138
Nuns Walk, Demesne Road,
Holywood
(18) 5885 yards

Kilkeel G.C.
(069) 3762296
Mourne Park, Ballyardle
(9) 6000 yards

Kirkistown Castle G.C.
(02477) 71233
Cloughey, Newtownards
(18) 6157 yards

Mahee Island G.C.
(0238) 541234
Comber, Belfast
(9) 5580 yards

Royal Belfast G.C.
(0232) 428165
Holywood, Craigavad
(18) 6205 yards

Royal County Down G.C.
(03967) 23314
Newcastle
(18) 6968 yards
(18) 4100 yards

Scrabo G.C.
(0247) 812355
Scrabo Road,
Newtownards
(18) 6000 yards

The Spa G.C.
(0238) 562365
Grove Road, Ballynahinch
(9) 5770 yards

Warrenpoint G.C.
(06937) 73695
Lower Dromore Road,
Warrenpoint
(18) 6215 yards

CO. FERMANAGH

Enniskillen G.C.
(0365) 25250
Enniskillen
(9) 5476 yards

CO. LONDONDERRY

Castlerock G.C.
(0265) 848314
Circular Road, Castlerock
(18) 6694 yards

City of Derry G.C.
(0504) 46369
Victoria Road, Londonderry
(18) 6362 yards (Prehen)
(9) 4708 yards (Dunhugh)

Kilrea G.C.
(026) 653 397
Drumagarner Road, Kilrea
(9) 4326 yards

Moyola Park G.C.
(0648) 68392
Shanemullagh, Castledawson
(18) 6517 yards

Portstewart G.C.
(026) 5832015
Strand Road, Portstewart
(18) 6784 yards (Strand)
(18) 4733 yards (Town)

CO. TYRONE

Dungannon G.C.
(08687) 22098
Mullaghmore, Dungannon
(18) 5914 yards

Fintona G.C.
(0662) 841480
Fintona
(9) 6250 yards

Killymoon G.C.
(06487) 62254
Killymoon, Cookstown
(18) 6000 yards

Newtownstewart G.C.
(06626) 61466
Golf Course Road,
Newtownstewart
(18) 6100 yards

Omagh G.C.
(0662) 3160
Dublin Road, Omagh
(18) 5800 yards

Strabane G.C.
(0504) 882271
Ballycolman, Strabane
(18) 6100 yards

IRELAND

CO. CARLOW

Borris G.C.
(0503) 73143
Borris
(9) 6026 yards

Carlow G.C.
(0503) 31695
Carlow
(18) 6347 yards

CO. CAVAN

Belturbet G.C.
(049) 22287
Belturbet
(9) 5180 yards

Blacklion G.C.
(0017) 53024
Toam, Blacklion
(9) 6000 yards

County Cavan G.C.
(049) 31283
Drumelis
(18) 6037 yards

Virginia G.C.
(049) 44103
Virginia
(9) 4520 yards

CO. CLARE

Dromoland Castle G.C.
(061) 71144
Newmarket-on-Fergus
(9) 6098 yards

Ennis G.C.
(065) 24074
Drumbiggle Road, Ennis
(18) 5714 yards

Kilkee G.C.
(Kilkee) 48
East End, Kilkee
(9) 6058 yards

Kilrush G.C.
(Kilrush) 138
Parknamoney, Kilrush
(9) 5478 yards

Lahinch G.C.
(065) 81003
Lahinch
(18) 6515 yards (Championship)
(18) 5450 yards (Castle)

Shannon G.C.
(061) 61020
Shannon Airport
(18) 6480 yards

Spanish Point G.C.
(065) 84198
Miltown, Malbay
(9) 6248 yards

CO. CORK

Bandon G.C.
(023) 41111
Castlebernard, Bandon
(18) 6101 yards

Bantry G.C.
(027) 50579
Donemark, Bantry
(9) 6436 yards

Charleville G.C.
(063) 257
Charleville
(18) 6380 yards

Cobh G.C.
(021) 811372
Ballywilliam Cobh
(9) 4800 yards

Cork G.C.
(021) 353451
Little Island
(18) 6600 yards

Doneraile G.C.
(022) 24137
Doneraile
(9) 5528 yards

Douglas G.C.
(021) 291086
Douglas
(18) 5651 yards

Dunmore G.C.
(023) 33352
Clonakilty, Dunmore
(9) 4180 yards

East Cork G.C.
(021) 631687
Gortacrue, Midleton
(18) 5602 yards

Fermoy G.C.
(025) 31472
Fermoy
(18) 5884 yards

Glengarriff G.C.
(027) 63150
Glengarriff
(9) 4328 yards

Kanturk G.C.
(029) 50181
Fairy Hill, Kanturk
(9) 5918 yards

Kinsale G.C.
(021) 772197
Ringnanean, Belgooly, Kinsale
(9) 5580 yards

Macroom G.C.
(026) 41072
Lackaduve, Macroom
(9) 5850 yards

Mallow G.C.
(022) 22465
Balleyellis, Mallow
(18) 6559 yards

Mitchelstown G.C.
(025) 24072
Gurrane, Mitchelstown
(9) 5550 yards

Monkstown G.C.
(021) 841225
Parkgarriffe, Monkstown
(18) 6000 yards

Muskerry G.C.
(021) 85297
Carrigrohane
(18) 6350 yards

Skibbereen G.C.
(028) 21227
Skibbereen
(9) 5890 yards

Youghal G.C.
(024) 2787
Knockaverry, Youghal
(18) 6206 yards

CO. DONEGAL

Ballybofey & Stranorlar G.C.
(074) 31093
Ballybofey
(18) 5913 yards

Ballyliffin G.C.
(Clonmany) 74417
Ballyliffin, Clonmany
(18) 6611 yards

Bundoran G.C.
(072) 41302
Great Northern Hotel, Bundoran
(18) 6328 yards

Donegal G.C.
(073) 34054
Murvagh, Donegal
(18) 6842 yards

Dunfanaghy G.C.
(074) 36238
Dunfanaghy
(18) 5450 yards

Greencastle G.C.
(077) 81013
Greencastle
(9) 2693 yards

Gweedore G.C.
(075) 31140
Derrybeg, Letterkenny
(9) 6234 yards

Letterkenny G.C.
(074) 21150
Barnhill, Letterkenny
(18) 6299 yards

Nairn & Portnoo G.C.
(075) 45107
Nairn & Portnoo
(18) 5950 yards

North West G.C.
(077) 61027
Lisfannon, Fahan
(18) 5895 yards

Otway G.C.
(074) 58319
Saltpans, Rathmullen
(9) 4134 yards

Portsalon G.C.
(Portsalon) 59102
Portsalon
(18) 5949 yards

Rosapenna G.C.
(074) 55301
Rosapenna
(18) 6254 yards

CO. DUBLIN

Balbriggan G.C.
(01) 412173
Blackhall, Balbriggan
(9) 5952 yards

Ballinascorney G.C.
(01) 512516
Ballinascorney
(9) 5322 yards

Beaverstown G.C.
(01) 436439
Beaverstown, Donabate
(18) 6000 yards

Beech Park G.C.
(01) 580522
Johnstown, Rathcoole
(18) 5600 yards

Corballis G.C.
(01) 450583
Donabate
(18) 4898 yards

Carrickmines G.C.
(01) 895 676
Carrickmines, Dublin
(9) 6044 yards

Castle G.C.
(01) 904207
Rathfarnham, Dublin
(18) 6240 yards

Clontarf G.C.
(01) 315085
Malahide Road, Dublin
(18) 5608 yards

Deerpark G.C.
(01) 322624
Deerpark Hotel, Howth
(18) 6647 yards

Donabate G.C.
(01) 436059
Balcarrick, Donabate
(18) 6187 yards

Dublin Sport G.C.
(01) 895418
Kilternan, Dublin
(18) 5413 yards

Dun Laoghaire G.C.
(01) 801055
Eglinton Park, Dun Laoghaire, Dublin
(18) 5950 yards

Edmonstown G.C.
(01) 931082
Rathfarnham, Dublin
(18) 6177 yards

Elm Park G.C.
(01) 693014
Donnybrook, Dublin
(18) 5485 yards

Forrest Little G.C.
(01) 401183
Cloghran
(18) 6400 yards

Foxrock G.C.
(01) 895668
Foxrock, Torquay Road, Dublin
(9) 5699 metres

Grange G.C.
(01) 932832
Whitechurch, Rathfarnham, Dublin
(18) 5517 yards

Hermitage G.C.
(01) 264549
Lucan
(18) 6000 yards

Howth G.C.
(01) 323055
Carrickbrae Road, Sutton, Dublin
(18) 6168 yards

The Island G.C.
(01) 436205
Corballis, Donabate
(18) 6320 yards

Killiney G.C.
(01) 851983
Killiney
(9) 6201 yards

Lucan G.C.
(01) 280246
Lucan
(9) 6287 yards

Malahide G.C.
(01) 450248
Coast Road, Malahide
(9) 5568 yards

Milltown G.C.
(01) 976090
Lower Churchtown Road, Dublin
(18) 6275 yards

Newlands G.C.
(01) 593157
Clondalkin, Dubiln
(18) 6184 yards

Portmarnock G.C.
(01) 323082
Portmarnock
(18) 7103 yards

Rathfarnham G.C.
(01) 931201
Newtown, Dublin
(9) 6250 yards

Royal Dublin G.C.
(01) 336477
Bull Island, Dollymount, Dublin
(18) 6858 yards

Rush G.C.
(01) 437548
Rush
(9) 5655 yards

St Anne's G.C.
(01) 336471
Bull Island, Dublin
(9) 6104 yards

Skerries G.C.
(01) 491204
Skerries
(18) 6300 yards

Slade Valley G.C.
(01) 582207
Lynch Park, Brittas
(18) 5800 yards

Woodbrook G.C.
(01) 824799
Bray
(18) 6541 yards

CO. GALWAY

Athenry G.C.
(091) 94466
Derrydonnell, Oranmore
(9) 5448 yards

Ballinasloe G.C.
(0905) 42126
Ballinasloe
(9) 5844 yards

Connemara G.C.
(095) 21153
Ballyconneely, nr Clifden
(18) 6700 yards

Galway G.C.
(091) 22169
Blackrock, Salthill
(18) 6193 yards

Gort G.C.
(091) 31336
Gort
(9) 5688 yards

Loughrea G.C.
(091) 41049
Loughrea
(9) 5798 yards

Mount Bellew G.C.
(0905) 79259
Mount Bellow
(9) 5564 yards

Oughterard G.C.
(091) 82131
Gurteeva, Oughterard
(9) 6356 yards

Portumna G.C.
(0509) 41059
Portumna
(9) 5776 yards

Tuam G.C.
(093) 24354
Barnacurrahg, Tuam
(18) 6321 yards

CO. KERRY

Ballybunion G.C.
(068) 27146
Ballybunion
(18) 6542 yards (Old)
(18) 6477 yards (New)

Ceann Sibeal G.C.
(066) 51657
Ballyferriter, Tralee
(9) 6222 yards

Dooks G.C.
(066) 68205
Glenbeigh, Dooks
(18) 5850 yards

Kenmare G.C.
(064) 41291
Kenmare
(9) 5900 yards

**Killarney Golf
& Fishing Club**
(064) 31034
Mahoney's Point, Killarney
(18) 6677 yards (Mahoney's Point)
(18) 6798 yards (Killeen)

Parknasilla G.C.
(064) 45122
Parknasilla
(9) 5000 yards

Tralee G.C.
(066) 36379
West Barrow, Ardfert
(18) 6800 yards

Waterville G.C.
(0667) 4102
Waterville
(18) 7184 yards

CO. KILDARE

Athy G.C.
(0607) 31727
Geraldine, Athy
(9) 6158 yards

Bodenstown G.C.
(045) 97096
Bodenstown, Sallins
(18) 7031 yards

Cill Dara G.C.
(045) 21433
Cilldara, Kildare Town
(9) 6196 yards

Clongowes G.C.
(045) 68202
Clongowes Wood, College Naas
(9) 5743 yards

Curragh G.C.
(045) 41238
Curragh
(18) 6565 yards

Naas G.C.
(045) 97509
Kerdiffstown, Naas
(9) 6233 yards

CO. KILKENNY

Callan G.C.
(056) 25136
Geraldine, Callan
(9) 5844 yards

Castlecomer G.C.
(056) 41139
Castlecomer
(9) 6985 yards

Kilkenny G.C.
(056) 22125
Glendine, Kilkenny
(18) 6374 yards

CO. LAOIS

Abbey Leix G.C.
(0502) 31450
Abbey Leix, Portlaoise
(9) 5680 yards

Heath G.C.
(0502) 46622
Portlaoise
(18) 6247 yards

Mountrath G.C.
(0502) 32558
Mountrath
(9) 5492 yards

Portarlington G.C.
(0502) 23115
Garryhinch, Portarlington
(9) 5700 yards

Rathdowney G.C.
(0505) 46170
Rathdowney
(9) 5416 yards

CO. LEITRIM

Ballinamore G.C.
(078) 44346
Ballinamore
(9) 5680 yards

Carrick-on-Shannon G.C.
(078) 20157
Carrick-on-Shannon
(9) 5922 yards

CO. LIMERICK

Adare Manor G.C.
(061) 86204
Adare
(9) 5430 yards

Castleroy G.C.
(061) 335753
Castleroy
(18) 6089 yards

Limerick G.C.
(061) 44083
Ballyclough, Limerick
(18) 5767 yards

Newcastle West G.C.
(069) 62015
Newcastle West
(9) 5482 yards

CO. LONGFORD

Co. Longford G.C.
(043) 46310
Dublin Road, Longford
(18) 6028 yards

CO. LOUTH

Ardee G.C.
(041) 53227
Town Parks, Ardee
(18) 5833 yards

County Louth G.C.
(041) 22329
Baltray, Drogheda
(18) 6728 yards

Dundalk G.C.
(042) 21731
Blackrock, Dundalk
(18) 6740 yards

Greenore G.C.
(042) 73212
Greenore
(18) 6150 yards

CO. MAYO

Achill Island G.C.
(098) 43202
Keel, Achill Island
(9) 5420 yards

Ballina G.C.
(096) 21050
Mosgrove, Shanaghy, Ballina
(9) 5182 yards

Ballinrobe G.C.
(092) 41659
Ballinrobe
(9) 2895 yards

Ballyhaunis G.C.
(0907) 30014
Coolnaha, Ballyhaunis
(9) 5852 yards

Belmullet G.C.
(097) 81093
Belmullet, Balhina
(9) 5714 yards

Castlebar G.C.
(094) 21649
Rocklands, Castlebar
(18) 6109 yards

Claremorris G.C.
(094) 71527
Claremorris
(9) 5898 yards

Mulrany G.C.
(098) 36185
Mulrany, Westport
(9) 6380 yards

Swinford G.C.
(094) 51378
Swinford
(9) 5230 yards

Westport G.C.
(098) 25113
Carrowholly, Westport
(18) 6950 yards

CO. MEATH

Headfort G.C.
(046) 40148
Kells
(18) 6393 yards

Laytown & Bettystown G.C.
(041) 27534
Bettystown, Drogheda
(18) 6254 yards

Royal Tara G.C.
(046) 25244
Bellinter, Navan
(18) 6343 yards

Trim G.C.
(046) 31463
Newtownmoynagh, Trim
(9) 6266 yards

CO. MONAGHAN

Clones G.C.
(Scotshouse) 17
Hiton Park, Clone
(9) 550 yards

Nuremore G.C.
(042) 61438
Nuremore, Carrickmacross
(9) 6032 yards

Rossmore G.C.
(047) 81316
Rossmore Park, Monaghan
(9) 5859 yards

CO. OFFALY

Birr G.C.
(0509) 20082
The Glenns, Birr
(18) 6216 yards

Edenberry G.C.
(0405) 31072
Boherbree, Edenberry
(9) 5791 yards

Tullamore G.C.
(0506) 21439
Brookfield, Tullamore
(18) 6314 yards

CO. ROSCOMMON

Athlone G.C.
(0902) 2073
Hodson Bay, Athlone
(18) 6000 yards

Ballaghaderreen G.C.
(No tel.)
Ballaghaderreen
(9) 5686 yards

Boyle G.C.
(079) 62594
Roscommon Road, Boyle
(9) 5728 yards

Castlerea G.C.
(0907) 20068
Clonalis, Castlerea
(9) 5466 yards

Roscommon G.C.
(0903) 6382
Mote Park, Roscommon
(9) 6215 yards

CO. SLIGO

Ballymote G.C.
(Ballymote) 3460
Ballymote
(9) 5032 yards

County Sligo G.C.
(071) 77134
Rosses Point
(18) 6600 yards

Enniscrone G.C.
(096) 36297
Enniscrone
(18) 6511 yards

Strandhill G.C.
(071) 68188
Strandhill
(18) 5523 yards

CO. TIPPERARY

Cahir Park G.C.
(062) 41474
Kilcommon, Cahir
(9) 6262 yards

Carrick-on-Suir G.C.
(051) 40047
Garravoone, Garrick-on-Suir
(9) 5948 yards

Clonmel G.C.
(052) 21138
Lyreanearle, Clonmel
(18) 6330 yards

Nenagh G.C.
(067) 31476
Beechwood, Nenagh
(18) 5911 yards

Roscrea G.C.
(0505) 21130
Roscrea
(9) 6059 yards

Thurles G.C.
(0504) 21983
Thurles
(18) 6230 yards

Tipperary G.C.
(062) 51119
Rathanny, Tipperary
(9) 6074 yards

CO. WATERFORD

Dungarvon G.C.
(058) 41605
Ballinacourty, Dungarvan
(9) 6282 yards

Lismore G.C.
(058) 54026
Lismore
(9) 5460 yards

Tramore G.C.
(051) 81247
Tramore
(18) 6408 yards

Waterford G.C.
(051) 74182
Newrath, Waterford
(18) 6237 yards

CO. WESTMEATH

Moate G.C.
(0902) 31271
Moate
(9) 5348 yards

Mullingar G.C.
(044) 483
Belvedere, Mullingar
(18) 6370 yards

CO. WEXFORD

Courtown G.C.
(055) 25166
Courtown Harbour, Gorey
(18) 6398 yards

Enniscorthy G.C.
(055) 33191
Knockmarshall, Enniscorthy
(9) 6220 yards

New Ross G.C.
(051) 21433
Tinneranny, New Ross
(9) 6102 yards

Rosslare G.C.
(053) 32113
Strand, Rosslare
(18) 6485 yards

Wexford G.C.
(053) 42238
Mulgannon, Wexford
(9) 6038 yards

CO. WICKLOW

Arklow G.C.
(0402) 32492
Arklow
(18) 5770 yards

Baltinglass G.C.
(0508) 81350
Baltinglass
(9) 6070 yards

Blainroe G.C.
(0404) 68168
Blainroe
(18) 6681 yards

Bray G.C.
(01) 862484
Ravenswell Road, Bray
(9) 6250 yards

Coollattin G.C.
(055) 29125
Coollattin, Shillelagh
(9) 5966 yards

Delgany G.C.
(404) 874536
Delgany
(18) 5249 yards

Greystones G.C.
(01) 876624
Greystones
(18) 5900 yards

Wicklow G.C.
(0404) 67379
Dunbar Road, Wicklow
(9) 5536 yards

Woodenbridge G.C.
(0402) 5202
Arklow
(9) 6104 yards

Royal County Down

6

1990
A YEAR OF GOLF

JANUARY

Royal Ashdown Forest

Looking at the image above it isn't difficult to appreciate why in January the nineteenth hole so often becomes the most popular retreat at golf clubs the length and breadth of the country. Not a million miles from Royal Ashdown Forest grown men who ought to know better do battle more with the elements than with each other at Rye for the annual President's Putter.

Some January days can, of course, be very mild, and then is the time to venture forth onto the links, suitably armed with the season's new broom-handled putter and the Payne Stewart plus-fours . . . .

A change of scenery is needed, and in the different worlds of Australia and South Africa the golf seasons are in full flow. The end of the month sees the South African Open, though gone, alas, are the days when the name Gary Player was inscribed on the trophy almost before the first ball was struck. In the United States the USPGA Tour tees off in Southern California. The first event is the Tournament of Champions at Carlsbad and it is followed by the Tuscon Open, the Bob Hope Classic and the Phoenix Open. This is America's 'Desert Tour', or the 'Johnny Miller Tour', as it used to be termed in the mid-1970s.

Meanwhile, back in Britain, much of the chatter at the nineteenth revolves around discussions as to who is going to win the major championships in the following season. At the time, Augusta and April seem light years away.

FEBRUARY

The Emirates Golf Club, Dubai

At a time when the majority of British golfers are trying their darnedest not to shiver and slice their way along February's frozen fairways, the European Tour makes an early start in (hopefully) sunny Portugal. In 1989 it teed off in the Canary Islands: the Tenerife Open staged at Golf Del Sur, beneath the spectacular gaze of Mount Teidi. The Tenerife Open has been moved forward a month, and in 1990 the season is ushered in by the Atlantic Open to be played at the Estela Golf Club just north of Oporto. Later on in the month the Tour visits the even more unlikely setting of Dubai for the Desert Classic. Woodhall Spa in Lincolnshire is often described as a golfing

oasis – the Emirates Golf Club is the real thing.

Elsewhere in the world, the Asian Tour also gets underway with the Philippines Open, followed by the Hong Kong Open. The US Tour visits equally exotic locations, namely Hawaii, and on the mainland, the Monterey Peninsula and the superb Pebble Beach course for the AT&T (formerly Bing Crosby) Pro-am.

Arguably the biggest event in February is the Australian Masters at Huntingdale near Melbourne, a tournament which has been dominated in recent years by Greg Norman.

MARCH

Sunset at Sawgrass, home of the Players Championship

March brings a new tournament to the European calendar, the first American Express-sponsored Mediterranean Open. The venue chosen for 1990 is Las Brisas, a course where only four months previously the World Cup of Golf was played – or sort of played – amid torrential rain. From mainland Spain the tour moves to Majorca and then later in the month visits the beautiful city of Florence for the Volvo Open.

From Florence to Florida, this is where the US Tour drops its anchor for the whole of March. There are four tournaments here, including the prestigious Doral Ryder Open and the even more prestigious Players Championship. The latter is regarded by some (especially by those who, like Tom Kite, have won it) as golf's fifth Major. Perhaps such claims were put into proper perspective by Sandy Lyle, who, after winning the championship in 1987, was asked by an American reporter, 'what's the difference between the Players Championship and the British Open?' 'About 120 years,' replied Lyle.

By the middle of the month the professional tour in Australia is drawing to a close, despite it still being summer down under; the twin lure of the American dollar and the Japanese yen proves too strong a temptation for Australasia's leading players. The Japan PGA Tour runs from March through to December, while in the same quarter of the globe the Open Championships of Thailand, Indonesia, Malaysia and Singapore all take place in March.

APRIL

Gene Sarazen gets the Masters underway

Oh to be at Augusta in April! The Masters is surely the most exciting golf tournament in the world. Year after year the final nine holes on the Sunday afternoon seem to produce as much heart-stopping drama as the rest of golf's major championships put together. The excitement started back in 1935, when Gene Sarazen, pictured above some fifty years on, holed his second shot on the par-five 15th hole for a double-eagle and went on to win the tournament in a play-off.

A quick glance at the history of the Masters in the 1980s reveals ten highly memorable occasions. In 1980 it was a first green jacket for Severiano Ballesteros, the youngest ever champion; in 1981 Watson edged out Nicklaus; and 1982 was the year of the Walrus, Craig Stadler, who triumphed in a tense play-off. In 1983 it was Seve again, while 1984 threw up a most popular champion in 'gentle Ben' Crenshaw. 1985 produced the first ever Major win by a German, and in 1986 Bernhard Langer put a sixth green jacket on to the shoulders of Jack Nicklaus. 1987 was the year of the 'Mize Miracle', 1988 brought the first British win, and in 1989 it was a case of the Englishman following the Scotsman, Faldo snatching a famous victory in fast fading light.

Augusta week over, and with heart-beats returning to normal, the club golfer in Britain will be hoping that he or she can produce their best golf to snatch victory in the long-awaited Spring Medal. In April the best women golfers in Europe commence battle with one another on the WPG European Tour and most eyes will be on Marie Laure de Lorenzi to see if she can repeat her brilliant seasons of 1988 and 1989. As for their male counterparts: Jersey, Cannes and Madrid is where the action is to be found.

MAY

St Mellion

The first week of May heralds the first arrival of the Volvo Tour on British soil. The Benson and Hedges International has found a new date on the calendar and an exciting, not to mention exacting, new venue in St Mellion. The tournament has been played at St Mellion once before, in 1979, but that was in the days before the Jack Nicklaus Course had been built. Many commentators are predicting that if the weather is anything less than friendly a score of par or less should be good enough to win the event. At the end of the month another high-quality field is sure to assemble at Wentworth for the Volvo PGA Championship, won in such masterly fashion last year by Nick Faldo.

The Belgian and Italian Opens are sandwiched between the great spectacles at St Mellion and Wentworth, while on the other side of the Atlantic another famous Jack Nicklaus creation, Muirfield Village, provides the stage for the important Memorial Tournament. Most golfers in Europe will remember Muirfield Village as the scene of the historic Ryder Cup victory in 1987. It was early autumn then and Muirfield Village was at its stunningly beautiful best. After the Memorial comes the Colonial, and then it's back to Georgia for the Atlanta Classic. By now the Women's European Tour is in full swing, and in Japan a strong field is guaranteed to turn up to try to wrestle the Chunichi Crowns title from Greg Norman.

JUNE

Medinah's extraordinary 19th hole

June eternal. A warm sun and a rapidly diminishing handicap; is it too much to ask for? And how about a British winner of the US Open? After all it has only happened once in seventy years. Ian Woosnam came within a whisker of achieving glory in 1989, and nobody will be more determined to prevent Curtis Strange from scoring a magnificent hat-trick of victories this year – remember it was Strange who produced the finish of a lifetime to defeat Woosnam in the final Ryder Cup singles match at the Belfry. Whoever wins at Medinah will have to produce the kind of arrow-straight hitting that enabled Lou Graham to win his only major championship over the same course fifteen years ago. Ironically the week immediately following the US Open provides Woosnam with his own opportunity for a hat-trick of wins in the Irish Open. Portmarnock and Medinah – what a contrasting pair! In addition to the laid-back atmosphere of the Irish Open, the European Tour also visits Paris for the French Open and some rather stately surroundings at Moor Park (for the Wang Four Stars Pro-am) and Woburn (for the Dunhill British Masters), where the lions outnumber the birdies.

It is twenty years since Tony Jacklin won the US Open and sixty years since a player last won the British Amateur and US Open double in the same year. That man of course was the immortal Bobby Jones. It is safe to say that no one will ever achieve that particular double again – not that this will overly concern the winner of the Amateur Championship at Muirfield in early June.

JULY

St Andrews

The Open Championship is always a special occasion, but in 1990 it is a little extra-special, because the Open returns to St Andrews, the 'Home of Golf'. Mark Calcavecchia defends the championship he captured at Troon, and Ballesteros will be out to emulate Jack Nicklaus's achievement of winning successive Open Championships on the Old Course. The last time the Open was played at St Andrews, in 1984, the ending could not have been better scripted. Ballesteros and Watson, then the two greatest golfers in the world, were level playing the final holes at the end of a marvellous championship. Many felt it a fitting ending when Ballesteros holed a birdie putt on the 18th green to win.

Nicklaus and Lee Trevino have won five Open Championships between them, but as they also share a century of years in age nei-

ther is expected to finish ahead of the field at St Andrews. However, if both should remain in Scotland for an extra week's golf and play in the British Seniors Open at Turnberry, it isn't difficult to imagine those two giants of the game fighting it out head-to-head *à la* Watson and Ballesteros.

July 1990 is something of a Scottish festival of golf, for in addition to the Open at St Andrews and the Seniors Open at Turnberry there is also the Scottish Open at Gleneagles. While all this is happening, the US Tour is fairly quiet. July, however, is the month of the US Women's Open, Betsy King defends the title won in 1987 by Laura Davies, and it also sees the staging of the Curtis Cup at Somerset Hills, New Jersey, where the British and Irish team will be attempting to win the trophy for a record third time in succession.

AUGUST

Woburn

As the Open returns to St Andrews after a gap of six years, so the season's final major championship, the USPGA, returns to Shoal Creek, Alabama, after a similar length of absence. Lee Trevino won the PGA Championship of 1984, his sixth major win, and coming at the age of 44 it was something of a surprise bonus. That was an extraordinary week, however, for, sharing second place, thanks largely to a magnificent second-round 63, was 48-year-old Gary Player. The defending champion at Shoal Creek will be the unmistakable figure of Payne Stewart.

Coming the week after the 'PGA is the International at Castle Rock, Colorado, the US Tour's one non-stroke-play event, and then it is off to the World Series of Golf on the superb Firestone Course at Akron, Ohio.

It is an important month for Europe's women golfers, with the Ladies' British Open at Woburn. This is the premier event on the WPG European Tour, and the cream of Europe, in the shape of Marie Laure de Lorenzi, Laura Davies, Alison Nicholas and Kitrina Douglas, will be determined to bring the trophy back from America following Jane Geddes' thrilling victory at Ferndown last year.

The Volvo Tour scales some heights in August – quite literally, in fact – it begins the month in the interestingly named town of Bokskogens for the PLM Open, then visits Fulford and the Belfry for the Murphy's Cup and English Open respectively, and then climbs the Swiss mountains for the Ebel European Masters at Crans-sur-Sierre.

SEPTEMBER

Wentworth

September comes yet brings no Ryder Cup – how will we golfers survive! At least our thirst for match-play golf should be suitably quenched by taking a trip to Wentworth for the Suntory World Matchplay Championship. Like the Masters in April, the World Matchplay has a habit of producing spectacular nerve-jangling finishes. 1989 was one of the best: 3 down to Ian Woosnam with 7 holes to play, Nick Faldo played some tremendous golf to bring him back to only one down with 3 to play. He then stunned his Ryder Cup team-mate with a birdie-birdie-eagle finish to win the match on the 36th green. Faldo then promptly gave his entire winnings to charity.

Wentworth is far from the only bright light in September. Neighbouring Sunningdale hosts the Panasonic European Open, an event with an international roll of champions that includes Norman, Lyle, Aoki, Marsh, Kite and Woosnam. In September there is also the Lancôme Trophy in France which regularly attracts class fields, and at the end of the month more televised golf with the Epson Grand Prix at Chepstow.

Across the seas the Japanese Tour is still going strong, and right in the middle of the month the US Tour heads for Toronto for the Canadian Open Championship at Glen Abbey. It is an event which in recent years hasn't attracted the fields its status merits; Nicklaus, however, appreciates the challenge – he never misses – but then Jack built the golf course.

OCTOBER

Japan's new St Andrews

There can be few finer things in life than playing a leisurely round of golf in October, just when the autumnal shades are approaching their glorious best. For the world's golfing elite there is nothing leisurely about the game in October. In both Europe and America, the tours are playing out their final dramatic acts.

In 1989 it was still very much in the balance as to who would win the Order of Merit crown right until the final nine holes of the Volvo Masters at Valderrama before Rafferty pulled away from Olazabal. In America the decision went into extra time, when Payne Stewart and Tom Kite, first and second in

the money list before the Nabisco Championship began, tied after 72 holes. Tom Kite eventually went on to win the title and first place on the money list when Stewart missed a four-foot put.

Prior to journeying to Valderrama, the European Tour visits Portugal, Germany and, for the first time, Austria – the inaugural Austrian Open being staged near Salzburg. The month also sees the United States defending the Dunhill Cup at St Andrews; the start of the Australasian Tour and the most important tournament on the Japanese Tour, the Japan Open.

NOVEMBER

Grand Cypress, Florida

There are few more depressing sights on a British golf course than that of a tractor little more than three quarters of the way down a fairway, and a greenkeeper busy preparing the first temporary greens of winter.

By now, the clocks have gone back an hour and mid-week golf is out of the question for most of us. Thoughts immediately turn to warmer climes. The European season now over, many of the touring professionals from both men's and women's European Tours link up for the Benson and Hedges Team Trophy, won in 1989 by Miguel Jimenez and Xonia Wunsch. Needless to say, the event is staged in sunnier southern Europe.

Early in November Japan hosts the Four Tours tournament, a team event comprising six players a side from the European, US, Japanese and Australasian Tours. Much of the best tournament golf in November in fact takes place in Japan, with the Taiheiyo Masters, Dunlop Phoenix and Casio World Open all attracting strong international fields. In the southern hemisphere, there is the Australian PGA Championship; in Africa the Safari and Sunshine Tours; and in America the entire nation tunes in to watch the Skins Game.

Last but not least, there is the much beleaguered World Cup of Golf. As we at home curse the greenkeeper for doing his duty, let's pray that the weather in Florida is better than it was at Las Brisas in 1989.

DECEMBER

Kingston Heath

If temporary greens are the worst thing about winter golf, the second most annoying is the club bandit who pips you by a point for the Christmas turkey in the winter stableford. Strange as it may seem, club golfers also play for turkeys in Australia. As midsummer approaches in the lucky country, so the nation's premier golf tournament is held, the Australian Open Championship. Last year Peter Senior romped away from a high-class field to win by seven strokes at Kingston Heath near Melbourne. Senior joined an impressive list of past winners that includes Palmer, Player, Nicklaus, Watson and Norman.

For a few seasons now a million dollars have been on offer for the winner of the Sun City Tournament in Bophuthatswana. Ian Woosnam became the first golfer to pick up such a cheque in 1987. More Skins Golf takes place around the world in December – there was a time when to play for one's shirt was thought to be serious enough – and at La Manga in southern Spain, even more is at stake when Europe's young (and not so young) hopefuls try to win a tournament player's card.

The end of the year is always a time for reflection. For most golfers it is time to look back over all those 'what might have been if onlys'. Time to re-examine the swing, perhaps; time to think of a new excuse, the old 'struck the ball really well but couldn't hole a thing' may be wearing a bit thin. But above all it's time to congratulate oneself for having taken up such a marvellous and mischievous game in the first place. Happy New Year!

USPGA TOUR 1990

JANUARY
4-7 **MONY Tournament of Champions**, Carlsbad, California
11-14 **Northern Telecom Tucson Open**, Arizona
17-21 **Bob Hope Chrysler Classic**, La Quinta, California
25-28 **Phoenix Open**, Scottsdale, Arizona

FEBRUARY
1-4 **AT&T Pebble Beach National Pro-Am**, Pebble Beach, California
8-11 **Hawaiian Open**, Honolulu
15-18 **Shearson Lehman Hutton Open**, La Jolla, California
22-25 **Nissan Los Angeles Open**, Pacific Palisades, California

MARCH
1-4 **Doral Ryder Open**, Miami, Florida
8-11 **Honda Classic**, Coral Springs, Florida
15-18 **The Players Championship**, Ponte Vedra, Florida
22-25 **The Nestle Invitational**, Orlando, Florida
29-1 April **Independent Insurance Agent Open**, The Woodlands, Houston, Texas

APRIL
5-8 **Masters**, Augusta, Georgia
5-8 **Deposit Guaranty Golf Classic**, Hattiesburg, Mississippi
12-15 **MCI Heritage Classic**, Hilton Head, South Carolina
19-22 **K-Mart Greater Greensboro Open**, North Carolina
26-29 **USF&G Classic**, New Orleans, Louisiana

MAY
3-6 **GTE Byron Nelson Classic**, Irving, Texas
10-13 **Memorial Tournament**, Dublin, Ohio
17-20 **Southwestern Bell Colonial**, Fort Worth, Texas
24-27 **Bell South Atlanta Classic**, Marietta, Georgia
31-3 June **Kemper Open**, Potomac, Maryland

JUNE
7-10 **Centel Western Open**, Oak Brook, Illinois
14-17 **US Open**, Medinah, Illinois
21-24 **Buick Classic**, Rye, New York
28-1 July **Canon Greater Hartford Open**, Cromwell, Connecticut

JULY
5-8 **Anheuser-Busch Golf Classic**, Williamsburg, Virginia
12-15 **Bank of Boston Classic**, Sutton, Massachusetts
19-22 **British Open**, St Andrews, Scotland
26-29 **Buick Open**, Grand Blanc, Michigan

AUGUST
2-5 **Federal Express St Jude Classic**, Memphis, Tennessee
9-12 **USPGA Championship**, Shoal Creek, Alabama
16-19 **The International**, Castle Rock, Colorado
23-26 **NEC World Series of Golf**, Akron, Ohio
30-2 September **Greater Milwaukee Open**, Franklin, Wisconsin

SEPTEMBER
6-9 **Hardee's Golf Classic**, Coal Valley, Illinois
13-16 **Canadian Open**, Oakville, Ontario
20-23 **B.C. Open**, Endicott, New York
27-30 **Southern Open**, Columbus, Georgia

OCTOBER
4-7 **Texas Open by Nabisco**, San Antonio
10-14 **Las Vegas Invitational**, Nevada
17-20 **Walt Disney World/Oldsmobile Classic**, Lake Buena Vista, Florida
25-28 **Nabisco Championship**, Houston, Texas

NOVEMBER
1-4 **Asahi Glass Four Tours**, Yomiuri, Japan
7-10 **Isuzu Kapalua International**, Maui, Hawaii
16-18 **RMCC Invitational by Greg Norman**, Thousand Oaks, California
27-28 **Skins Game**, La Quinta, California
29-2 December **J.C. Penney Classic**, Largo, Florida

DECEMBER
6-9 **Team Championship**, Wellington, Florida